By the Same Author

Dajjal — The king who has no clothes

Blood on the Cross

The Journey of Ahmad and Layla

The Wives of the Prophet
may the blessings and peace of Allah
be on him and his family and companions.

Fatima az-Zahra

Asma bint Abi Bakr

The Difficult Journey

The Way Back

THE DIFFICULT JOURNEY

Ahmad Thomson

Published by
**Ta-Ha Publishers Ltd.
1, Wynne Road
London SW9 0BD**

©Ahmad Thomson 1994

First published in Great Britain in Muharram 1415 / June 1994 by

Ta-Ha Publishers Ltd
1 Wynne Road
London SW9 0BB

All rights reserved. No part of this book may be reproduced or utilised in any form or by any means, electronic or mechanical, without the permission in writing from the Publisher.

Typesetting by Ahmad Thomson

The English translations of the Qur'an appearing in the text are based on that of Muhammad Pickthall, *alehi rahma*.

British Library Cataloguing in Publication Data

Thomson, Ahmad

The Difficult Journey

1. Islam. Contemporary Islam

I. Title

ISBN 1 897940 19 X

Printed in Great Britain by Deluxe Printers. Tel: 081-965-1771

CONTENTS

Acknowledgements vii

Author's Note viii

Preface ix

LONDON 1

ATHENS 5

CRETE 23

ALEXANDRIA 25

CAIRO 33

HUMAYSARA 49

ASWAN 57

WADI HALFA 65

KHARTOUM 69

OMDURMAN 73

ABU HARAZ 85

TAYYABA 91

WAD MADANI 101

AL-MARRAHEH 103

KADDABAS 111

OMDURMAN 119

KUSTI 127

AR-RAHAD	131
EL OBEID	137
ZARIBA	141
EL OBEID	147
NYALA	153
JEBEL MURRA	157
DARIBE	163
KALUKITTI	177
NYERTATI	181
OMDURMAN	187
KHARTOUM	197
JEDDAH	199
MAKKA	207
THE HARAM	213
MINA	235
ARAFAH	237
MUZDALIFAH	247
MINA	251
MAKKA	255
MINA	261
MAKKA	267
Glossary of Arabic Terms	275
Bibliography	325

ACKNOWLEDGEMENTS

This book would not have been written had it not been for Shaykh Abdal-Qadir al-Murabit who showed me the beauty and majesty and truth of Islam and who sent me out on the Hajj.

It is dedicated to all those who helped along the way, and it is especially for all those who have been, or who hope to go, on the Difficult Journey.

My thanks are also due to all those who supported me while this book was being written, including Afsar Siddiqui, Muhammad Abdar-Rahman Saeed, Ahmad As-Suwaidi, Abdal-Aziz Al-Alayan, and Hamid Al-Jazayri, and particularly my parents, Hugh and Mary, my wife's parents, Paul and Jean, and especially my wife, Susan, whose patience and love helped me keep going.

Finally, I would also like to thank all those who have helped make it possible to have this book published, long after it had been written, especially Dr A A El-Kassas and Fouad Mattar. Thank you!

Ahmad Thomson
London
Spring 1994

Author's Note

Most of the definitions in the Glossary of Arabic Terms are taken directly or derive from the books listed in the Bibliography which should all be read in order to arrive at an understanding which is far beyond the scope of this book. They are from the overflowing wisdom of Shaykh Abdal-Qadir al-Murabit, by the permission of Allah and His Messenger, may Allah bless him and his family and his companions and all those who follow in his footsteps, and grant them peace.

PREFACE

As I sit facing Makka it is summer here in England. People are making the most of the warm days and the long evenings. As always, the weather is one of the main topics of conversation, along with what is happening at Wimbledon, and in the Test Match, and on the TV, and, of course who is currently doing what with whom.

Flowers are blooming in millions of gardens, thrilling to even more millions of summer rain drops, and a million loves are being born or renewed, or are dying or dead, with each passing moment. Far around us in the night sky, millions of stars shine out, their light flashing across millions of light years through space, filling those who gaze on them with wonder, unnoticed by those who are asleep.

Each one of us lives in a different world, in a different universe, each one true, in a subtle unified patterning that can only be described as perfect. We travel through life, learning as we go, and sometimes we pause, as the spinning earth swims through space at two hundred miles a second in a perfect orbit, with us pausing there somewhere on its fragile surface, resting on earth or water with fire beneath us and air around us and in us, and as we pause, sometimes we dive into the ocean of our memory and glide smoothly through recollections of past moments in our journey through life:

It was in the summer of 1977 that Abdal-Jalil, Mustafa al-Alawi and I set out to go on the Hajj, the pilgrimage to the House of Allah in Makka, the Difficult Journey as it is called, for this is one of the meanings of the Arabic word al-Hajj. It is a long time ago now since we first set out, and yet all these years later the journey still remains vividly clear, from start to finish, in my awareness. It was the journey of a life-time – and the key to unlock the meaning of one's whole life journey, as well as all the journeys made within it, for whoever makes this journey with understanding must surely realise that surely we come from Allah and surely to Him we return.

Ahmad Thomson
Summer 1990

In the Name of Allah the Merciful the Compassionate

By the morning hours
And by the night when it is most still,
Your Lord has not forsaken you nor does He hate you,
And truly what comes after will be better for you
than what has come before,
And truly your Lord will give to you
so that you will be content.
Did He not find you an orphan and protect you?
Did He not find you wandering and guide you?
Did He not find you destitute and enrich you?
So do not oppress the orphan,
And do not drive the beggar away,
And speak about the blessings of your Lord.

(Qur'an: 93.1-11)

LONDON

"What do you want?"

Shaykh Abdal-Qadir looked keenly at me and through me as he spoke, as if he already knew exactly what I wanted, but was just asking the question so that I would discover the answer for myself.

I looked into my heart. For the last six months I had been writing a book on the history of Islam in Spain with the help of Colonel Rahim, either cooped up in the British Museum Library or back at his small flat near Marble Arch for most of the time. Other than the occasional walk in Hyde Park, or a swim in the nearby swimming pool, I seemed to be living in books. I was tired of words, especially printed ones. I wanted action. I wanted adventure. I wanted to be out on the open road, travelling in the way of Allah.

"I want to go on Hajj – on foot," I replied.

"It would take far too long!" grinned Shaykh Abdal-Qadir with delight, and that seemed to be that.

❂   ❂   ❂

Miraculously, however, I soon found myself preparing to go on the pilgrimage to Makka. I would not be walking all the way as I had hoped, but there were still five months to pass before the time of the Hajj arrived, so it had been decided that Abdal-Jalil, Mustafa al-Alawi and I would go to the Sudan and travel there before making our way to Makka, insh'Allah. Our only instructions from Shaykh Abdal-Qadir were to visit the awliya and to sing the Diwan of Shaykh Muhammad ibn al-Habib wherever we went.

Within three weeks, the three of us were ready. The book, I thought, was completed, after having spent most of many of my nights awake and writing – although as it turned out, another third of it remained to be written on my return. We had three one-week-return tickets to Athens, visas to enter Egypt in our passports, and fifty pounds sterling between us. Somehow, we were not quite sure how, we hoped to be able to make our way over to Alexandria and then down through Egypt to the Sudan, trusting in the truth of Shaykh Muhiyy'ud-Din Ibn Arabi's words, "Whoever engages in travel will arrive!" and trusting especially in the generosity and mercy of Allah.

Since we had virtually no money, it was decided that the basis of our journey would be the saying of the Prophet Muhammad, may the blessings and peace of Allah be on him and his family and his companions and all who follow him and them with sincerity in what they are able until the Last Day, that whoever does the five obligatory prayers each day will be fed and clothed and sheltered by Allah. He had also once said that if you really trusted in Allah, then you would be like the birds who go out in the morning with nothing, and who return home to roost with nothing, and who have been fed during the day. It is one thing to know these sayings, and quite another thing to act on them. Insh'Allah in the days and weeks and months ahead, we would come to know their reality and truth.

Having said our goodbyes, we made our way to Gatwick Airport, each carrying a small travelling bag containing only the bare necessities. All our affairs were in order and all our debts had been settled. There were no loose ends or half completed transactions to hold us back. If we were to suddenly die, all that would be necessary would be to wash and bury our bodies and say the funeral prayer over us, before distributing our meagre possessions to our relatives. What few possessions we owned, we carried with us. We did not have bank accounts or travellers cheques or credit cards. Our only insurance was trust in Allah. We were very poor – and we were very rich. We had no possessions to hold us back or weigh us down, and the whole world lay before us. The only commitment we had was to be in Makka in a few months' time on the 8th of Dhu'l Hijjah, the day that the rites of the pilgrimage begin. As the Prophet Muhammad once said, may Allah bless him and grant him peace, the whole world is the possession of the one who has no possessions and the belonging of the one who has no belongings.

❂   ❂   ❂

We looked at the busy summer time holiday traffic passing through Gatwick Airport in amazement. It was all so efficient, so well-regulated, so predictable, so meticulously computerised. If there were to be a sudden long-lasting power failure, everyone would be left stranded, helpless, aimless, almost unable to move once the computers and visual display units and conveyor belts were lifeless. Everyone except us, it seemed, appeared to be in a trance, not only oblivious of even the possibility of such an occurrence, but also entirely caught up and distracted in what they were doing, which was either going somewhere on holiday or business, or helping people to go somewhere on holiday or business. It was as if we were the only people in the whole airport who were going on the pilgrimage to Makka. It was as if no one else was aware of the all-pervading presence of Allah. It was as if we were the only three people there that afternoon who did wudu and prayed the shortened, joined, travelling prayers of dhur and asr in a quiet corner, amidst the continual toing and froing of travellers who were too busy combining pleasure with business to pause, and reflect, and remember, what is on the other side of death. Allah.

Having checked in, we made our way up onto the roof garden and waited for the time to pass, watching the people and 'planes come and go, eating our chocolate coated snacks and sipping our coffee, until at last the call for our flight came over the public address system loud and clear. Shouldering our bags, we descended the stairs, passed through customs, strolled through the departure lounge and along the long corridor, glimpsing the last of that gentle English summer through the plate glass windows, and then we were aboard the 'plane and settled in our seats and soon we were up in the air, with England rapidly fading away behind us in the distance. There was no turning back. This was a one way journey. I had been on many journeys in the past, but never on one quite like this one. Somehow it had an altogether different feel about it.

Once we were cruising at our designated altitude, the usual flight rituals unfolded. A small meal was served, followed by the duty frees trolley. We were on a cheapo cheapo package flight, and our fellow passengers were busy stocking up on their full allowance, determined to enjoy to the full their annual one or two week break away from their daily routine of work and play. We had no need for alcohol or nicotine now, although they had been part of our lives in the days before we had embraced Islam, and instead talked amongst ourselves and gazed out at the beautiful cloudscape which hung in the sky beneath our craft. Soon the sun had set swiftly behind us as we sped towards the deepening dark blue of the rapidly approaching night. We did tayyamum, attracting curious glances from those whose seats were nearest to us, and prayed maghrib and isha together, remaining seated and facing roughly in the direction of Makka. Insh'Allah we were now on the way to see with our own eyes what we had been facing each day when we stood and bowed and prostrated and sat in prayer, but there was still a great deal of ground to cover before we finally entered Makka and saw the black cube of the Ka'aba right in front of us. As we sped through the night without appearing to be really moving, I could feel a cold gradually taking hold of my throat and nasal passages, but I did not care in the least. At least we were now on our way, diving into the unknown, and feeling marvellously alive and young. How glad I was to be on that 'plane!

ATHENS

Almost before we had fully realised that we were actually on our way, we had touched down at Athens airport and passed through customs. We watched our fellow passengers a trifle enviously as they were whisked off to their hotels by courtesy coaches, and finally found ourselves being driven through the warm Mediterranean night by a smiling half drunk with joy taxi driver, who told us with complete and utter certainty that we were going to have a good time. I relaxed at these words and gazed out in wonder at the full moon that shone on a more rugged and temperate landscape than the one we had just left behind. We were in a different world!

The taxi driver drove us straight to an inexpensive hotel which had a room with three beds, and having collected his fee for having brought us there, disappeared into the warm night with a smile and a wave. Although it was now well past midnight, we were still wide awake and eager to have a look around, for none of us had visited Athens before, and indeed Mustafa had never been outside the British Isles. Strolling out into the streets, we found the best open air coffee shop in town, and soon we were relishing our cappuchinos and rich gateaux like millionaires in an almost entirely deserted square whose peace and silence were only momentarily broken by a group of drunken late night revellers who staggered past, laughing and shouting incoherently in Greek as they made their way unerringly back to base. It really did feel so good to be alive. Tomorrow we would run out of money and have nowhere to stay, and no doubt my cold would reach the uncomfortable stage, but tonight we had fed well, it was lovely and warm, and the moon was full. We had done all the prayers within their time. Allah would provide. We returned to the hotel, climbed thankfully into our beds, and, suddenly tired, fell fast asleep.

Having showered and prayed subh and eaten breakfast, we left the hotel and made our way through the busy streets of day time Athens to its main park, not quite sure what to do next, half dazzled by the bright sun, sweating in the unaccustomed heat, and feeling somewhat jet-lagged. Our exuberance of the night before had disappeared and we were now faced with what Shaykh Zamzami used to call 'los nittos grittos'.

We did have the addresses of two Muslims whom Abu'l Qasim had met on a ferry in the Mediterranean some two years earlier, and were not certain whether we should try and look them up or go to Pirraeus harbour with the intention of finding a yacht that was going to Alexandria and needed a crew. If we could find such a vessel, then we could work our passage across to North Africa.

As we pondered on what to do next, we relaxed in the shade in the park, feeling sleepy and indolent, and spending most of what little money we had left on cold drinks which had been produced locally by a company called EV.

Midday came and went, and having done wudu – using the convenient trickle of water from a leaking water outlet, and ignoring the red-faced keeper who shouted at us and waved his arms in anger – we prayed dhur and asr on the lovely green grass. Abdal-Jalil had asked me to lead the prayer, and as my forehead came to rest on the ground in sajda, there was a sudden sharp stinging sensation just above my left eye. I had been stung by a bee or a wasp. Ignoring the pain as best I could, I completed the two prayers while my forehead swiftly began to swell. Shaykh Abdal-Qadir once wrote: "The sufis say that the common people get the sting and they do not get the honey, the elite get the honey and they do not get the sting, but the elect of the elite get the sting and the honey and they do not care."

As soon as we had finished doing the prayer, a Sudanese Muslim who had been walking past and seen us came over to us and invited us to his house for a meal. As we accompanied him through the streets of Athens, we learned that he was a student there and that he shared a house with several other Muslim students and manual workers from Egypt and the Sudan. Soon we were all sitting round a table at their house, enjoying a simple meal of bread and cheese and olives. During the meal, one of the men at the table excused himself, saying that if he did not leave immediately, he would be late for work. He worked at EV, the factory which produced the soft drinks which we had recently sampled in the park.

During the meal, Abdal-Jalil showed our host the two names and addresses that Abu'l Qasim had given to us before we had left England. "Ah," he said, recognising them both, "Ramadan is not in town today, and Umar will probably be at this cafe whose address you have here. If you want, I will take you there."

The cafe turned out to be one of the main meeting places for all the Muslims in Athens. Umar was indeed there, and having bought us a Greek yoghurt and a coffee each, and having listened to our idea about trying to find a yacht that was going to Alexandria and needed a crew, he said that he reckoned it was worth a try. Umar took us down to the right bus-stop, put us on the right bus – thrusting enough money in my hand, with a quiet 'Bismillah', to pay for the fares and buy us supper as we boarded it – and wishing us well he waved us goodbye with a flashing gold and silver filled smile.

Soon we were out of Athens and in Piraeus, walking around a very posh yacht marina. After an hour of asking uninterested yacht owners if they were about to sail over to Alexandria and needed a crew, it had become patently obvious that this improbable state of affairs did not actually exist. We were at a loss as to what to do next and decided to call it a day. The sun had just set, it was time for the prayer and we were hungry again. We retraced our steps to a deserted waterfront cafe which we had spotted on our way to the marina, purchasing some food on the way, and having prayed maghrib and isha, we sat at one of the empty tables and ate our simple supper, as the freshening evening breeze tugged playfully at the paper bags and our clothes. By the time we had finished eating, it was dark. We peered over the edge of the concrete platform on which the deserted open air cafe stood. The rocks below were large and relatively flat and a good few feet away from the water's edge. "It looks like there's nothing else for it," said Abdal-Jalil. "This is where we sleep tonight."

There was no one else about to observe or stop us. We clambered down to the rocks below in the darkness, and bedded down as best we could on the unyielding rocks. Fortunately, Abdal-Alim had given me a striped cotton rug before we had left England, so at least we had something to lie on. Soon we were fast asleep, lulled by the lapping sound of the dirty harbour water as the harbour lights twinkled all around us, their reflections dancing on a thousand waves.

❂ ❂ ❂

We awoke the next morning, bleary-eyed and stiff, and surrounded, to our horror, by dried out human excrement, which we had been unable to see in the darkness of the night before. "That's life," remarked Abdal-Jalil. "One moment you're in a nice comfortable hotel, the next moment you're in a pile of shit!"

We clambered back onto the concrete platform, prayed two rakats each to make up for subh which we had missed, and reviewed our situation. Clearly we would have to return to Athens. There we could either try and sell the return half of our 'plane tickets, or else we would have to try and find work, perhaps at EV. We had just enough money for one person to catch the bus back into Athens. Abdal-Jalil, who was the Amir of our party, decided that I should be the one who initially returned to Athens. I was to try and find Ramadan and explain our situation to him and see whether or not he could help us. Meanwhile, he and Mustafa would wait in Pirraeus.

I bid them farewell, found my way back to the bus-stop and boarded the bus back into Athens, my tongue moving rapidly as I silently made dua after dua, as most people do when in this kind of situation.

❂ ❂ ❂

As it turned out, I found Ramadan's small flat with little difficulty, and by Allah he was at home, freshly showered and smartly dressed, and concerned at my slightly dishevelled appearance. I explained our predicament, embarrassed to be laying our need at his doorstep. He listened sympathetically, gave me an open, welcoming smile and said, "Never mind, you are guests of Allah. You can come and stay here with me until you get yourselves sorted out. Let's go and collect Abdal-Jalil and Mustafa immediately. They must be wondering what's happening!"

Ramadan drove us out to Pirraeus in his smart little car, picked up a somewhat sun-struck Abdal-Jalil and Mustafa, and returned with us to his flat as if he had all the time in the world to help us. An hour later, we had all showered and changed into clean clothes, and were drinking freshly made coffee as we chatted to Ramadan, may Allah give him the Garden. He was so spontaneously generous to us, and did not begrudge helping us in the least.

That evening we returned to the Muslims' Cafe, and dined on foules mesdames – North African field beans spiced with cumin, tahini and olive oil – salad and fresh bread, surrounded by Muslims who were mainly from Egypt and the Sudan and who were mostly employed as cheap labour in the factories of Athens. Soon we were smiling and laughing and trying to answer myriads of questions simultaneously, as the jukebox blared out Arabic love songs, especially those of Umm Kalthoum, in the background, and, every so often, a recitation from the Qur'an.

The contrast between this evening and the one before it could not have been more marked. Life after Pirraeus seemed possible after all. Before bedding down for the night in Ramadan's sitting room, it had already been decided that tomorrow we would try and sell the return halves of our air tickets, for we were determined not to use them ourselves. If we were unable to raise sufficient funds by these means, then we would try and find work at EV, the soft drinks factory. Apparently it was hard work for not very much pay, but at least they did not require you to have a work permit. Before leaving London, Colonel Rahim had told me to give him a ring if we were in difficulty, and this was yet another option we could try, although I did not particularly wish to exercise it, as I knew that he had very little money.

The next day dawned bright and we set off early with renewed optimism. Somehow we still expected Allah to provide for us without our having to work very hard for our provision! After several fruitless hours spent in the hippy part of town, we still had not sold the return halves of our air tickets. Reluctantly I telephoned Colonel Rahim who seemed surprised to hear my voice so soon, but who said he would send whatever he could raise to such and such a bank as soon as he could.

Having done what we could for the day, we sat at the table of a side-walk cafe and sipped cold water which was not only very refreshing but also was free, watching the world hurry by us and feeling rather helpless. Suitably refreshed, we decided to take a look at the Acropolis while we happened to be in that neck of the woods, and by the time we had climbed up to this ancient site we were very thirsty once again. Hordes of tourists came and went unceasingly, and the guides tirelessly gave their version of events in a dozen or more languages, thankful perhaps that the ancient Greeks had so thoughtfully provided them with a means to earn their living. Certainly it was a very beautiful edifice, and one thing was clear: The ancient Greeks had built far better buildings than the steel and concrete monstrosities that were being produced nowadays – and they were long gone.

● ● ●

The next day we tried again to sell our tickets, but again without success. We went to the bank, but no funds from England were waiting there for us. The day after that was exactly the same, and on arriving back at Ramadan's flat to spend our third night with him, we were told that his wife would be joining him the next day and that it would no longer be possible for us to stay at the flat once she was back. However there was a Youth Hostel not far away, where we could stay until we had made better arrangements. Generously, Ramadan gave us enough money to pay for a couple of nights at the hostel, and the next morning we bade him farewell, thanking him for all that he had done to help us.

When we arrived at the hostel, it turned out to be full up, but we were directed to another one in a less salubrious part of town, where we were able to pay for a bed each for the next two nights. Both this day and the next followed the same pattern as the two before them. We would go to the bank, only to be told that there was no money waiting for us, walk about for a while, stopping for an iced water whenever we had grown thirsty, and then return to the bank shortly before it closed for the day, only to receive the same answer. It was only when I had returned to England six months later that I learned that Colonel Rahim had wired some money to Athens, but to a different bank to the one I had asked that it be sent! However this was just as well, for it meant that in the end we were obliged to act positively, rather than taking the easy way out and crying "Help!" at the first sign of difficulty.

By the second night at the hostel – the seventh that we had spent in Athens – we had no money and were extremely hungry and weak. "This is no good!" exclaimed Abdal-Jalil. "Let's go and see if anyone has dropped any money on the pavement." It seemed a very long shot indeed, but we tried it, silently imploring Allah to show us a little more of His endless generosity. A hundred yards down the busy city street, we found a large watermelon lying in the gutter. It was only slightly cracked, and must have fallen off the back of a lorry! Gratefully we picked it up, with the minimum of debate as to whether it was alright to do so, and returned to the hostel with our booty. Having cleaned it up as best we could, we cut it up into large generous slices, sharing it with two Japanese travellers whose beds adjoined ours, and who supplemented the feast with a large bag of mini Milky Ways. That night hunger did not keep us awake.

The next morning we checked out of the hostel, and, having received our usual answer from the bank, we decided that there was only one thing for it: We would have to try and find work at EV. The factory was on the outskirts of the city, and as we walked through Athens towards it, the time came for our return flight to take off. The time passed. I imagined the 'plane on its way back to England – and I was glad that we weren't on it, glad that we hadn't chickened out. "Well," I said, "We won't be needing these any more then, will we?" And I tossed our now useless return tickets into a nearby litter bin. We had burned our boats. There was no way back. We could only go forward!

Much to our surprise, we were given jobs immediately at EV, and were told to start the next day on the early shift which began at eight in the morning and ended at eight in the night. Long hours for not much pay, but insh'Allah we hoped somehow to be able to save enough money to reach Alexandria.

We returned to the Muslims' Cafe and explained what had happened to the manager, Muhammad, who was a quiet and well mannered man. Help was immediately forthcoming. There was a room with its own shower and toilet at the back of the cafe which we were welcome to use, as the man who usually lived there was away travelling. Since we were guests of Allah, travelling fi sabili'llah, we need not pay rent. He would lend us some money to tide us over until we received our first week's pay from the factory.

Gratefully we thanked our generous host and moved into the small dimly lit room which was just big enough to hold the three of us. It was the fifth place we had stayed at in just over a week. As we sat and relaxed, I opened my English translation of the Qur'an which I had brought with me at random. It fell open at the following verse from Surat'al-Kahf:

> And when you withdraw from them
> and that which they worship
> except Allah,
> Then seek refuge in the cave.
> Your Lord will spread for you of His Mercy
> And will prepare for you a pillow in your difficulty.
>
> (Qur'an: 18.16)

For the next three weeks the Muslims' Cafe became our home, and we nearly always had our evening meal of foules mesdames, salad and bread, followed by Greek yoghurt with honey and coffee, at one of its tables, glad to have finished another long day's work at the factory and to be in the company of Muslims again. The cafe was always full of life. There were the regulars, most of whom worked in the factories, and there were the travellers, most of whom worked on the ships which docked at Piraeus for a few days before continuing on their way. Everyone accepted us, and wished us well.

We soon discovered that the cafe had a basement which was easily accessible via some wide stairs from the ground floor, and which was not being used. It was empty except for a few dilapidated tables and chairs, and I guessed that it must have been used as an overflow room in more prosperous days gone by. It would clearly make a good mosque, and having sought and received Muhammad's permission, we had soon cleaned the place thoroughly, white-washed the walls, and painted the Divine Name in Arabic – Allah – on the wall behind which lay Makka. In no time at all the dingy basement had become a bright mosque, swept clean and ready for use.

❁   ❁   ❁

The factory was dirty and noisy and old. Each day, except for Friday which we had chosen as our day off, we would ride the bus that passed nearby the factory, and clock in. The factory was in continual production, twenty-four hours a day seven days a week, and anyone who had been working there for a considerable length of time was simply quite mad. The three of us formed part of the human link between the conveyor belt that monotonously delivered the crates of used empties which had been unloaded from the lorries below, and the bottle-washing machine. As the crates arrived, we would grab one each and check each bottle inside it, removing any metal tops or collars which were still on them, before stacking the completed crate near the man in charge of the bottle-washer. He in turn would load the bottles into the bottle-washing machine, and then, once they had been thoroughly washed, stack them onto the conveyor belt which took them on to be refilled with various coloured liquids, topped, labelled, re-crated and stacked back onto the continuously moving conveyor belt which delivered the crates of unused fulls to be loaded on the waiting lorries outside.

From the moment that we entered the room that housed all this activity, our ears were filled with the constant rattle of bottles and hum of machinery, glass against glass and glass against metal. No one could pause for an undesignated breather, as this would cause a bottle-neck in the process. It was just possible for each of us to slip off, one at a time, to do the prayer on a piece of cardboard round a corner, when the time for the prayer came. Halfway through the shift, we had a twenty minute meal-break, during which we would eat whatever lunch we had brought with us. We were free to drink as much of the factory's produce as we wanted, but after a few days we were drinking water only, just like all the other employees who had been there any length of time. Nearly all the employees were from Egypt or the Sudan, and I wondered what could have possibly made them want to come and put up with EV.

I had always vowed instinctively never to work in a factory, and now I could see exactly why.

We lived in a twilight world at EV. Some natural daylight managed to find its way through the dusty opaque glass that filled a couple of token windows, and this was supplemented by inadequate artificial strip lighting. The constant clatter and rattle of moving bottles made it impossible to hold a conversation, and all communication, which was kept to a minimum, consisted either of shouts or sign language. Accordingly I passed much of the time singing my heart out, sometimes singing my favourite pop songs, sometimes reciting what little Qur'an I knew by heart, sometimes singing from the Diwan of Shaykh Muhammad ibn al-Habib, and sometimes repeating the various forms of dhikr which Shaykh Abdal-Qadir had given me to do, such as 'Astaghfiru'llah' – 'I ask forgiveness of Allah', and 'Husbuna'llhu wa ni'am'al-wakil' – 'Allah is enough for us and He is the best guardian', and 'La ilaha il' Allah' – 'There is no god except Allah', and 'Allahumma salli ala sayyedina Muhammadin'abdika wa rasulika'nabiyyi'al-ummi wa ala alihi wa sahbihi wa salem taslima' – 'O Allah, bless our master Muhammad, Your slave and Messenger, the unlettered Prophet, and his family and companions and grant them peace.' By constantly doing dhikr, my heart was always still and at peace, and somehow I was shielded from the awfulness of the place. Shaykh Abdal-Qadir once said that the effect of reciting 'Astaghfiru'llah' on the heart is like sweeping away dust with a brush, and that the effect of repeating the prayer on the Prophet on the heart is like washing clothes by hand, and that the recitation of 'La ilaha il' Allah' purifies one's innermost secret.

Seated at the bottle-washing machine on our first day at the factory – and indeed on most of the days that we were there – with a cigarette hanging loosely but securely from the corner of his mouth for much of the time, was Ibrahim from the Sudan. He greeted us like long lost friends, and showed us the ropes, and after our first day's work invited us round to his small flat for supper. In the days that followed we became firm friends, and of all the people who came to the Muslims' Cafe, it was Ibrahim who helped us the most in converting the abandoned basement into a mosque, and when we held the first jumua prayer there the next day – probably the only jumua prayer I will ever have led – Ibrahim was the only person present besides ourselves. Thankfully the numbers did start to increase thereafter, especially once the most knowledgeable man in the Athens Muslim community had been appointed as Imam.

❂   ❂   ❂

It was after our first jumua prayer that Muhammad, the manager of the cafe, informed us that we would have to leave our room by the next evening, as its usual occupant would be back from his travels by then and would want to move back in. Ibrahim, who had overheard his words, did not hesitate an instant: "That's alright," he beamed, "You can come and stay with me! Welcome! Marhaban! Ahlan wa Sahlan!"

There is no time like the present, and two hours later we had already packed our few belongings, tidied up the room at the cafe and moved into Ibrahim's flat. It was at the top of a three storey building and had its own little stairway up onto the roof. Since the flat only consisted of one small room, a small kitchen and a small shower and toilet room, it was decided that it would be best if we slept up on the flat roof underneath the stars. I was delighted at this arrangement, since I disliked being cooped up in confined spaces, especially in ones made of concrete and situated in hot climates, since the result is always an oven-like environment that leaves one feeling like a Tandoori chicken. The building was relatively high up on the slopes of Athens and there was little traffic in its vicinity, so the warm night air was fresh and we had a lovely view over the sparkling city lights as the moon and stars shone down on us from a clear unclouded Mediterranean summer sky. After the confined, noisy, sweaty atmosphere of the factory, it was sheer bliss to sit up there on the roof and look out over the city, before stretching out and gazing up at the stars until one fell asleep.

That night we all had supper at Ibrahim's flat, glad that we had been obliged to move out of the cafe. When one door shuts, another always opens. As we ate our simple but tasty meal and thanked Ibrahim yet again for his generosity and kindness, he smiled. "Actually," confessed Ibrahim, "About three months ago I had a dream that three strangers came to stay as my guests. I did not understand it at the time, but of course now its meaning is very clear!"

We marvelled at the all-embracing knowledge of Allah. Events appear to happen unexpectedly out of the blue as far as we are concerned, when they are already in the knowledge of Allah long before they have occurred, since everything is from Him:

Allah is the Creator of you and your actions.

(Qur'an: 37.96).

Our conversation turned to our plans for the future, and Ibrahim produced a small atlas, turning to the pages which displayed the maps of Egypt and the Sudan. North Africa still seemed very far away to us, but looking at the maps and listening to Ibrahim talking about his home and family back in the Sudan made these places seem a little more real and not so far away and out of reach. As we talked around the map of the Sudan, we spotted an isolated green patch in the middle of the desert, right over in the west. "What is that?" I asked.

"That is the Jebel Murra – the Mountains of Time," replied Ibrahim. "We call them the jewel of the Sudan."

"In that case," said Abdal-Jalil, "I wonder who the jewel of the Jebel Murra is? Insh'Allah we will go there and find out!" My heart jumped at the prospect, and although I was now enjoying this part of the journey, especially now that my cold had cleared up, I longed for the next stage of the journey when, insh'Allah, we would be travelling in Africa.

● ● ●

The days passed in swift succession, as we toiled away at EV and spent as little of our hard-earned money as possible. With the exception of a day-trip out of Athens to the seaside – where we spent the day swimming and sunbathing and trying to remove the black spines of a sea anemone from Abdal-Jalil's right foot – we remained in the city, working and resting and often chatting with the friendly and varied clientele of the Muslims' Cafe.

After we had been at the factory for nearly three weeks, and at Ibrahim's flat for about two, his landlady appeared one morning to talk about 'the problem' – which was our presence at the flat. Apparently some of the people who lived in the taller apartment blocks across the road from us had seen us doing the prayer on the roof and felt threatened by it. Despite Ibrahim's protestations that this was not a problem, she kindly but firmly made it clear that she wanted us out of the flat by the end of the week, before affectionately reminiscing about her visit to Alexandria as a little girl, when an old man in a white robe and turban had swept her off her feet and into his arms, saying, "Ya Habibi! ya Habibi!" – O my Beloved! O my Beloved! – again and again. The kind old lady's face broke into a lovely smile. "Ya Habibi! Ya Habibi!" she chuckled, again and again, the memory still evidently very clear in her heart.

It was clear that Allah was moving us on, and we did not try to resist. That afternoon we went for a long walk, right out of the city and up into the hills overlooking Athens. The heat no longer bothered us and we were all in good health, although Mustafa was still finding it all a little too much, this being his first journey out of England. I knew exactly how he felt. I had come to England from Africa when I was eighteen, and nine years later I still had not become entirely accustomed to the British and their ways!

Having found a secluded spot, we held a short gathering of dhikr, singing from the Diwan of Shaykh Muhammad ibn al-Habib for an hour or so, and then doing a long strong hadra – which is the invocation of the name of Allah al-Hayyu done standing. Al-Hayyu means the Living, the Alive, the One Who gives Life. Having completed the hadra, we sat down in a small circle, and I recited the ayat'al-Kursi in the calm serenity that always follows the invocation of Allah, when one is very aware of the all-pervading presence of Allah. The meaning of this verse of the Qur'an indicates the absolute knowledge and power of Allah:

> Allah – there is no god except Him,
> the Living the Self-subsisting.
> He is not diminished by the years
> and He does not sleep.
> To Him belongs what is in the heavens
> and what is in the earth.
> No one can intercede without His permission.
> He knows what comes before them
> and what comes after them.
> And they do not encompass anything of His knowledge
> except as He wills.

> His throne extends over the heavens and the earth.
> And He is not fatigued in preserving them.
> And He is the Exalted the Tremendous.
>
> (Qur'an: 2.255)

We considered our situation, aware that we were living on a knife-edge. After a short discussion it was all decided. We would collect our pay on Friday, after the jumua prayer, and then give in our notice. Normally, of course, we would have given a week's notice, but in view of Ibrahim's landlady's ultimatum, we had no other choice. Once we knew exactly how much money we had, we would try and catch a ferry to Alexandria, hoping that we had earned and saved enough to pay for our fares. "It's amazing!" said Abdal-Jalil. "It actually feels like we are travelling along the siraat al-mustaqim!" I knew exactly what he meant, as I recalled the Prophet's description of the siraat al-mustaqim – the straight path – which he had once described as being narrower than the edge of the finest sword.

❂   ❂   ❂

Everything unfolded as planned. We worked our last day at EV on the Thursday, bidding "Yasu" to the man at the gate for the last time, collected our pay on the Friday, for we were paid weekly, and then handed in our notice. I hurried to the travel agents which we had already decided to use, discovered that there was a ferry leaving for Alexandria the next day, and asked what was the cheapest fare possible. On being told, I quickly and roughly calculated that we had just enough money and asked for three tickets. As the lady examined our passports and made out the tickets, I checked my calculations and realised, with a sinking feeling, that I had miscalculated the total cost. We did not have quite enough money to pay for our tickets! I did not know what to say. And then, much to my surprise, the lady smiled and asked for even less than the amount that I had first calculated. I paid her immediately, thanking her profusely. Miraculously she had decided to give us three tickets at the reduced student rate, even though none of us had student cards and even though I had not even considered the possibility, let alone mentioned it.

That night we went to the Muslims' Cafe a little earlier than usual to say our goodbyes. The newly appointed Imam of the mosque, who had led his first jumua prayer that day, had invited us to a meal at his home that evening, and having said goodbye and thankyou to everyone at the cafe we were taken round to his flat. Ramadan, who had been out of town on business for the last few days, was there, and we thanked him especially. His kindness and generosity when we were down and out in Pirraeus had made everything else possible. He himself was overjoyed on our behalf that everything had worked out alright. "Al-hamdulillahi wa shukrulillah!" – Praise to Allah and thanks to Allah – he exclaimed, pointing heavenwards, and giving us an Egyptian five piastre piece each. "This is to spend in Egypt!" We all laughed, for they were only worth about five English pence each.

The meal at Muhammad's flat – everyone affectionately called him 'Mimi' – was a feast. There was meat, which we had not tasted for a month, and vegetables, and rice, and foules mesdames, and salad, and bread, and fruit, followed by good strong coffee. Before we left, Muhammad gave us each a fresh clean change of clothes, and a good strong hug, wishing us a good journey and an acceptable Hajj at the end of it. Strengthened by the food and warmed by his friendliness, we made our way back to Ibrahim's flat and gazed out over Athens at night for the last time, before falling fast asleep.

Ibrahim had Saturday morning off, and came down to the docks at Pirraeus to see us off. We had a coffee together, and then with the last of our money bought some dried bread, oranges and water. It was time to leave and we were sad to go. We had come to enjoy our existence in Athens and the warmth and friendliness of the people at the Muslims' Cafe, and especially the gentle, good-natured company of Ibrahim. Having said goodbye and thankyou, for the Prophet said that if you do not thank people then you have not thanked Allah, we boarded the ferry. Moments later it sounded its siren and sailed majestically out of the harbour – with the three of us aboard! Miraculously we were on our way once again, penniless but extremely well, standing at the rails of the ship and watching the outline of the mainland grow smaller and smaller, as the wide expanse of the sunny Mediterranean opened itself up to us.

◦ ◦ ◦

Once we were well out to sea, we sat down on the striped cotton rug that Abdal-Alim had given me before we left England, and enjoyed a simple meal of dried bread and oranges and water, with the deck beneath us vibrating from the thrust of the ship's engines. There was a young man from England hovering nearby, and we invited him to join us and share our food. It transpired that he too was bound for the Sudan. Having approached numerous companies in his search for sponsors, he was now equipped with a landrover and two months' supply of food as well as all sorts of traveller's accessories, even down to water-purifying tablets. I did not envy him in the least. Somehow, travelling the way we were travelling, knowing that we were utterly dependant and reliant on Allah, was far more adventurous and exciting. He, on the other hand, did not envy us in the least, glad that he had the apparent security of his own transport and food and money supplies.

Before leaving our company, he imparted a great secret to us: "I hear there is a password that they use in North Africa that is said to open all sorts of doors. I don't know what it means, but I have it written down here somewhere. A lorry-driver in Morocco told me it. Perhaps it will be of use to you!" Almost looking over his shoulder to make sure no one was looking, he pulled out his note-book and looked through it. "Ah! Here it is! The password is ... `La ilaha il'Allah – Muhammad ar-Rasulu'llah'! Do you know what that means?"

"Certainly," we replied smiling at each other. "It means `There is no god except Allah – Muhammad is the Messenger of Allah'. It is the beginning and end of all true knowledge and wisdom. If it were not for this password we would not be here now!"

"I see," he said, not seeing at all, but nevertheless writing down the translation in his note-book. "Well, thank you very much. See you around. Hope you have a good journey." And with that he disappeared out of our lives.

○ ○ ○

That evening, after praying maghrib and isha out on the finely foam sprayed wind swept deck, we took shelter in the TV lounge. The next two hours were spent watching Barbara Dickson singing Beatles songs.The programme was very enjoyable, but somehow very strange. After our month in Athens which had been spent largely in the company of Muslims from North Africa, it was difficult to relate to the whole conceptual framework to which the songs belonged. Although the Beatles pop song genre was very much a part of the culture in which we had been brought up and from which we had recently come, it was alien to the culture we were now approaching. On reflection it became clear to me that our month in Athens had been in order to give us time to acclimatise to this change gradually, so that when we finally arrived in North Africa, the impact would not be so marked and there would be less danger of any of us suffering from the culture-shock bends.

Once the programme was over, we had another meal of dried bread, oranges and water, and then tried to catch what sleep we could on the passenger seats that were available. The moon was full once again and we were on the move again, tanned, healthy, accustomed to the mid-summer Mediterranean heat and ready for anything. Only Allah knew where we would be when the next full moon came round. After watching the frothing wake of the ferry in the moonlight for a long while, I found myself a space and slept until morning, when, shortly after praying subh and eating the last of our dried bread and oranges, we steamed into Heraklion harbour in Crete.

CRETE

Once the ferry had docked, we shouldered our small travel bags and disembarked. We had to change ferries here, and the ferry for Alexandria did not leave until six o' clock the next morning. Longingly we eyed the waterfront cafes. A good hot cappuchino and cake would have been just what the doctor ordered, but we had no money. We would have to do without. We decided to walk westwards out of Heraklion in the hope of finding a beach where we could rest and maybe even have a swim. We had not slept very much the night before, partly out of excitement, and partly because ferry passenger seats always seem to have been designed with the specific intention of keeping any one who sits on them uncomfortable and wide awake. Feeling a little the worse for wear, we walked out of Heraklion with the sun already feeling hot on our backs. It was going to be a hot day.

After passing through what appeared to be the poor part of town, we finally left Heraklion behind us, and after a mile or two eventually came to a beach where the water did not seem to be dirty. After washing in the sea and doing wudu, we prayed dhur and asr, and then began to look for shelter from the fierce sun. The only possible source of shade in sight was what appeared to be a deserted building on the other side of the coast road. We approached it cautiously and peered inside through the dirty window panes. There was nothing there other than a few planks of timber and large mounds of sawdust. Surely no one would mind if we sheltered there until the heat of the afternoon was over. We tried the door. It was unlocked. Thankfully we entered into the building's cool shade, and, overcome with tiredness we sank down onto the soft wood sawdust and fell asleep. After what must have been only a few minutes, I surfaced momentarily and opened an eye. The breeze that drifted slowly through the building had slowly been covering us with a fine coating of sawdust, so that we were almost a part of the mounds on which we lay. I smiled and sank slowly back into oblivion.

❀   ❀   ❀

When I next awoke, it was to find a large smiling bearded face looking into mine, with an even larger tray stacked high with freshly cut water-melon held before it. Brushing the sawdust from my clothes, I woke Abdal-Jalil and Mustafa, slightly alarmed that we were trespassing. Although we had no language in common, however, the man made it clear that we were most welcome, his weathered face forever smiling as he invited us to eat. As we thankfully sank our teeth into the cool juicy thirst-quenching water-melon, our host disappeared, only to return a few moments later with more food, a steaming bowl of meat stew and big hunks of fresh crusty bread. We would have loved to have eaten the stew, but concluded that it was probably made with meat that was not halal. Reluctantly we tried to explain that we were Muslims, and would only eat the meat of animals which had been killed in the name of Allah by cutting the jugular vein so that all the blood – which contains many impurities – could drain from the carcase. Trying to explain what halal meat is in sign language is not an easy matter – although not as embarrassing as asking where the toilet is in sign language – but our easy-going host understood that we were unable to eat the stew for whatever reason, and, without appearing to be in the least bit offended, he disappeared with the dish and then shortly reappeared with yet more food, cheese and oranges this time, which we thankfully ate with the bread until we were satisfied. As we ate, all his children appeared, seven of them, and after solemnly greeting us were soon larking about in the sawdust, laughing and playing without a care in the world.

By now it was late afternoon, and we decided that it would be best to return to Heraklion so as to be sure that we were there to catch the ferry early the next morning. Having thanked our generous host we returned the way we had come, convinced that he must be the hidden wali of Crete. Having found a patch of grass near the harbour jetty, we passed the night talking or snoozing, and shortly after subh our ship arrived, we boarded it and off it sailed, next stop Alexandria.

ALEXANDRIA

Having spent the day basking in the sun, and the night sleeping as best we could, daylight found us again with the North African coast clearly in view. As we approached Alexandria, the sea abruptly changed colour ahead of us, from deep Mediterranean blue to milky brown. It was as if a line had been drawn from east to west, and the sea coloured differently on the other side. I realised that this must be the water from the river Nile, and that what we were seeing was what is described in the Qur'an: Two seas, one salt, one sweet, which meet but do not mix.

We watched the harbour of Alexandria come closer and closer, gazing in anticipation at the longshot view of the ancient city with its tall graceful palm trees, until it was time to go below and complete the immigration formalities. Fortunately our passports were stamped while we were still on board the ferry. The remaining customs and immigration formalities were to be conducted once we were ashore. We were slightly apprehensive about this part of the proceedings, since it would probably be necessary to inform the customs officials where we would be staying and to prove that we had sufficient funds to finance our stay, neither of which we could do. We would just have to see what happened.

Our passports were routinely stamped, the ship docked, and we disembarked. Fortunately, the building in which the remaining customs and immigration formalities were to be conducted was a good half a mile's walk away along the quay. Every two hundred yards or so, there was a road which led off into the city, but there were guards posted at each entrance, and it was clear that there was going to be no easy escape into the city that way. As we drew closer and closer to the building in which the officials might turn us back, I recited Surat' al-Fatiha, the opening Sura of the Qur'an, which means the Opening, or the Victory, and asked Allah for an opening out of our situation:

In the Name of Allah the Merciful the Compassionate

> Praise to Allah, Lord of the worlds,
> the Merciful the Compassionate,
> King of the Day of the Life-Transaction.
> Only You we worship and only You we ask for help.
> Lead us on the straight path,
> the path of those whom You have blessed,
> not of those with whom You are angry,
> and not of those who are astray.
>
> Amin.
>
> (Qur'an: 1.1-7)

As if in answer to my prayer, an opening literally appeared before our eyes, for suddenly there in front of us was a hole in the wall, placed strategically between two of the guarded access roads and a good quarter of a mile from the customs and immigration building. We paused, looked around us, and when no one appeared to be looking, zipped through the hole in the wall like escaping convicts, to find ourselves on the road that led from the customs building into Alexandria.

Nonchalantly but swiftly we hurried down the road towards the city, expecting to hear official sounding shouts behind us every second of the way, but thankfully not hearing them. In no time at all we had been swallowed up in Alexandria's busy streets. We had arrived! Al-hamdulillahi wa shukrulillah!

We decided that the best and first thing to do was to go to the tomb of Shaykh Abu'l-Abbas al-Mursi, one of the exalted teachers in the long line of teachers that stretched, without a break in the chain of transmission of wisdom, from the Prophet Muhammad, may the blessings and peace of Allah be on him and all his true followers, to our teacher, Shaykh Abdal-Qadir. Stopping the next old man with a beard and turban who passed by us, we asked for directions and were delighted to find that Shaykh Abu'l-Abbas was buried very close by. On our way there, we stopped and bought some bread with the few piastres which Ramadan had given to us in Athens, which already seemed far away and a long time ago.

Our simple meal was soon eaten, and minutes later we had found the mosque inside which this great wali of Allah is buried, done wudu, greeted the Shaykh, and done two rakats, the customary courtesy on entering a mosque. We sat back and basked in the peace of the mosque, grateful, elated and tired. We were here at last, at the top of Africa, in a land where the way of Islam was an accepted social norm and not the exception to a general ignorant rule. I literally sighed with relief.

We spent the rest of the day resting and catching up with ourselves, not exactly sure what to do next, but in no particular hurry, soaking in the baraka of the presence of Abu'l-Abbas al-Mursi's ruh, which is undeniably there. The baraka of the awliya is a subtle energy which emanates from the ruh which is pure light. Whoever is near the ruh of a wali, whether it be in his body or in his grave or in a true dream, experiences its baraka, just as those who stand in the sunlight feel its energy, and just as those who dive in the ocean feel its wetness.

Although there was a constant flow of people in and out of the mosque, no one approached us or bothered us, and it was during this resting space that we decided that we must visit the tomb of Shaykh Abu'l-Hasan ash-Shadhili, the renowned teacher of Abu'l-Abbas al-Mursi, although we did not have the faintest idea where he was buried. Insh'Allah we would be guided to where his tomb was, and this was one of the many favours that we asked of Allah that day.

After the times for dhur and asr, which we prayed behind the Imam of the mosque, had come and gone, several people came over and questioned us – who we were, where we had come from, where we were going. A couple of them asked us if we needed anything, but then looked rather uncomfortable when we said that we did, and we soon found that it was best to hide our need, whether it was real or imagined. As the Prophet once said, poverty is beautiful when it is secretly hidden, and ugly when it is openly displayed. Accordingly, when any one else asked us if we needed anything, we would say, "No thank you, everything is fine, alhamdulillahi wa shukrulillah," secure in the knowledge that Allah was perfectly aware of our needs, and increasingly firm in the expectation that He would satisfy them. As Allah once said on the tongue of the Prophet Muhammad in a hadith qudsi, "I am in the expectation of My slave." As always, I was aware that there is usually a large difference between what we want and what we need, but this did not prevent me from placing a very great expectation in my Lord, Allah.

After maghrib, for which the mosque was virtually full, an energetic old man wearing the distinctive red and white turban of Al-Azhar University walked directly up to us, sat down, and started reciting Surat Ya Sin, which is often called the heart of the Qur'an and which ends with this very direct statement:

> Surely His command when He intends a thing
> is only that He says:
> "Be!"
> and so it is.
> So glory to Him in Whose hand
> is the dominion over all things,
> and to Him you will be brought back.
>
> (Qur'an: 36.82-83)

We sat down and joined in the recitation as best we could, although none of us knew the whole Sura by heart, reminded that we were completely helpless in the decree of Allah, and wondering what was going to happen next. After the recitation was completed, he greeted us, welcomed us, asked us the usual questions, and then left.

The adhan for isha followed soon afterwards, and after we had prayed it the same man reappeared. He explained that in a couple of hours the mosque would be locked up for the night until it was time for the dawn prayer, and that no-one was allowed to sleep in the mosque overnight. However, he had prepared some straw mats for us outside where we could sleep without becoming cold, and there was some food there now if we would like to have something to eat. Gratefully we accepted his invitation, for our last square meal had been two days ago, in Crete, and we were feeling a little faint from hunger.

He led us out of the mosque, and round to one of its outside walls, where the mats and food awaited us. Having made sure we now had everything we needed, he bid us good night, brushing aside our thanks with a "Welcome! You are guests of Allah!" and leaving us surrounded by a group of young men who eagerly asked the questions which we had already answered so many times and which we had become resigned to answering again and again. What were our names? Where did we come from? Where were we going to? How long had we been Muslims? What had made us embrace Islam? Did we have any brothers or sisters? Were they Muslim? They were? – What made them embrace Islam? Were our parents Muslim? They weren't? – Why not? – Had we told them about Islam? And so on, until I for one began to feel a little irritated in my tiredness. The Prophet did not usually talk very much after isha, and I tried to do likewise, concentrating on our simple but most enjoyable meal, and keeping my replies to a minimum. They were questions we were to be asked again and again, by nearly all except the very wise, sometimes out of genuine interest and sometimes just for something to say. Interestingly enough, the answer to the same question often varied, depending on who had asked it. At last we were left alone to have a much needed sleep, and soon we were out for the count, totally relaxed in the balmy warm night air.

The next morning we changed out of our western clothes and into our robes and turbans. Since we no longer needed our western clothes, we decided to try and sell them, in the hope of raising enough money to pay for our fares to Cairo. We wandered along the palm tree lined streets, asking shop-owners if they wished to buy our clothes. They were not in prime condition to say the least, and we were not at all surprised to discover that no one was particularly interested in purchasing them. The manager of a garage was just rummaging through them, when Abdal-Jalil asked if we could have some water to drink, for it was much hotter in Alexandria than it had been in Athens, and our bodies were still in the process of readjusting, which meant that we still became terribly thirsty very easily.

A young man who happened to be there said that he would go and fetch some and left. He returned soon afterwards with three large glasses filled with ice-cold water which we gratefully drank while the manager shrugged his shoulders and said that there was nothing worth buying in this lot. "I know where you can sell your clothes," said the young man. "Follow me." We downed the last of our water, and followed him.

The young man led us through the streets of Alexandria, through streets where the buildings on either side became increasingly more dilapidated and shabby, to what must have been one of the poorest areas of Alexandria, in which his parents lived together with their five children in a tiny two-roomed flat. A simple meal was immediately prepared for us by his mother as soon as we had arrived, while he disappeared for about half an hour. When we had all eaten until we were satisfied, we got down to business. Several neighbours appeared, and a light-hearted auction began, amidst much joking and laughing and mock-serious bargaining, for no one could take the matter seriously. Within forty minutes, we had sold all our western clothes, and now only possessed the robes and turbans we were wearing and a couple of changes of underclothes. Everyone was happy with the deal. Our customers had clothes which they would never have otherwise been able to afford, and we had enough money to pay for our fares to Cairo.

Our ever-attentive host informed us that the train would be leaving for Cairo and offered to take us to the station. We said goodbye and thankyou to everyone, all squeezed in that tiny flat, and followed the young man through the winding back streets of Alexandria, across a dusty park with a few dusty palm trees, and into the main railway station. Having bought us our tickets with our money, he gave us the change, made sure we were on the right train, and bid us Ma salaama with a wave and a smile, as if this was the sort of thing he did every day.

A few minutes later, the wooden slatted seats feeling very hard through our thin cotton robes and the sweat covering our entire bodies in the airless third class compartment, we pulled slowly out of Alexandria and crawled out of the city and through the rich date plantations and luscious green fields of the Nile delta, with the large red sun now hanging low in the sky as the earth continued its measured turn. It was hot and dusty in the train, although once we had picked up a little speed there was the semblance of a breeze in the air. The compartment was crowded but muted, for making even the most trivial conversation was an effort. Everyone sat in silence, mopping their brows, and waiting for the journey to come to an end. It was a far cry from the British Rail service that had whisked us smoothly and swiftly from Victoria to Gatwick in another world.

On the way to Cairo, we stopped for a few minutes at Tanta, where the man who had been sitting opposite us and with whom we had exchanged a few words was due to alight. He repeatedly asked us to break our journey at Tanta and stay with him as his guests. We could continue our journey in a couple of days. We were tempted to accept his invitation, especially since another great wali, Shaykh Ahmad al-Badawi, is buried there, but our sights were set on the Sudan, and Cairo was the next stop. We declined apologetically, determined to travel ever further beyond the point of no return, and soon we were trundling south again through the darkness of our second North African night.

CAIRO

It was already growing late when we slowly and finally pulled into Cairo. The poor street lighting glimmered in a haze of dust that had been left hanging in the air after another busy day. I had never seen anywhere so full of people before in my life. The whole city was choc-a-bloc with people. Where did they all sleep, I wondered, and how did they all get fed? We made our way through the hustle and bustle of Cairo train station and out into the city, walking a short way to stretch our legs, and stopping at a street vendor's stall to have a drink of kirkadi, a deep red ice cold drink made from dried out succulent desert flowers. In all my travels I have always drunk the same water as the locals drink, without any serious side-effects, and this journey was no different.

Having quenched our burning thirst, we paused to decide on the next step. We had the address of a well-known doctor in Cairo, Dr. Abdal-Munim Abu Fadl, whom, again, Abu'l-Qasim had met on his travels, and although it was late, we decided to see if he was in. We tracked down the whereabouts of the address with little difficulty, for it turned out to be the address of his clinic, which was situated fairly centrally, and, thank God, he was still there, although fortunately he had no more patients to see that day.

Dr. Abu Fadl, whose name literally means 'father of over-flowing generosity', welcomed us as if he had been expecting us and had only stayed on late at his surgery especially to see us. He sent his assistant out to bring some food for us, which turned out to be the inevitable and ever enjoyable foules mesdames, and asked after Abu'l-Qasim and everyone else whom we knew in common with evident warmth and affection. After we had all had tea together, Dr. Abu Fadl said we were welcome to spend the night at the clinic, and indeed to stay as long as we wanted. There were shower and toilet facilities, and the padded benches in the waiting room would be very comfortable to sleep on. It was so hot, that we had no need of any kind of bedding. Gratefully we accepted his offer of hospitality, and after he and his assistant had bid us good night, we all showered away the dust and sweat of the journey, before camping out in the waiting room, clean, well-fed, comfortable and content.

❂ ❂ ❂

We awoke next morning, excited and refreshed. The sounds and sunlight of Cairo flooded into the room as soon as we opened the shutters, and having washed and prayed two rakats each to make up for the dawn prayer which we had missed, we made our way down the large inner stairway and let ourselves out into the bright brand new day. Dr. Abu Fadl had given us a key to the front door, and arranged to meet us on Saturday, since the clinic would be closed today and tomorrow, today being Thursday and tomorrow being the day of the jumua. We found a simple cafe nearby, and decided what to do next, as we tucked into our coffee and croissants.

We had been given two other addresses by Abu'l-Qasim, one of a businessman who had contacts in the Sudan, and the other of a man who was the khalifa, or muqaddem, of Shaykh al-Fayturi Hamudah in Libya. We wanted to visit both of them, and decided to visit the businessman first of all, assuming that his office would be open today even though it was a Thursday. We walked through the crowded streets of Cairo, which seemed to have a mosque wherever you looked, gazing about us with interest. It was as if we were in a time warp, for many of the modern buildings had been built in the 1920s and 1930s, and many of the people who were dressed in western clothes still seemed to be following the fashions of that era. Simultaneously, the myriads of people who still dressed in robes and turbans if they were men, or long dresses and head shawls if they were women, gave the place an ageless, timeless look. This was emphasised by the sounds of the Qur'an being recited which continually filled the air. Admittedly what we were hearing were recorded tapes being played through loud speakers, rather than actual live people, but the overall effect was not like anything any of us had experienced before. I wished my knowledge of the Qur'an and the pure Arabic language was better, for if one could have understood all the ayat of Qur'an continually floating in the air, it probably would have been wonderful. As it was, I was clearly reminded of the fact that anyone who does not understand the Qur'an in the original Arabic – its outer and inner and gnostic meanings – is basically pretty ignorant, however much he or she knows. However much we know, we only know a little.

The man we visited was clearly a very successful businessman. He dealt in large trucks, the new camels of the desert, and his large showroom displayed the latest in the Mercedes range of heavy goods vehicles. Abu'l-Qasim had told Abdal-Jalil that a few years previously this man had wished to build a mosque with his surplus profits, as an investment for the future, but where, he wondered, could he build a mosque in a city already so full of mosques? His dilemma had been solved one night, when he had met Shaykh Abu'l-Abbas al-Mursi in a clear dream and had been told that if he wanted to build a mosque, then he should build one near the tomb of Shaykh Ahmad ibn Ata'illah, which is exactly what he had done. Shaykh Ahmad ibn Ata'illah was perhaps the most well-known follower of Shaykh Abu'l-Abbas al-Mursi, whose tomb we had visited two days earlier in Alexandria. Just as Shaykh ash-Shadhili had transmitted his knowledge and wisdom to Shaykh Abu'l-Abbas al-Mursi, so Shaykh Abu'l-Abbas al-Mursi had transmitted his knowledge and wisdom to Shaykh Ahmad ibn Ata'illah.

As soon as we entered the man's office, it was clear that he was no ordinary businessman. His lips were constantly moving in silent dua and dhikru'llah. A continual stream of visitors and paperwork flowed round his desk, interspersed with numerous 'phone calls which he answered in a quiet down to earth manner, and in the midst of this quiet but concentrated activity, he ensured that we were brought tea, asked us what we wanted and then suggested that we visit the zawiyya of Shaykh Abdal-Bourhani, who was a Shaykh in the Sudan with fuqara all over North Africa. He did not know exactly where the Cairo zawiyya was situated, other than that it was very close to the mosque of Sayyedina Husayn. Our conversation did not last more than five minutes, but it was to determine the way our journey unfolded all the way down to Khartoum. Our guide of the moment, who did not wear a beard or robe or turban, but an ordinary off the peg suit, was clearly not only a wali of Allah, but also a man who was much in demand. We excused ourselves during the next momentary lull in activity, wished him peace, and passed out of his life, gradually making our way through the ever crowded streets towards the mosque of Sayyedina Husayn.

○   ○   ○

We arrived at the mosque of Sayyedina Husayn, one of the grandsons of the Prophet Muhammad, just in time for maghrib. The Imam's voice was especially sweet and melodious as he recited the Qur'an from the depths of his heart, and the mosque was packed with people. It is said that Sayyedina Husayn is buried here, although there is also a tomb in Kerbala where he was originally martyred. Not knowing for sure where he is buried, I approached the tomb after the prayer and greeted him, making dua not only for him, but also for his brother Sayyedina Hasan, and indeed for all those who are descended from the Prophet Muhammad, may Allah bless him and his family and grant them peace in both worlds.

We eventually emerged from the mosque, surrounded by people on every side, and started to look for the zawiyya of Shaykh Abdal-Bourhani in the dusk. No-one we asked had even heard of it. Suddenly a majdhubba – a woman who is drunk with the Light of Allah – appeared as if from nowhere and pointed over our shoulders: "Zawiyya! Zawiyya!" she screeched, and then disappeared back into the crowd. We made our way towards the direction in which she had pointed, until we arrived at a row of doorways which all seemed the same. Suddenly the majdhubba appeared out of the darkness once again, this time pointing at one door in particular: "Zawiyya! Zawiyya!" she screeched once more, and was gone.

We knocked at the door and waited. It was soon opened by a young man with a withered arm. "Is this the zawiyya of Shaykh Abdal-Bourhani?" enquired Abdal-Jalil. It was indeed. Unfortunately the muqaddem, Hajj Mustafa, was not in at the moment, but was at his house in another part of Cairo. It would be best if we visited him there after the jumua tomorrow. The young man, whose name was Muhammad, invited us in for tea, and having written down Hajj Mustafa's address for us, took us back to the mosque to pray isha, after which we stopped off at a simple restaurant for some food and then returned to the surgery, more than ready for a good night's sleep.

◆ ◆ ◆

We awoke early the next morning to the sound of a thousand adhans as the slumbering city roused itself to worship the Creator of the Universe. Having done the prayer, we prepared for the jumua, each of us having a ghusl and putting on clean clothes. We had decided to go to the jumua prayer at the very famous Al-Azhar Mosque, the centre of one of the earliest universities in the world, which in fact turned out to be not very far from the Sayyedina Husayn mosque. After the jumua, insh'Allah, we would try and find Hajj Mustafa, although from what Muhammad had said, it appeared that he lived quite a way away.

We retraced our steps back to the Sayyedina Husayn mosque and on to the Al-Azhar Mosque, stopping along the way for a bite to eat and a glass of freshly crushed sugar cane juice which was extremely sweet. Immediately childhood memories of chewing sugar cane in the African bush flashed back through my consciousness, and for a moment I was just a little boy again in bare feet and a pair of shorts without a care in the world. It is amazing how powerful scents and tastes and sounds can be in triggering off memories of the distant past.

Having spent the last of the proceeds of our Alexandrian jumble sale on this refreshing treat, we entered the huge mosque of Al-Azhar in good time for the prayer, and having prayed two rakats, we made ourselves comfortable on the ancient carpets and recited the Qur'an or did dhikr until it was time for the jumua to begin. The mosque was lovely and cool, and it took a while for our eyes to adjust after the brightness and heat of the world outside. It was difficult to believe that only a week ago we had prayed the jumua prayer with a handful of people in our little basement mosque in Athens. As the time for the prayer drew closer, the mosque gradually filled up with every conceivable kind of person, many of them with the look of men who had spent their whole life remembering Allah. Every way of life leaves its mark on the one who lives it. Finally the adhan was given and the Imam began the khutba, after which everyone rose to do the jumua prayer, as they had been doing for virtually the last fourteen centuries. No wonder the mosque had the feel of a place where God has been continuously glorified and worshipped. How different it was to being inside a church or a cathedral. I remember Shaykh Abdal-Qadir once saying that in the time of the crusades, the Christians used to send spies to live amongst the Muslims, and in order to escape being observed they naturally had to live like Muslims, only to find that their quality of life was considerably enhanced as a result. "The Christians back in medieval Europe just couldn't understand why the spies never wanted to come back!" had laughed Shaykh Abdal-Qadir.

After the jumua prayer was over, we were approached by a tall smiling Sudanese man in a huge dazzling white turban and flowing djelaba. Having ascertained that we were bound for the Sudan, he shook his head and gave us a flashing confident smile: "You'll never do it. They won't let you in at the border." And then, contradicting himself, he said, "Please do call in and visit me if you get there. I am the chief of police in Omdurman. Everyone knows where I live." So saying, he produced an important piece of plastic with his colour photograph and official status preserved beneath it. As we said goodbye to him, I thought "This is one man whom we definitely won't visit!" The last time I had accepted an invitation from a policeman in a Muslim country, I had ended up in prison for three days, suspected of being a spy, because the chief of police, who was dedicated to emulating the example of his former French colonial masters, simply could not understand how anyone from the West could possibly have wanted to embrace Islam. We never saw him again.

We emerged from the peaceful coolness of the Al-Azhar Mosque into the blinding heat of the early afternoon sun, longing for a cold drink, but penniless once more. For the next couple of hours, we walked and walked, growing hotter and hotter, stopping every so often to ask passers by if we were heading in the right direction for Hajj Mustafa's address. "Please Allah," I begged, as my tongue began to feel like a piece of old leather, "Please don't make it too difficult." I busied myself with dhikru'llah as we walked on through the intense heat, remembering the ayat in the Qur'an which refer to the jumua prayer:

> O you who trust, when the call is heard for the prayer
> on the day of the jumua,
> Hasten to the remembrance of Allah
> And leave your trading.
> That is better for you, if only you knew.
> And when the prayer is ended,
> Disperse in the land and seek the bounty of Allah,
> And remember Allah much so that you will be successful.

(Qur'an: 62.9-10)

"We sure could do with some of Allah's bounty right now," I thought, as we walked on and on through the hot dusty streets.

Finally we arrived at Hajj Mustafa's door. He answered it himself, welcomed us, sat us down and placed large glasses of deliciously cold orange juice in our hands. He and his large family had been just about to eat, and as soon as we had quenched our thirst, space was made for us at the meal table, and what food there was was shared between everyone there. It was lovely. Roast chicken, vegetables and rice were followed by large dripping chunks of juicy red water melon. Life was possible once again!

As we ate, we explained who we were and what we hoped to do. Hajj Mustafa listened attentively, nodding his head in approval every so often, and became visibly excited when he heard that we wished to visit the tomb of Shaykh ash-Shadhili, who, as with our Shaykh, Shaykh Abdal-Qadir, had been one of the main teachers in the line of transmission of knowledge and wisdom from the Prophet Muhammad through to his Shaykh, Shaykh Abdal-Bourhani. He clapped his hands in delight. "You are our guests from now on!" he exclaimed. "Please stay at the zawiyya while you are in Cairo. When it is time to visit Shaykh ash-Shadhili's tomb, some of the fuqara will go with you. After that you can visit Shaykh Abdal-Bourhani in Khartoum. Do not worry about money! You are our brothers and you are guests of Allah! We will clothe you and feed you and pay for your train fares! Allah is Generous!" We were overwhelmed by his generosity and his welcome. And how well his promises were kept. This is true brotherhood in Islam.

After we had finished our meal, refreshed and replenished once more, Hajj Mustafa drove us back to the zawiyya himself, and instructed Muhammad, the young man who had first answered our knock at the zawiyya door, to look after us and be our guide in Cairo. His first task was to take us to a tailor who was to make a robe for each of us. Having made sure our every need was taken care of, Hajj Mustafa bid us farewell for the time being and disappeared back into the afternoon traffic.

Having called in at a tailor, who measured us up on the spot and had our new robes ready twenty-four hours later, we returned to the surgery and collected our few belongings, leaving the key with an explanatory note to Dr. Abu Fadl in a prominent place. We were back at the zawiyya in time for maghrib. After the prayer, we had a simple meal with a few of the fuqara, prayed isha, and then bedded down on the thin yet comfortable mattresses which had been provided for us. What a day it had been!

○ ○ ○

During the week that followed, we spent the time visiting several Shaykhs while we waited for our Sudanese visas to be issued by the Sudanese embassy, and in the process saw a great deal of Cairo. Muhammad was our constant companion for much of the time, and although we had no money – and did not ask for it from anyone – we were never hungry or thirsty for very long. Two of the Shaykhs whom we visited were very ill. Shaykh Hafidh was swathed in bandages, and slept much of the time that we sat quietly with him. He instructed one of his fuqara to bring us some mint tea which we gratefully drank, and having sung some Diwan, we quietly took our leave. Shaykh Salih had a high fever when we visited him. He was lying on a low bed surrounded by fuqara chanting "La ilaha il'Allah", and having shook each of our hands, he sank back on the bed, plainly exhausted and in great pain. There was nothing we could do to help him, other than asking Allah to heal him, and so after only a very short time we departed. Muhammad also took us to meet Shaykh Abdal-Haleem, the head of the Al-Azhar University, who received us in his office with kind dignity. He asked us if there was anything that we needed, and when asked by Abdal-Jalil to write a letter requesting all Muslim authorities to grant us safe passage, wrote one out on the spot. He asked us if we had any other questions, and I asked if temporary marriages were permitted. I already knew what his answer would be, but had recently read some of the **Travels of Ibn Batuta**, and was still wondering how he seemed to have managed to have a new wife wherever he went and keep within the limits of the Shari'a. The Shaykh Al-Azhar looked at me very seriously. "It is haram," he said.

Perhaps our most memorable meeting in Cairo was with Khalifa Ibrahim, the representative of Shaykh al-Fayturi, who was in Benghazi, in Cairo. Just as all the world's political leaders have representatives in different countries, so do all the world's true spiritual leaders. Just as the world's embassies are characterised by formality and protocol, so the world's zawiyyas are characterised by sincere courtesy and good behaviour.

Khalifa Ibrahim was the epitome of sincere spiritual courtesy, towards both the Creator and the creation. His father was descended from Sayyedina Hasan and his mother was descended from Sayyedina Husayn, and, like all people descended from the Prophet Muhammad, he possessed a nobility and radiance which commanded immediate recognition and respect. Khalifa Ibrahim took us to visit many of the descendants of the Prophet who are buried in Cairo, knocking at the entrances to their tombs and then waiting before entering, as if he would not move until he actually heard their greeting and invitation to draw closer in the unseen. At each tomb that we visited, he would give us something to drink, either some of the perfumed water that was there for whoever was thirsty, or else a bottle of coke from a nearby street vendor. In the evening we went to his simple zawiyya in the poor part of town for an evening of dhikr, in which we and his fuqara sang from the Diwans of both Shaykh Muhammad ibn al-Habib and Shaykh al-Fayturi, may Allah be pleased with them. Shaykh Abdal-Qadir once wrote that the singing of the Diwan "opens the seekers to a flowing and delightful condition in which the most exalted and purest experience of Divine Love is known." After a long strong hadra and a short simple meal, Khalifa Ibrahim asked the three of us to sing three more qasidas from the Diwan which we did and he taperecorded, before returning with us to the Sayyedina Husayn mosque. There he bought us some warm milk to drink at a nearby cafe, made dua for us, and then bid us "As-salaamu-alaikum wa rahmatullahi wa barakatuhu", embracing us firmly but warmly before disappearing into the crowds. Khalifa Ibrahim was a most courteous and humble man, and his face was so kind and luminous. We were like pigeons in his hands, fed and reassured, with our ruffled feathers all smoothed out, before being released for our onward flight.

❂ ❂ ❂

As well as visiting some of the living awliya in Cairo, we also decided to visit Al-Muqatim, where many of the awliya from the past are buried. Al-Muqatim, which literally means 'the place which has been cut out', is an extraordinary place, a city of the 'dead' –

although of course it is well known that when the body dies, the ruh, that is the spirit, does not die, for it is made of indestructible light. Much of Al-Muqatim has literally been cut out of the hills that used to surround Cairo in the past, although it now surrounds them, and many of the graves and tombs there have walls and roofs over them, so that from a distance it looks like just another suburb, with perhaps a lot less traffic than usual. It is only when you are actually there that you realise what it really is: a huge graveyard.

The first time that we went to Al-Muqatim, it was late in the afternoon, after asr. The first tomb we visited was that of Shaykh Muhammad al-Baqri. We were only inside the room which houses his tomb for about ten minutes, but in that short time the man who looked after the tomb had prepared a meal for us. The adhan for maghrib had just echoed all around us, so having done the prayer, we ate the meal, sitting outside on a woven palm leaf fibre mat. "I feed everything that lives around here," explained our host, tossing a little of the food we were eating into a nearby ditch and sprinkling a little sugar on one end of the mat for a small group of advancing ticks. "I feed everything – not only the people who come to visit the Shaykh, but also the cats and dogs and birds who pass by, and even the rats and ants in the ditch – everything!" He smiled benevolently, and stressed how important it was to be kind to one's parents: "Even if they are not Muslims, even if they are Kaffirs, you must honour them and be good to them. Even if they are harsh with you, you must not be harsh with them – because they looked after you when you were helpless. When I was at the Al-Azhar University, memorising the whole of the Qur'an by heart, people looked up to me and respected me, but my father still used to beat me if he thought I was being impolite or was not working hard enough, but I never became angry with him because he was my father, and because I loved him, even though he used to beat me."

We chatted on for half an hour or so, and then continued on our way, chancing upon the tomb of Shaykh ibn al-Farid, the Sultan of the Lovers of Allah, almost by accident, for at that time we did not even know that he was buried there. We stopped to make dua for him, and as always when visiting a wali, I asked Allah to give me what he had given him. As we were leaving, the keeper of the tomb handed us a most beautiful and exotic flower with delicate petals and an intoxicating perfume. It was as if the Shaykh had given it to us himself.

At last we arrived at the tomb of Shaykh Ahmad ibn Ata'illah, and the beautiful mosque which had only recently been built there by a wealthy businessman who loved Allah and His Messenger and His awliya. There were some old fuqara there doing dhikr together in a circle, and having greeted Shaykh Ahmad ibn Ata'illah and prayed two rakats, we sang some Diwan and then joined them until it was time to pray isha. After this we started to make our way back to the zawiyya, only to be re-routed by a man whom we met who offered to show us the tomb of Shaykh Ali Wafa, another of the teachers of our teacher who had written ravishing qasidas about the gnosis of Allah before dying while he was still relatively young. The tomb is housed in a large low-roofed building, and is surrounded by several tombs in which some of his close family and fuqara are buried. The place was clean and free of dust, and there were new straw mats on the floor. We could not resist the temptation, and sat ourselves down to sing yet more Diwan and do yet another hadra. By the time we had finished, it was very late, and we did not really have a clue how to find our way back to the zawiyya. Fortunately our guide was still with us, and he offered to show us the way back, guiding us through the quiet darkness of Al-Muqatim until we reached the land of the living once more.

On our way back to the zawiyya, our guide stopped by a relatively small mosque, and pointed through its entrance towards a simple tomb: "Imam Shafi'i," he said, "Imam Shafi'i." I was glad that we had been guided here, for Imam Shafi'i had been one of the most knowledgeable men about the Shari'a in his day. He had been one of the most well-known students of Imam Malik, memorising the entire Qur'an by heart by the age of seven, and **Al-Muwatta** of Imam Malik by the age of fifteen. One of his best known students had been Imam ibn Hanbal, who, along with Imam Malik, Imam Shafi'i and Imam Abu Hanifa became eventually recognised as one of the four major reliable transmitters of the Shari'a of Islam. We entered the mosque and having prayed two rakats, made dua. By now it was nearly dawn, so we waited for the adhan, prayed subh, and then continued on our way through the growing early morning light until we at last reached the zawiyya, more than ready for some rest, tired, drunken with dhikr and illuminated.

○   ○   ○

The adab of visiting the awliya is very fine, whether they are alive or in their graves, for although they are distinctively filled to overflowing with divine light, they can never be worshipped, and duas cannot be directed to them. It is, however, permissible and of great benefit to visit them, to greet them, to make dua to Allah for them and for others and for oneself, to do dhikru'llah in their presence, such as reciting the Qur'an or doing the prayer on the Prophet Muhammad or calling on Allah by His most beautiful Names, to bask in the baraka that unarguably surrounds them and then to leave them. The advantage in visiting them when they are still in their bodies is clear: They can teach you and guide you on the path that leads to gnosis of Allah, provided of course that they have the idhn, that is the permission, to do so. Idhn is from Allah and His Messenger.

❂ ❂ ❂

On another afternoon, we suddenly decided that we really should go and visit the pyramids while we had the opportunity to do so, and see the legacy of those who had so ignorantly and yet so cleverly opposed the prophetic teaching of Moses, peace be on him, with our own eyes. Clearly, visiting the tombs of the Pharaohs would be the antithesis of visiting the tombs of the awliya, since the former had rejected Allah and His Messengers, whilst the latter had accepted Allah and His Messengers. Light characterises those who accept. Darkness characterises those who reject. Everything lies in its opposite. Everything is known by its opposite.

We made our way to 'Freedom Square', a ghastly bare edifice of concrete walkways and imprisoning steel railings, whose name reminded me of the story of **The Emperor's Clothes** and whose appearance reflected the political situation in Egypt at the time, and eventually tracked down the right bus stop. Soon we were on our way, in a bus that became steadily more packed full of people as it went along, and then quickly emptied out as we began to reach the limits of the sprawling city. The three main pyramids were now clearly visible in the distance, lit up by the setting sun.

We did not arrive at the pyramids until just after sunset. Having prayed maghrib in the dusk, we looked at the mighty pyramids in wonder. They loomed high above us in the semi-darkness, their shape – which is the most stable form there is – clearly outlined against the dark blue sky. There was no one else in sight, not even a solitary camel to ride. Tourist time was clearly over for the day, and if we had wanted a souvenir right then, only the pebbles on the ground would have sufficed. We walked from one pyramid to the next, and around each one, almost gasping at the height and size of the huge stone blocks with which they had been constructed. I had been told that they had been built with the use of the jinn – some of whom are immensely powerful – and levitation, since the Pharaohs were well-versed in magic and the occult, and certainly, when faced with the raw magnitude of the pyramids, this seemed a far more plausible explanation of how this remarkable feat of engineering had been accomplished, rather than the usual scenario of thousands of weak and ill-fed slaves hauling these huge blocks of granite up ramps of earth on rollers made of tree trunks, which surely would have been crushed to splinters under the weight of such heavy blocks of stone.

We made our way to the Sphinx, which was in the process of being lit up by the lurid green and red and yellow lights of a son et lumiere show that no one else except ourselves was present to witness, the dramatic and poetic yet boring commentary in French evoking the memory of Napoleon's escapades in this part of the world, as the empty sounds echoed off into the empty darkness. I recalled the Asterix version of these events, as I looked at the inscrutable smiling face of the Sphinx with its chipped nose, and smiled. I still have not ascertained to this day whether or not it was Napoleon who fired a cannon at its face and so caused the damage, or whether it is just the result of the ravages of time and weather.

At one point, we started trying to climb the Great Pyramid, intending to do a hadra once we had reached its peak, but soon realised how difficult a climb it would be, especially since it was now very dark and besides which, robes are not the best garb in which to climb. Furthermore, the last bus would be leaving within the hour and we did not wish to miss it. Contenting ourselves with a short strong hadra at the pyramid's base, and a swift recitation of some Qur'an, we returned to the bus stop in good time and caught the bus back into town, first past the shanty towns of the very poor and then past the illuminated hotel casinos of the very ignorant, until finally we were back at just one of the zawiyyas of the very contented.

○ ○ ○

After we had spent a few days at the zawiyya, our passports were returned to us with the necessary visas for the Sudan now stamped in them. We were now ready for the next stage of the journey. Having visited Dr. Abu Fadl and his wife Zahara for supper, during which we thanked them both so much for having helped us so readily at a particularly difficult stage in our journey, and after a night of dhikr with Hajj Mustafa and his fuqara, we bade farewell to him and Muhammad and all the other fuqara who had kept our company in the zawiyya, and whom we had accordingly come to know well. Accompanied by three of the fuqara, of whom a short, plump, for ever smiling man called Hajj Ahmad was the leader, we were driven to the train station in a taxi, and soon the six of us were aboard a train which was bound for Aswan, to the east of which lay Humaysara, the place where Shaykh Abu'l Hasan ash-Shadhili is buried. In an almost unbelievably short space of time our intention to visit the tomb of this great saint, which we had made at the tomb of Shaykh Abu'l-Abbas al-Mursi in Alexandria, was becoming a reality. By the grace of Allah, our duas were being answered.

○ ○ ○

This train journey was very different to the one we had experienced when travelling from Alexandria. We sat in a cool air-conditioned compartment, wearing the new white robes for which Hajj Mustafa had so generously paid, eating regular well-cooked meals, as the train meandered southwards down through Egypt, in no particular hurry, always keeping near to the life-giving Nile and sometimes passing near some of the famous sites that tourists seek, but in which we were not interested. After many hours we arrived at our destination, a small town just north of Aswan, in which there was a Bourhaniyya zawiyya. Here we stayed and here I learned Surat al-Kafirun by heart from one of the fuqara, while we were waiting for Hajj Ahmad to arrange a taxi to take us to Humaysara. The meaning of this Sura is unequivocal, for it indicates a fundamental difference which cannot be fudged over through compromise:

In the Name of Allah the Merciful the Compassionate

> Say: O you who reject,
> I do not worship what you worship,
> and you do not worship what I worship,
> and I will not worship what you worship,
> and you will not worship what I worship.
> To you your way of life, and to me my way of life.
>
> (Qur'an: 109.1-6)

Hajj Ahmad returned to the zawiyya with a bigger smile than usual on his face. Everything was arranged. We would leave tomorrow morning early, immediately after we had prayed the dawn prayer and had our breakfast. Insh'Allah we would arrive safely!

HUMAYSARA

Our driver, who was ready and waiting for us when we emerged from the zawiyya in the early morning light, was a fat and cheerful fellow, forever cracking jokes and laughing, with the local radio blaring out Arabic music into the interior of the cab, as we headed out eastwards away from the Nile, with the sun just rising directly before us and dazzling us with its brilliance, and the inhospitable desert wastes of the Eastern Sahara stretching out in every direction. The patchy tar road soon became a patchy dirt road, and then just a patchy track through the stony desert. The car could not travel very fast, and yet it still managed to jolt us about uncomfortably in the steadily growing heat. If we opened the windows for air, we were smothered in dust. If we closed them to avoid the dust, we roasted. Gradually we fell silent. It was going to be a long, difficult journey.

Mid-day came and went. We stopped to pray dhur and asr, both of them shortened and joined now that we were on the move once again and doing travelling prayers, and had a simple meal of dates and bread and luke-warm water. This was rough country. It is said that it is never easy to reach a great wali, and that the greater a wali is, the more difficult the journey is to reach him. If this were true, I thought, then Shaykh ash-Shadhili must be a very great wali!

Deeper and deeper into the desert we travelled, hot, dusty and bumpy. A couple of times along the way, where the road forked, there were tombs of awliya. We stopped at each one, greeted their occupants, made dua and then continued our journey. It was as if each tomb was a kind of checkpoint charlie where our credentials had to be checked and cleared before we could safely continue our journey without the car breaking down.

Finally, when the sun was now mercifully low in the sky, and Abdal-Jalil and Mustafa and I had revived sufficiently to sing some Diwan, we rolled into Humaysara, Hajj Ahmad asking the taxi driver to stop by the first human being we saw, to whom he generously handed a high denomination note. Having thus made our good intentions evident, we followed the road towards the mosque and the tomb of the great Shaykh, as I reflected on the meaning of the qasida which we had just been singing:

REFLECTION

Reflect upon the beauty of the workmanship
with which the land and sea are made,
and openly and secretly busy yourself
with the attributes of Allah.

In the self and on the horizon
is the greatest witness
to the limitless perfections of Allah.

If you were to concern yourself
with the physical bodies and their perfection of form
and their inner connection, like a string of pearls:

If you were to concern yourself
with the secrets of the tongue and its articulation,
and its expression of what you conceal in your breast:

If you were to concern yourself
with the secrets of all the limbs
and the ease with which they obey the heart:

If you were to concern yourself
with the turning of the hearts to obedience,
and how they sometimes move to disobedience:

If you were to concern yourself
with the secrets of the oceans and its fish,
and its endless waves held back by an unconquerable barrier:

If you were to concern yourself
with the secrets of the winds,
how they bring the mists and clouds which bring down rain:

And if you were to concern yourself
with the secrets of all the heavens, and
the Throne and the Footstool and the spirit of the Command:

Then you would believe in tawhid with a firm belief,
and you would turn from illusions, doubt and the other.

You would say:
'My God, You are my desire and my goal
and my fortress against evils, injustice and deceit.

You are my hope in providing for my needs,
and You are the One who rescues us
from evil and wickedness.

You are the Compassionate,
the Answerer to whoever calls upon You,
and You are the One who makes up for the poverty of the poor.

To You, O Exalted,
I have raised my pleas,
so hasten the Opening and the Secret, O my God,

By the rank of the one who is hoped for
on the Day of grief and distress, and the Day
of the coming of the people to the Place of Gathering.

May the blessings of Allah be upon him
as long as there is a gnostic who concerns himself
with the lights of His Essence in every manifestation,

And upon his family and Companions
and every one who follows his glorious sunnah
in prohibition and command.

(Diwan of Shaykh Muhammad ibn al-Habib)

Humaysara was an extraordinary place. We had travelled all day through the desert, without seeing another living being, and yet here, in the middle of nowhere, suddenly there was life: A tomb, a mosque, a small village, and people whose sun-bleached clothes had been bleached by the sun still further, people who looked as if they were from another world. I reflected on the account which Hajj Mustafa had given us in Cairo of how Humaysara had come to exist:

● ● ●

Like many great walis, Shaykh ash-Shadhili knew when he was going to die. When that time was close, he summoned his closest murid, Abu'l-Abbas al-Mursi, and told him to prepare two camels for a long journey.

"What for?" asked Abu'l-Abbas.

"You will see in Humaysara." replied his Shaykh.

The two men left Alexandria and made the long journey down to the south, following the Nile until Shaykh ash-Shadhili said that it was time to branch eastwards. When they had arrived in the middle of nowhere, they stopped. "This is Humaysara," said Shaykh ash-Shadhili. "In a few days I will die here. I want you to wash my body and bury it here. Do not worry about water. A small caravan of people will pass by just after I have died. They will have water and will help you. You must not ask them who they are or where they are from. When you have said the funeral prayer for me and have buried my body, they will leave. When they have gone, then return to Alexandria."

Shaykh Abu'l Hasan ash-Shadhili spent the rest of his life on the top of a small hill immersed in the remembrance of Allah. In a few days he died, and everything happened as he had foretold. Having buried and prayed for his master, Shaykh Abu'l-Abbas al-Mursi returned to Alexandria. At a later stage, those who came to visit his tomb discovered two wells nearby, one with salty water and one with sweet water. Eventually some people settled there, and the place became known as Humaysara.

Thankfully the car came to a halt outside the mosque of Humaysara, and thankfully we alighted from it, our bodies still gently vibrating with the jolting they had received. It was almost time for maghrib, and we prepared for the prayer, doing wudu with the salty water, and drinking the sweet water. After the prayer, we approached the simple tomb with the plain carved wooden grill around it, and greeted and made dua for its occupant. The place was immensely silent. There was no electricity and no traffic. It was very peaceful. I was very conscious of being alive, and very aware of how amazing it is to be alive.

Later, after we had prayed isha, we feasted on the goat which some of the villagers had killed and cooked for us, sitting on the thick rug that lay on the floor of the guest house which had been built for people such as ourselves. After we were replete, we sat outside in the chilly desert night, quenching our thirst from waterskins that held the cool sweet water of Humaysara, and gazing in wonder at the myriads of stars that filled the desert sky. We were in the last two or three days of the lunar month of Shaban, the month before Ramadan begins, and so there was no moon, even somewhere below the horizon – just millions and millions of shining stars in a clear, clear sky in the vastness of space. There was a deep silence all around us which gave one the same feeling that you experience when you swim in mid-ocean, aware of the great depths that stretch down below your flimsy floating body. It was so beautiful and peaceful and protected. No wonder it was a difficult place to reach. How different it was to any of the capitals of the 'civilised' world! Having drunk our fill, we retired to the sleeping room in the guest house, and snuggled up in the thick warm blankets that had been provided for us, glad to be horizontal and still, and in a moment, we were deeply asleep, tired after a long day's travelling.

We awoke to the penetrating sound of the adhan for subh. Some people love it and some people hate it, but either way, it certainly wakes you up! Fortunately, I have always loved the sound of the adhan, even from the days before I had embraced Islam when I first heard it in Iran and Morocco, without having the faintest idea what its words meant:

> Allah is greater. Allah is greater.
> I witness that there is no god but Allah.
> I witness that there is no god but Allah.
> I witness that Muhammad is the Messenger of Allah.
> I witness that Muhammad is the Messenger of Allah.
> Come to the prayer. Come to the prayer.
> Come to success. Come to success.
> Prayer is better than sleep. Prayer is better than sleep.
> Allah is greater. Allah is greater.
> There is no god but Allah.

We arose immediately, the cold dawn air soon waking us up, and the cold salty water making us fully alert as we did wudu. The stars which had shone so brightly during the night were now beginning to glimmer and fade in the first light of dawn. After doing the dawn prayer and reciting our wird, which took about twenty minutes, by the tomb of Shaykh ash-Shadhili, we made dua for the Prophet and his family and his companions and all his sincere followers, especially for all the teachers who formed the human chain of transmission of knowledge and wisdom between the Prophet Muhammad and our teacher, Shaykh Abdal-Qadir al-Murabit. We prayed for all the genuine Shaykhs who teach with idhn and for all their fuqara, and we prayed for all the Muslims who follow the Prophet with sincerity in what they are able. Lastly, we prayed for ourselves, renewing our intention to go on the pilgrimage to Makka, and asking Allah to make it possible, and to give us a good time along the way, protecting us from the evil that He had created, and exposing us to the good that He had created, and always putting us in the company of the ones that He loves. Having completed our dua, we returned to the guest house, and after enjoying a simple breakfast of bread and tinned jam and tea, we strolled outside and watched the day unfold in Humaysara.

As the sun rose, we watched all the livestock, mainly camels and goats with their young, being watered at the two wells. Since all the water had to be pulled up by hand, not a drop was wasted. This was an art which by now we were beginning to acquire, and even the memory of the taps which I carelessly used to leave running in England would make me shake my head in disapproval.

After watching this pleasant scene for a while, we decided to climb the hill on the top of which Shaykh Shadhili had spent his last days on earth. There were two paths from which to choose, one which went straight up to the top, and another which zigzagged more gradually up the steep hill-side. We took the path which went straight up, which is always the way I like to do things, as I silently reflected on the ayat in the Qur'an which talk about 'the steep ascent':

> And what will tell you what the steep ascent is?
> It is to free a slave and to feed in the day of hunger
> An orphan near of kin, or some poor wretch in misery,
> And then to be of those who trust,
> And who counsel one another to be patient,
> And who counsel one another to be merciful.
>
> **(Qur'an: 90.12-17)**

Having reached the top of the hill, which was in fact much higher than it had at first seemed, we looked around us with awe. The rugged hilly desert stretched away majestically in every direction to the horizon. Other than the small village below, there was not a single sign of life to be seen. I tried to imagine what it must have been like for Shaykh ash-Shadhili as he sat there alone, invoking Allah continuously, and waiting with perfect patience for his time to come.

Having returned to the mosque before it grew too hot, we spent much of the rest of the day sitting next to Shaykh ash-Shadhili's tomb doing dhikr and resting. Dhur and asr came and went, and after maghrib we had a gathering of dhikr. It was Thursday night, laylat-al-fuqara or laylat-al-jumua as it is sometimes called, and the atmosphere was laden with baraka. We sang from the Diwan and did some of the dhikr to which Shaykh Abdal-Bourhani's fuqara were accustomed, and completed the gathering with a combined hadra, which alternated between the form which we knew and the form which Hajj Ahmad and the other two fuqara knew. There was no competition or conflict between us. The forms of remembrance may vary, but the One who is remembered is One:

In the Name of Allah the Merciful the Compassionate

**Say: He is Allah, the One,
Allah, the Everlasting.
Nothing is born from him
And He was not born from anything.
And He is not like any thing.**

(Qur'an: 112.1-4)

After isha, we retired to bed. Ramadan was in the air. In that pure place you could almost sense its approach and feel its baraka in the wind that blew gently from the east, or was it from the Garden itself?

We had to leave the next day, since our ferry down the Aswan Dam was due to leave on the Saturday, and as soon as we had prayed the jumua prayer, we were off, seeking the bounty of Allah once more and elsewhere. We bid "As-salaamu-alaikum wa rahmatullahi wa barakatuhu" to our generous hosts, and then set off back the way we had come, our driver humbled and turbanned, with a recording of some of the Qur'an playing in the taxi's cassette player. On the way back we stopped for a drink at a well which I had not noticed on our outward journey. I watched with admiration as a wiry camel trader filled his old paraffin tin from the rough rubber bucket without spilling a drop, his family waiting silently nearby in the sparse shade of an acacia tree.

As is the case with many journeys, the return journey seemed much shorter than the outward journey, and we were safely back at the zawiyya in time for isha. There were many fuqara there, and when the Imam began to lead the tarawih prayers, which are only done during the blessed month of Ramadan, almost immediately after the prayer, I realised that the new moon of Ramadan must have been sighted, and that the month of fasting had begun. This was confirmed during the feast which was unexpectedly laid before us after the tarawih prayers were over, as everyone prepared themselves for the first day's fasting. We were told that the ferry for Wadi Halfa would be leaving from Aswan after asr the next afternoon, and that we would be taken there in good time to catch it.

That night I smiled with gratitude in the midst of the peace that always comes with Ramadan. It was hard to believe that this time a fortnight ago we had been in Athens, wondering whether or not we would be able to enter Egypt. Now we were just about to leave it!

ASWAN

Although Muslims are allowed not to fast during Ramadan if they are travelling – provided that they make up the days they have missed at a later stage – the Qur'an does say that it is better for you if you do fast. Accordingly we decided to fast while we travelled, even though this might entail some hardship at times. I had always tried to avoid being in debt whenever possible, and besides which, I had always found it so much easier fasting during Ramadan than at any other time of the year, that making up days missed at a later stage always seemed to involve more difficulty than actually fasting difficult days in Ramadan, even in those exceptional situations when one was not obliged to do so.

It usually takes one's metabolism two or three days to accustom itself to the fasting pattern, especially if one does not fast regularly all the year round, and accordingly we took things very easy on our first day of fasting, resting quietly in the zawiyya until it was time to drive to Aswan to catch the ferry. It was the hottest time of the year in the Sahara, and my previous four fasts of Ramadan had taken place in a much cooler environment. As is often the case when one is faced with a new experience, I was a little apprehensive as to whether I would be able to survive fasting in such heat, and was very careful to breathe through my nose and not my mouth so as to avoid losing precious moisture. As with all my other anxieties before earlier months of Ramadan, my fears turned out to be largely unfounded, and as before, I was able to conclude from experience rather than through rational thought, that the One Who has made the fast of Ramadan obligatory, has also made it possible.

After dhur it was time to be on our way. Hajj Ahmad and the other two fuqara from Alexandria were also starting out on their journey back up north that day, and we shook hands firmly and embraced each other, united not only by our way of life, but also by the journey that we had shared together. They had been so generous to us, both with their money and with their selves, and had shown what true brotherhood is.

Two of the fuqara from the zawiyya at which we had been staying drove us into Aswan, past the mighty wall of the Aswan Dam, and up to the departure point for the ferry at the edge of the lake which lay on the other side of it. I had been to Lake Kariba during my childhood, but this was a much larger expanse of water, and I would not like to be around when the time finally comes for the wall to go. As we said goodbye and thank you, one of the fuqara handed Abdal-Jalil a Sudanese five pound note, which he accepted thankfully. This was the only money we had, and we had no idea how much the tickets for the ferry would cost.

All the people who were waiting to board the ferry began to move forward, and we just joined the general movement, silently reciting Surat'al-Fatiha, and asking Allah to put us on board that ferry. We passed through customs, had our passports routinely stamped, and walked up the shaky gang-plank on to the dilapidated Victorian paddle steamer that had definitely seen better days. No one stopped us, and no one asked to see our tickets. Lashed to the main boat was another smaller boat, with a sheltered area in the middle of the deck. This was already full up, mainly with families surrounded by large bundles of possessions and a few live chickens clucking away in their woven cages. There was room on its flat roof, but it was still very hot, and we would simply fry up there. Making our way up to the front of the boat, we were surprised to find an empty space up against the outside panelling of the sheltered area. Thankfully we sat down, a little shaky at the knees, and once we had regained our strength, we managed to rig up an awning by tying my striped rug to some convenient stays. This gave us the shade that we needed, for it was hot, very hot, the hottest time of the year, and we were parched!

It turned out that we had been among the first to board the ferry, and for the next hour or two, more and more passengers crowded on to the two boats, the men mostly wearing white djelabas and turbans and the women dressed in colourful swathes of brightly patterned cloth. After what seemed a long time, the ferry slipped its moorings and set off southwards down the vast Aswan Dam, crowded with people and low in the water, with its giant paddle swirling the waters purposefully behind us as the tired engines tried their best to move us in the right direction. The three of us sat at the bows with the lake stretching out before us, and the

Aswan 59

sun on our right now beginning to sink low into the western Sahara. It was very beautiful, and very natural. In this setting travel by 'plane seemed odd and uncommon, with its computerised standardised routines that ensure the swiftest of passages with maximum efficiency and the minimum of inconvenience. Here on the ferry, no one was in a hurry, and there was plenty of time to enjoy each moment. Insh'Allah we would arrive without the engine breaking down.

At last the sun finally disappeared altogether, and scooping up the lake water from the bow wave which was only about a foot below deck level, we each did wudu and then prayed maghrib and isha on our little patch of deck. Although we had neither food nor water, we did not have to worry about our provision. A small group of people, who, like us, had chosen to fast, invited us to join them in their meal, which we gladly did, sitting together crosslegged in their corner of the deck and gratefully quenching our thirst and only eating a little, for we were so thirsty that we did not feel at all hungry.

Shaykh Abdal-Qadir once said that outwardly the fast of Ramadan is like an illness, while inwardly it is a journey. I wondered where we would be by the time the end of Ramadan had arrived. Insh'Allah we would be in the heart of the Sudan. As the new moon appeared low over the western horizon for a while and then sank beneath it, followed closely by the evening star, I relaxed in the darkness as we chatted together, refreshed and cool beneath the stars, with the steady throb of the engines making the two boats shake and vibrate. The impossible had happened! We were well and truly on our way to the Sudan in the all-pervading baraka of Ramadan, and it had all unfolded in such a wonderful way that I personally could never have planned this adventure, even if I had owned the whole world. Allah's plan always turns out to be better than one's own plan.

Still thirsty, we tracked down the man who was making and selling tea. A fellow passenger refused to let us buy our own, and gratefully we sipped the glasses of strong black sweet tea that he handed us, answering the usual questions in a good natured manner, now that all our needs had been met. Later, we stretched out on the flat roof of the sheltered area, with the lake all around us and stars all above us, and fell fast asleep to the exciting sound of the throbbing engines and the churned up waters, undisturbed by the noise made by the other people in our floating village.

We awoke before dawn, chilled into wakefulness by the cold desert night, but, not realising just how hot the day would be, we hardly drank anything. It was a mistake which we did not repeat again. As the day unfolded and the sun rose higher in the sky, reflected a million times in a million little wavelets on the lake's surface, it grew hotter and hotter, until even the people who had always lived in the Sahara were finding it hot. Our make-shift awning was only partially successful in giving us shade, and there was no escape. Poor Mustafa did not know what had hit him, and for all our previous experience of warm climates, Abdal-Jalil and I were not much better prepared. It was a long hot day. The sun seemed to hang in the sky forever. We grew thirstier and thirstier, dazzled by the sparkling waters of the lake into which we longed to plunge.

We chugged on slowly but surely through the day and the heat, only stopping once, at a small island, to give the man who lived there some provisions. Apparently he was the weatherman, and knew the lake well. Insh'Allah there would be no storms during the next day or so, so it was safe to continue. On we went, and it seemed as if the sun would always be there, always shining down on us, and not for the first time I longed for one of those cold, wet, windy, English days that everybody always seems to complain about. In the end I had no choice but to become completely submitted to the situation, to accept that I was dried out and thirsty, and then of course I was able to enjoy it, once I no longer had any expectations of it being other than what it was.

At last the sun set. Again we were invited by some of those who were also fasting to share their food and drink. Gratefully we sank our teeth into cool juicy red watermelon chunks, soaking up glass after glass of water like sponges that had not seen water for years. In vain our more experienced hosts warned us not to drink too much, for otherwise we would not feel like eating anything and would grow weak. This was something we would learn in the days ahead, but on that particular evening the mercy of Allah that pervades the first third of Ramadan especially was definitely manifesting itself in the form of cool wet water. The Prophet Muhammad, may the blessings and peace of Allah be on him, said that those who fast have two rewards: One when they break their fast, and one when they meet their Lord.

As always during Ramadan, the difference between the day and the night was strongly emphasised, and now that we were free to eat and drink again, the day that we had endured already seemed long gone. We were grateful for it, for if we had not fasted during the day, we would not have enjoyed the delights of the night nearly as much. We chugged on through another deliciously cool night, and on waking up before dawn, made sure that we were fully tanked up with water before the call to prayer echoed out across the lake, signalling the start of our third day's fasting. As a result, we all had to go to the toilet an hour or two later, but at least we did not start the day off feeling thirsty as we had done the day before.

We had no idea how long our journey on the ferry was going to last, and by now time had become very elastic anyway, so that sometimes even a few moments seemed to stretch on forever. As it happened, we arrived at Wadi Halfa late that morning, and soon the ferry was tied up alongside the simple jetty, the gang-plank was in place, and everyone was gathering their belongings together and readying themselves to disembark. It was at this point that the ticket collector suddenly appeared and asked us for our tickets, about which, in the excitement of the journey and the difficulty of the fasting, we had completely forgotten. Abdal-Jalil proffered our Sudanese five pound note, but it was not enough. The full fare for the three of us was eight pounds. The only article of any value that we had was my striped rug. I asked the ticket collector to wait a few minutes while I tried to sell it, and approached a fellow traveller, asking him if he would like to buy it. He looked at it, told us to wait, and disappeared into the crowd.

While we waited, the ticket collector continued collecting fares from the other passengers, returning now and then to see what was happening. He was most apologetic about the whole matter, especially once he had realised that we were Muslims and were fasting, but he was only doing his job. We were just reassuring him and telling him not to worry about it, when our fellow traveller reappeared, his cupped hands full of loose change. "Bismillah," he said, giving it to us with a large smile, and refusing to accept the rug that I tried to give to him in return. When we counted the money up, it amounted to just over three pounds.

We gave the ticket collector all our money which he graciously accepted, and disembarked, thankful that that hurdle was behind us, but slightly apprehensive about what would happen next. On entering the small hot crowded customs building, we had to fill in a declaration stating how much money we had and where we were going to stay. This did not take long to complete. We had no money and no address to give. We handed our forms to the placid looking customs official. Silently I recited Surat'al-Fatiha. Surely, having come this far, and having tasted such generosity from virtually everyone we had met, we would not be turned back now.

The customs official looked at us, at our passports, at our declarations, and back at us again. "No money?" he said.

"Yes," we replied, "No money."

He paused significantly, looking at our documentation once again, perhaps not quite sure what to do about us, and in that moment a bearded turbanned man on the other side of the barrier called out, "Shaykh Abdal-Bourhani!" in a clear strong voice.

"Yes!" I replied, "Shaykh Abdal-Bourhani!"

"Shaykh Abdal-Bourhani?" queried the customs official.

"Yes," we all replied together, "Shaykh Abdal-Bourhani."

"Good," he said firmly, stamping our passports and letting us through the barrier, as if there was nothing more to say.

The man who had opened the way for us, greeted us warmly. He was the muqaddem of the Bourhaniyya zawiyya in Wadi Halfa, and had received a message from Hajj Mustafa in Alexandria that we were on the ferry. The train for Khartoum, he explained, did not leave until after isha that evening. Until then we could rest at his house. Gratefully we climbed into his landrover, and bumped along the dirt road to Wadi Halfa. Once again, the day had become extremely hot, and we felt drained of energy, tired and thirsty. As if he were reading my thoughts, the kind muqaddem turned towards me as we bumped along the uneven road. "Don't worry, we will pay for the train tickets." A few minutes later, all our anxieties about our provision now completely dispelled, we were lying flat out in our generous host's house, thankful for the breath of wind that stole past the curtains through the open window and over our hot tanned faces. Al-hamdulillahi wa shukrulillah! We were in the Sudan and we were still alive. Just!

WADI HALFA

The rest of the day passed like a slow dream, and finally, when sunset came, we thankfully broke the fast with dates and fresh iced lime squash, sitting out in the courtyard on woven palm leaf mats. After praying maghrib and isha, we were given meat and vegetables and a kind of unleavened bread made from durra that was formed like thick folded pancakes. This was followed by fruit and then hot sweet milky tea, served in what looked like Harrod's best china. As always, ease had suddenly followed hardship, and once again we were contented and grateful. Our host did not know very much English, and our Arabic was still very poor, so our conversation was very simple and limited, but it did not matter. It was so good just to be in his company. We sat outside in the cool of the evening and relaxed.

After we had finished our tea, it was time to catch the train, and in no time at all we were comfortably seated in our second class compartment, chatting with our most generous host, until the train finally began to chuff slowly out of the station, whereupon he bid us farewell and jumped off the slowly moving train with a kind smile and one last "As-salaamu-alaikum." We were off! I hung out of the window looking at the loose sprawl of the new Wadi Halfa, for the old Wadi Halfa was now buried deep beneath the waters of Lake Aswan, excited like a child to be behind a steam engine once again. The last time I had been on a steam engine had been in Russia, and it seemed an age ago. So much had happened since then. Insh'Allah this time tomorrow we would be in Khartoum!

I was wrong. Half an hour later the ancient steam engine started to have difficulties, and began to move more and more slowly until at last the decision was taken to return to Wadi Halfa for essential repairs. It was well past midnight when we chuffed slowly out of Wadi Halfa once again, with much clanking and creaking, and headed out once more into the depths of the desert and the fourth of Ramadan.

○   ○   ○

We must have drifted off to sleep, for when we awoke at dawn, everything was silent and still. The train was not moving. The ageing steam engine had finally broken down completely, and we would have to wait until a replacement engine had arrived from Khartoum before we could continue our journey. For the time being we were stranded in the middle of the Nubian desert, somewhere between Wadi Halfa and Abu Hamad. We prayed subh out on the fresh clean cool sand beneath the perfect dome of the sky, and then began to wait, not knowing how long we would have to wait, but pretty certain that it would be quite a while.

We waited and waited as the sun moved imperceptibly higher and higher in the sky and the day grew hotter and hotter, the lone and level sands stretching far away in every direction. By noon the carriages had become ovens, and sitting outside in the sun was not any cooler. We found that the best place to be was lying between the tracks on the sleepers in the shade beneath the carriages, although even here the slight breeze that wafted in from the desert was still very hot. It was not the best of conditions in which to fast, but even if we had decided not to fast, we had no food or drink or money with us, we had no wish to beg, and so it was easier just to close down all systems and continue fasting. I recalled my Shaykh's words: "If you ever have any anxiety about your provision, then fast for the day, and just see what happens when maghrib comes!"

At last, at some point during the afternoon, when there was enough shadow on the eastern side of the train to be able to sit in it and be protected from the sun's rays, our replacement engine arrived, and soon we were on our way, chuffing through the vast expanse of sand that surrounded us. The flat desert reminded me of the descriptions I had read of what it will be like on the Last Day, when the oceans have all dried up, and the mountains have disintegrated into dust and dissolved like clouds, so that all that remains is a vast silvery plain of sand, on which all the people who have ever lived will be brought back to life and gathered together and then separated between the Garden and the Fire.

Later on in the afternoon, we rejoined the Nile, which had been looping out to the west of us and back all the while as we chuffed steadily southwards, stopping briefly at Abu Hamad to let some people off and more people on. It was refreshing to see green again, green plants and green date palms, and animals, camels and goats, and people, people who belonged to this kind of life, life sustained by the waters of the Nile. Life! I remember reading that the Prophet said that the Nile is one of the rivers of the Garden. We watched with interest at the busy activity which filled the station, which was more like a market place than anything else. Amidst the coming and going of travellers, people were busy selling fresh dates and fruit and bread, or brewing up milky tea or fresh coffee over small portable earthenware charcoal stoves. Others lugged large buckets filled with bottled drinks and large chunks of ice, shouting out their wares. Business was brisk and lively, and after our delay in the hot desert, the drinks and fresh fruit merchants must have done especially well. As the train slowly made its way southwards, stopping off at every little station that we passed, the same scene greeted us again and again. It was so good to see this dynamic pattern of life flourishing, so different to the carefully monitored and regulated pattern of life on British Railways, where the only food you could buy was factory food from the dining car or station cafeteria, carefully packaged in plastic and served by someone in a uniform.

By the time the sun finally set on what must have been one of the longest days of my life, we were parched and hungry. Again, however, just before maghrib, some fellow fasters from another carriage, whom we had not even met or noticed, invited us to join them and share their food and drink as soon as the sun had set. This was to be a familiar pattern throughout our travels in the Sudan. Everyone shared their food with each other. How different to the commuter trains of the civilised high-tech north, where people are often far too busy being busy to even be aware of another's hunger other than their own, or too conditioned to consider feeding a fellow human being who is not connected by family, friendship or business ties.

Having prayed maghrib and isha, and quenched our thirst and eaten our fill, we trundled on through the night, hot and dusty and sweaty, through Atbarah and onwards through the night, enjoying the adventure of it all in spite of the hardship. None of us had ever been on a journey quite like this, where nothing was planned and anything could happen, and where there was simply none of the illusion of security that advance bookings and travel insurance and credit cards and travellers cheques sometimes provide. Never had I felt so helpless and so free. I could not 'prove' that Allah would provide, but I was certain that He would. On and on we travelled in our ancient carriage in the night, until finally, in the early morning sunlight, we rolled into Khartoum, tired and dusty, but there!

KHARTOUM

After leaving the station, we looked around us with interest at the new world in which we had just arrived. Khartoum was certainly very different to Cairo, more spread out, less crowded, more raw, and not so busy. We walked down the wide tree-lined streets with their low buildings and open ditches on either side. They reminded me of Tehran, although of course the Tehran I had visited in the days before I had embraced Islam had been a far more sophisticated city, both in the ancient and in the modern sense of the word.

Gradually we made our way towards the zawiyya of Shaykh Abdal-Bourhani, asking directions from passers-by whenever we were unsure of our whereabouts. Fortunately, it turned out to be not too far away, and finally we arrived in the late morning, tired and travel-worn and almost speechless with the heat, for like mad dogs and Englishmen, we had been out in the noon day sun.

Since it was the hottest time of the day, and because the majority of people were fasting, everyone was resting, and having reached the zawiyya at last, that is exactly what we did, incapable of doing, or even saying, anything else. As at Wadi Halfa, we had been expected – although with all the delays on the track no one had been sure when we would be arriving – and there were beds waiting for us, which, after a gloriously cold shower – making sure all the while not to let any water through my lips or down my throat – were most welcome. The fuqara who greeted us and made us welcome could see that we were tired, and as soon as our basic needs had been met, they left us in peace to rest. We had been travelling continuously across rough terrain and in difficult circumstances for over a week now, and our metabolisms were still adjusting not only to the fasting pattern, but also to fasting in such a hot climate. It was good just to lie there in the shuttered guest room of the zawiyya, on a clean white sheet, cooled by the gentle breeze created by a slowly moving fan that hung from the ceiling overhead.

✿   ✿   ✿

For the next three days we just rested in the zawiyya, doing the daily prayers whenever their time fell due, and breaking the fast with Shaykh Abdal-Bourhani's fuqara each evening. As with his fuqara in Egypt, they were friendly and attentive to our needs and for ever concerned with the remembrance of Allah. On our second evening there, the Shaykh, who by now was a very old man, came to lead the isha and tarawih prayers. After these prayers were over, he gave a talk to his fuqara, who clearly loved and respected him, and then we were briefly introduced to the man whose far-reaching influence had certainly been one of the main factors in making our journey from Cairo to Khartoum via Humaysara possible. He greeted us warmly and smiled in welcome. His life had probably begun during the era when British troops had slaughtered thousands of Muslims in order to establish their supremacy in his country, and now, near the end of his life, we were probably the first British Muslims he had met.

"What have you come for?" he asked.

"We are on our way to do the Hajj in Makka, insh'Allah," I replied, "but in the meantime we would like to visit the awliya in the Sudan. We are here because we would like to drink from your cup."

The old man nodded his head in approval and understanding.

◦ ◦ ◦

The next evening we were invited to break the fast at Shaykh Abdal-Bourhani's home. About fifteen of us sat round the woven palm leaf mat on which a feast had been prepared, spread out on the small patch of lawn in his garden. During the course of the meal, the Shaykh handed me a large earthenware mug filled with a cool white drink which is made from dried beans. He waited to make sure that I had drunk all of it, nodded, and then continued with his meal, may Allah have mercy on him.

◦ ◦ ◦

Having spent three days at the zawiyya, we said goodbye and thankyou. There were no strings attached to Shaykh Abdal-Bourhani's generosity, for as the Prophet Muhammad once said, Allah is between the hand of the giver and the hand of the receiver.

Shaykh Abdal-Bourhani and his fuqara had been giving freely from what Allah had freely given them, certain in the knowledge that the result would be good for all concerned. It was Allah who should be thanked. However, we thanked the Shaykh and his fuqara, for as the Prophet said, whoever does not thank people has not thanked Allah.

OMDURMAN

About two years before we had set out on our journey to Makka, a Shaykh from Omdurman, Shaykh Al-Fattih Qarib' Allah, had visited our Shaykh's zawiyya in London while he was over in England to have an operation on his knees. He had said that our Shaykh and his fuqara must visit his zawiyya and would be most welcome to stay as his guests should they ever come to the Sudan. Accordingly Shaykh Al-Fattih Qarib' Allah's zawiyya was our next port of call.

The zawiyya was a very peaceful place, situated in a quiet backstreet of Omdurman, where many of the buildings were fashioned from the traditional sun-baked mud and straw rather than kilnfired bricks and concrete. The main entrance opened into a large sandy courtyard which had leafy trees round its edges. At one end of the courtyard was a large thick-walled mosque. At the other end was a square building which turned out to be the guest house. Between the mosque and the guest house, and set back, was a silver domed building that looked like a crude missile, although in fact it was the tomb of Shaykh Al-Fattih Qarib' Allah's father, who, when asked whether it was true that he could fly, had answered, "Yes, it is true. – But that is only the station of a fly!" On the far side of the guest house, and near the tomb, were the toilet and washing facilities. Behind the guest house, and in its own walled garden, was a large two-storeyed house, which was the house of Shaykh Al-Fattih Qarib' Allah. The whole place was imbued with calm and serenity. It was clearly a place where people were united in their remembrance of Allah, and separated from their differences and anxieties. I never witnessed one argument or complaint from anyone the whole time that we were there.

We were received like royalty by Shaykh Al-Fattih Qarib' Allah and his fuqara, even though we were poor and ignorant people. Of all the people who came to and went from the zawiyya, we must have been the three who knew the least about Allah and His Messenger and the prophetic way of life, and yet we were treated like honoured guests. Having been taken to see the Shaykh as soon as we had arrived, who rose to his feet to welcome us in spite of the great pain which his knees were still giving him, we were invited to stay as long as we liked and shown to the large airy guest room in the large sandy courtyard. It could not have been more different to the factory in Athens, which, only a month ago, had filled our world. Instead of the endless rattling of glass bottles on the conveyor belt, the air was filled with the sound of bird-song, as busy sparrows flew here and there, from tree to tree, and under the eaves of the various buildings, and even into the shady guest house itself.

We spent the last two or three days of the first third of Ramadan resting at the zawiyya, feeling that at last we had arrived at a place at which we could indeed stay as long as we liked without causing too much inconvenience to anyone. The Prophet Muhammad said that the first third of Ramadan is the mercy of Allah, and we had certainly tasted mercy in abundance. During the day we would spend much of our time just lying on our beds, resting or sleeping, for the Prophet said that even the sleep of a fasting man is blessed. We would pray dhur and asr in the mosque, the sand in the courtyard always far too hot to cross in bare feet, and usually it would be Shaykh Al-Fattih who led the prayer, his frail but firm body always immaculately clothed in a white robe and turban, and his fine aristocratic features always illuminated with light as he looked out onto the world with a gentle yet uncompromising gaze.

The period between asr and maghrib is always a good time for dhikru'llah, especially during Ramadan when the heart is at its most receptive as a result of the fasting process, and I would usually spend much of this time quietly reciting the Qur'an in a quiet corner on the woven palm leaf mat covered floor of the mosque. Just before maghrib, mats would be laid out on the sandy courtyard outside and covered with dates and cool drinks, including two drinks made from dried beans, one white, which I had already tasted at Shaykh Abdal-Bourhani's home, and the other a dark brown, which we called Sudanese coke because of the similarity of its taste to the 'real thing'. As the call to prayer echoed from hundreds of mosques, the courtyard would fill up with fuqara, and as soon as the adhan had ended, we would all break our fast together. After about ten minutes, we would pray maghrib, standing on the still warm sand of the courtyard, and then a proper meal, usually consisting of meat and bread and vegetables and fruit, would be served. Anyone who was not eating anywhere else could always be sure of a meal at the zawiyya with the fuqara.

After a while, when everyone's thirst and hunger had been neutralised, the adhan for isha would sound out through the night air, the numbers of men in the courtyard would increase still further, and then it would be time to pray the isha and tarawih prayers, standing in the clean cool sand facing Makka, swaying imperceptibly to the sound of the Qur'an like long grass in a gentle breeze, with everyone's white robes and turbans glistening white in the moonlight and the starlight. It was very beautiful and very peaceful.

Once the night prayers were completed, and everyone had drunk their fill of sweet milky tea or water, we would retire to our beds to sleep until dawn, some of the fuqara simply wrapping themselves up well in their burnooses and curling up asleep in the sand. Usually we would be awakened before dawn to have a welcome pot of milky tea and some biscuits, and having brushed our teeth and done wudu, we would pray subh when the time came, perhaps do dhikr until the sun rose, and then have a nap for an hour or so, with yet another day's fasting carefully under way.

This was the pattern of life at the zawiyya during Ramadan, and it refreshed us greatly. We did not, however, spend every day resting, and once we had regained our strength, we spent much of the second third of Ramadan, during which one is exposed to the forgiveness of Allah, visiting other Shaykhs in both Omdurman and Khartoum, and, in the process, drinking in all the new sights and sounds of the world about us which were somehow intensified and purified by the deep clarity and peace that always pervades the month of fasting. Wherever we went and whomever we visited, we were always graciously welcomed and generously fed, until the fact that we had no money was no longer a cause for concern or reason for being preoccupied. Sometimes we broke the fast with whoever we were visiting, sometimes we broke it at the zawiyya or with Shaykh Al-Fattih Qarib'Allah himself, and sometimes we were almost kidnapped by people who insisted that we must share their food with them. On one occasion, for example, there was a most violent thunder storm shortly before maghrib, and we were forced to shelter from the lightning and the rain in what appeared to be a deserted half built mosque. When the time came for maghrib, however, about twenty people appeared to do the prayer in the one part of the building that had a roof, and when we had done the prayer, they insisted that we eat with them.

One of our unexpected hosts who was called Abu Tarbush and his friend, Abu Bakr, then invited us to break the fast with them a couple of days later at Abu Bakr's home, which we did, feasting on the sumptuous array of food which was placed before us, and then, as always singing several qasidas from the Diwan of Shaykh Muhammad ibn al-Habib, much to the delight of Abu Tarbush who not only understood them but also was intoxicated by them. "Again! Again!" he would laugh. "Sing that one again!" Later on, after we had prayed the isha and tarawih prayers at a local mosque, and, it seemed, been greeted by virtually everyone who was there, we went to Abu Tarbush's house, where I was surprised to find that his eldest son was someone I had already met in London several months previously. He appeared to be ashamed of his father's outward poverty and lack of a western education, and even apologised angrily for what he perceived as his father's shortcomings, but I for my part could only feel pity for the son who had not been given the gift of understanding the Diwan and the deeper meanings of the Qur'an like his wise old father.

As well as visiting the living, we also visited the 'dead', and one of our first forays outside the seclusion of Shaykh Al-Fattih's zawiyya was to visit the Mahdi's tomb, which, like so many of the tombs in the Sudan, was crowned with a striking silver missile-like dome which might take off at any moment. Next to the tomb was a small museum which contained, amongst other things, one of the banners which the Mahdi's army had displayed during their battles with the invading British forces. The bold Arabic lettering on it, now faded with time, read:

La ilaha il'Allah
Muhammad ar-Rasulu'llah
Ahmad al-Khalif'ar-Rasulu'llah

which means:
There is no god but Allah
Muhammad is the Messenger of Allah
Ahmad is the Representative of the Messenger of Allah

There was also a collection of the swords and spears and bows and arrows with which the Muslims had fought, as well as a few of the large drums which they had beaten as they went into battle. A few official photographs showed battlefield scenes littered with bodies covered in flies, and nearby was a mounted cutting from the Times in which the use of the Maxim machine-gun against the Muslims was assessed. Apparently it had been very satisfactory, the machine-guns mowing them down like hay and winning the day. I marvelled at how, ultimately, the Mahdi's army had managed to overcome this brute technology.

In another display case, was a letter which the Mahdi had written to General Gordon on having been sent numerous gifts in an attempt to buy his co-operation. The translation of the letter is roughly as follows:

In the Name of Allah the Merciful the Compassionate

Dear General Gordon,

Each day you are straying further and further away from the straight path. Know that it is Allah Who is the King of this land, and not you or I.

Thank you for your gifts.

This is to let you know that I am coming with my army.

Peace on whoever follows guidance.

Ahmad.

Having crossed the western desert of the Sudan on foot, the Mahdi and his army had then defeated General Gordon at Khartoum. I was intrigued by this fearless man who had only feared Allah and nothing in His creation, and who, it is said, was always smiling whatever his situation. I admired his courage and trust in Allah. Although I am English, I found myself firmly on the side of the Muslims whose lands had been so arrogantly invaded by the Victorian Empire builders, in much the same way that I would have sided with the Saxons when they were invaded by the Vikings. Nearly a year later, I was to pray maghrib on a patch of lawn in one of the gardens that border the Thames Embankment, to find, on completing the prayer, that I was standing just a few yards away from the statue of Gordon of Khartoum. How times and people change!

When we entered the building which houses the tomb of the Mahdi, I could not help wondering whether or not there was in fact anyone buried there, since I could not detect any of the baraka which one usually experiences at the tombs of the awliya. I was later told that when Lord Kitchener's army finally overcame Khartoum and Omdurman, the Mahdi's body was dug up by the British forces, and the head cut off so that it could be taken back to Queen Victoria so that an inkwell could be made from the skull, while the rest of the body was dumped in the Nile. I was told that the headless body was then retrieved from the Nile, and the head intercepted at Wadi Halfa by a spy who managed to retrieve it and return it to Omdurman. The reunited body and head, it is said, were then secretly reburied in the original grave without the British finding out. Only Allah knows the truth of the matter, but it certainly did seem to me that there was no ruh in the vicinity.

Outside the tomb and the museum, in the small walled area that surrounds them, was a middle-aged man listening to a recording of the ratib, or wird, which the Mahdi and his close followers used to recite in the morning and in the evening. It sounded very strong and beautiful, but I never heard it actually being recited by a living person during the whole time that we were in the Sudan. It was as if his was a force which had had its time and then come to a close, perhaps to re-emerge somewhere else in someone else, in a different form. There can be no doubt that the Mahdi was an amazing being, and certainly I was told more than once that, like Shaykh Uthman dan Fodio who had fought the British in Nigeria, the Mahdi used to meet the Prophet Muhammad in dreams and visions, and was guided by him in his military tactics. Apparently it was for this reason that he came to be called 'al-Mahdi' which means 'the rightly-guided one', by other people, and not because he chose it for himself. Only Allah knows.

A great deal of water had flowed down the Nile since those days, and the situation now was very different. The British had come and departed, leaving their system behind them, and still there were Shaykhs and fuqara and zawiyyas and people who travelled in search of knowledge of Allah and His Messenger. There were still wise people in this part of the world, and we longed to visit them and learn from them before they disappeared off the face of the earth.

As our bodies became more accustomed to the fast and to the heat, we spent less time resting and sleeping and more time taking advantage of the unique opportunity we had been given to learn and reflect and purify our hearts. We often joined in the gatherings of dhikr which were held in the mosque, usually in the late afternoon before maghrib and in the mornings after subh. The qasidas which the fuqara sang were very beautiful and very different in form to the Moroccan ones with which we were most familiar, although of course their meaning was very similar since they were concerned with praising the Prophet Muhammad and glorifying Allah and preparing the genuine seeker for gnosis of Allah.

Shaykh Al-Fattih Qarib'Allah was not always present at these gatherings of dhikr, although when he was, the assembly was always charged with a greater baraka. He would always ask the three of us to sing from the Diwan of Shaykh Muhammad ibn al-Habib during such gatherings, and when we were invited to break the fast with him at his house. It was a large house which was always filled with guests, all of whom were fed. After we had finished eating, and were rounding off the meal with hot sweet tea, he would give a smile and ask to hear a qasida or two, to which he always listened closely, with his lovely refined face both alert and relaxed at the same time. Every so often, he would nod his head and say "Haqq!" – "True!" – in his penetrating voice.

At the entrance to Shaykh Al-Fattih's garden were two large pointed earthenware containers full of cool water. These water carriers were to be found everywhere in Omdurman, especially at street corners, so that everyone was able to quench their thirst very easily wherever they happened to be for free. The thick earthenware containers always kept the water beautifully cool, even on the hottest of days. However Shaykh Al-Fattih's water had an added ingredient: Qur'an. Every day, one of the fuqara would write out some ayat of Qur'an on a luh, a wooden writing board, using homemade ink that was both soluble and palatable, and then wash off these ayat into the drinking water. Thus when you drank the water, you also drank those ayat of the Qur'an. Naturally during Ramadan, we did not have much opportunity to try out this special brew, but at a later stage, when Ramadan was over, we were able to drink our fill.

We came across this practice all over the Sudan, and many of the doctors, or hakims as they are called in Arabic, meaning a wise man, used Qur'an as a medicine. They would either recite specific verses over the patient, often touching or blowing on the affected part of the body; or they would write them on a luh or a plate and dissolve them in water, which the patient would then drink; or they would write the ayat on a piece of paper and then set it alight, asking the patient to bend their head over and breathe in the smoke. In all of these practices, different ayat would be used for different illnesses, for both prevention and cure. It was also a very common practice to wear talismans, that is specific ayat of Qur'an written on paper and sewn into protective leather containers which are then worn continuously round the neck or upper arm, except when going to the toilet or washing. The purpose of these talismans has always been to serve as a means of protection from any kind of evil or harm, especially those forms which come from the Unseen.

One evening, shortly after we had finished praying the tarawih prayers, we were suddenly and unexpectedly caught up in a funeral procession. Apparently one of the fuqara had just died and it was time to bury his body. The fuqara swept out of the courtyard and through the streets of Omdurman with the three of us in tow, chanting 'La ilaha il'Allah, La ilaha il'Allah, La ilaha il'Allah' in a strong firm voice. We swept through the courtyard and into the house where the freshly washed and shrouded body was resting. The chanting stopped, and having made dua for the dead man and his family, his body was lifted up on a simple wooden stretcher and carried swiftly to the graveyard as we all chanted 'La ilaha il'Allah, La ilaha il'Allah, La ilaha il'Allah' once more. The body was placed by the newly dug grave, we stood in rows and said the funeral prayer, and then he was buried on his right side facing Makka.

As Abu Hurayra once said, "Make your funerals speedy, for it is only good that you are advancing him towards, or evil that you are taking off your necks." The Prophet Muhammad once said, "A slave who is mumin is relieved from the exhaustion and suffering of this world to the mercy of Allah, and a wrong-acting slave is the one from whom people, towns, trees and animals are relieved." He also said, may Allah bless him and grant him peace, "When you die, your place will be shown to you in the morning and the evening. If you are one of the people of the Garden, then you will be with the people of the Garden, and if you are one of the people of the Fire, then you will be with the people of the Fire. You will be told, 'This is your place of waiting until Allah raises you on the Day of Rising.'"

It was a sobering event, and a reminder. As Allah says in the Qur'an:

Surely Allah has knowledge of the Hour.
And He sends down the rain
and knows what is in the wombs.
And no self knows what it will earn tomorrow.
And no self knows in what land it will die.
Surely Allah is Knowing, Aware.

(Quran: 31.34)

Another generous host in Omdurman was a young man called Abdal-Malik, tall, smiling and aristocratic, who traded in tyres. We met him at the crowded jumua prayer which was held every Friday in the zawiyya mosque, and were subsequently invited to break the fast at his house. It was only some ten minutes' walk away, past the local laundry which consisted of about five men under a small shelter who washed and ironed every article of clothing by hand for a very reasonable price. As always, we ate outside under the darkening sky after praying maghrib, grateful to be the fortunate recipients of such warm hospitality. Abdal-Malik spoke very good English, which was a great help, since our Arabic was still too poor to hold any conversation other than a very simple one. Apparently his Shaykh, Shaykh Jayli, lived in a place called Kaddabas, which was near Atbarah, but on the other side of the Nile. "He is a wonderful old man," said Abdal-Malik, with respect and love in his voice. "You really must visit him if you can. Just tell me when you are free to go, and I will pay for your train tickets and tell you how to get there."

We accepted his invitation and offer of help gladly, explaining that we would love to visit Shaykh Jayli, but that it would have to be at a later stage, after Ramadan, since we intended to spend the last third of Ramadan visiting Shaykh ar-Rayah who was the Shaykh of a Sudanese friend of ours who was studying in England, and who lived on the banks of the Blue Nile at a place called Abu Haraz. Abdal-Malik smiled indulgently. "That's fine," he said. "There is no hurry. You can go when it is convenient."

As the second third of Ramadan drew to a close, we informed Abbas, one of Shaykh Al-Fattih's sons, of our intention to travel to Abu Haraz, and asked him to ask his father to give us permission to make the journey. "Of course you will be able to go," laughed Abbas, "but you won't be able to leave until after the howliya." We had no idea what a howliya was, but the next evening, on the 21st of Ramadan, we found out!

The howliya turned out to be a festival of dhikr par excellence, to which, it seemed, all the Shaykhs and fuqara in Omdurman had been invited. By the time it was time to pray asr in the afternoon before the night in which the howliya was to take place, the courtyard and the mosque and Shaykh al-Fattih's house were all packed with people. After we had all prayed asr, the dhikr began, as everyone launched into singing well-known qasidas. The singing had not been going on for very long before Abbas attracted Abdal-Jalil's and my attention and beckoned us to follow him, which we did, out through the entrance to the courtyard and on to the dusty dirt road outside. We were just in time to see how quickly two large cows, which had been freshly killed for the occasion, can be cut up by people who know how. Within what seemed minutes, the carcases had been bled, skinned and carved up, their hides being pulled down in such a way as to serve as a clean ground covering on which the meat could be cleanly chopped up into pieces without becoming covered in dust. Once the meat had been reduced to manageable chunks, it was carried off to the kitchens in Shaykh Al-Fattih's house, and by the time maghrib had been prayed and it was time to break the fast, miraculously there was food for everyone present.

After isha and the tarawih prayers, the dhikr continued. It was like being at a fairground, and had all the excitement and sense of occasion that one feels at a fairground, only instead of there being different stalls and roundabouts, there were different gatherings of dhikr, each with their own particular hadra, which everyone was free to join as they wished. Everyone appeared to be intoxicated by the dhikr and radiant with light, as the night passed and the moon appeared and rose, without anyone feeling in the least bit tired. It was an extraordinary night, charged with energy and light, and in fact it seemed so out of the ordinary, that I felt sure that it must be Laylat'al-Qadr, the Night of Power, that very special night which occurs on one of the odd nights of the last ten days of Ramadan, and in which the Qur'an was first revealed to the Prophet Muhammad by the Angel Jibril, and which the Qur'an describes as being better than a thousand months:

In the Name of Allah the Merciful the Compassionate

**Surely We revealed it on the Night of Power.
And what will tell you what the Night of Power is?
The Night of Power is better than a thousand months.
The angels and the spirit descend in it
by the permission of their Lord with all decrees.
Peace there is until the rising of the dawn.**

(Quran: 97.1-5)

Laylat'al-Qadr is said to be a good time to make duas, and accordingly I spent most of the last third of the night making duas and praying, asking Allah for everything that I wanted, and – keeping our underlying objective in mind – especially for an acceptable Hajj and a place in the Garden.

Finally, as dawn approached, everyone paused to eat and drink a little more in preparation for the next day's fasting, and then, after praying subh, we all dispersed to have some sleep and rest. In fact we were not feeling at all tired, which was just as well, for later on that morning, before it had grown too hot, and having been given the names of three other Shaykhs to visit by Shaykh al-Fattih who also insisted that we must stay as his guests again on our return to Omdurman, we caught a truck taxi going to Wad Madani, the first stage on our journey to Abu Haraz and Shaykh ar-Rayah.

ABU HARAZ

Abu Haraz, which is situated some way up the Blue Nile south of Omdurman and Khartoum, is said to have a hundred Shaykhs buried there. Certainly the graveyard there is very large, and those below ground outnumber those above it. Having changed trucks at Wad Madani, we had been dropped off by a small tributary to the Blue Nile, crossed it in a small dug-out canoe, and then begun the walk to Abu Haraz. A young man had met us and offered to take us to Shaykh ar-Rayah's zawiyya which was situated at the far end of the village on the far side of the graveyard. After we had walked about a mile in the intense heat, Shaykh ar-Rayah's zawiyya, which consisted of a small cluster of very simple thatched huts carpeted wall to wall with clean sand, came into sight.

As we approached, I could hear the familiar and yet unexpected and somehow incongruous sounds of **Telstar** coming from a large radio. Next to the radio, under a tree, on a plaited raw-hide wooden-framed bed, lay a thin gaunt figure swathed in white cloth, resting like a cheetah in the heat of the afternoon. It was Shaykh ar-Rayah. He greeted us with a few words of welcome, told the young man to show us into one of the huts, which had three beds like his own – without any mattress or bed-linen, and stayed put. Thankfully we flopped out on the beds and rested. It looked like this was going to be one of our more thirsty days.

We had not been resting for very long, before the adhan for asr was given. A few fuqara had materialised, one of whom showed us where to obtain water and where the toilet was. The toilet was very basic, a squat affair surrounded by a grass fence and situated over a large enclosed pit, with a twelve foot natural gas outlet vent made from dozens of tin cans that had been opened at both ends and then soldered together. The smell was amazing. We were out in the wilds alright!

We did wudu wherever we fancied, the dry earth soon soaking up the water, using the briques which we had been given. These were beautiful water containers, cleverly fashioned out of old tin cans and pieces of tin soldered together to form elegant jugs with long spouts and flip-top tops and strategically placed handles.

As soon as everyone was ready to do the prayer, we lined up behind Shaykh ar-Rayah, standing on ageing mats in the shade of a large tree, and dived in. I have never prayed behind a man who prayed so swiftly and meticulously without praying too fast. Even Abdal-Jalil, who was never one to hang around or waste time, was taken unawares and had difficulty in keeping up with him. As soon as the prayer was completed, Shaykh ar-Rayah, who was clearly a man of few words, returned to his bed under the tree, and did not move from it until the next adhan. Of all the people whom I have met, Shaykh ar-Rayah is the one who most reminds me of Al-Muhassabih's saying, "What is life but five prayers a day and waiting for death."

When the time came to break our fast, our food that evening was very simple, tough but wholesome and washed down with the waters of the Blue Nile, which flowed silently past, about a quarter of a mile away from the zawiyya. Shaykh ar-Rayah said very little to us, but he taught us a great deal about simplicity just in the way that he behaved and lived. He was clearly detached from the world but always aware of what was going on around him. There was nothing ostentatious about him whatsoever, and one could only guess at the knowledge that must be concealed within his heart. The thin Shaykh was glorious in his poverty, a king dressed in rags, and yet although I admired him, and realised how similar in many ways his life must be to that of the first companions of the Prophet, I knew that I could never live in such raw simplicity, unless I had no other choice.

The following day we decided to visit the tombs of some of the Shaykhs who are buried in Abu Haraz, and made our way through the early morning under leafy trees to the graveyard. After greeting tomb after tomb, without having the faintest idea who was buried there, making prolific duas at every stop and sometimes singing a qasida or two and doing a hadra into the bargain, we soon realised that we had bitten off more than we could chew and that perhaps our youthful enthusiasm had been a trifle misplaced and could be pointed in a more fruitful direction. Having made one last all-embracing dua for all the people who were buried there, we retreated through what promised to be another very hot day back to the shade of our hut, suddenly feeling tired and thirsty. So often one has to go beyond the limit in order to discover what the limit is!

Later on in the day, just before asr, we were invited to visit some of the people who lived at the other end of the village. We strolled along the banks of the wide river, pausing to do wudu on our way, prayed asr with our hosts, and chatted until maghrib. Amongst other things, we were told a little about one of the Shaykhs from the past who had helped to establish Islam in this region. His name was Shaykh Tayyib and although he had lived in Abu Haraz at one time, he was buried at Al-Marraheh, which is on the Nile north of Omdurman, near the zawiyya of Shaykh Salih, who was one of the Shaykhs whom Shaykh Al-Fattih had said we should visit.

"No fly ever settled on Shaykh Tayyib," we were told. "Once a crocodile grabbed hold of one of his fuqara while the man was washing in the river. Shaykh Tayyib hit the crocodile with his tasbih, and it turned to stone. Look, this is what remains of its head." We were shown what looked remarkably like three quarters of a crocodile's head, made of stone, although it was cracked and chipped and what would have been the snout was missing entirely.

Our hosts were especially pleased when they heard that we had done wudu in the Nile. "We have a saying that if you do wudu in the Nile, then it means you will return to the Sudan again one day, insh'Allah," explained the eldest man there. "And we have another saying," he added with a beaming smile, "that when Allah created the Sudan, He smiled!" I am certain that his words were true, and certainly, three years later I found myself briefly back in the Sudan, this time on my way to Malaysia.

After maghrib and a tasty feast we prayed isha and the tarawih prayers in the simple nearby mosque, and then walked back to the zawiyya in the starlight by the silent waters of the Nile. The moon was rising a little bit later each night, and Ramadan was drawing inexorably to its close. Only another week of fasting remained, and now that we had become accustomed to the fasting pattern and, at least to some extent, the heat, we were enjoying the special calm and peace that is only experienced during these last few days, when one's appetites are tamed and one's ruh is shining. It is in this state that one has a taste of what it must be like in the Garden.

◉ ◉ ◉

That night, before dawn, we were awoken by the young man who had first led us to the zawiyya. He handed us three earthenware mugs of very smoky tasting warm milk which we found hard to drink. "You must drink it," he said. "It is from the Shaykh." So we did, knowing that whenever a wali gives you something to eat or drink, he is also giving you knowledge and wisdom along with it. Whenever a wali gives you food in the outward, it means in the inward that he is teaching you.

While we were eating our suhur, the meal which only the Muslims eat shortly before dawn on the day of a fast – for the original followers of Moses and Jesus who used to fast each year only had one meal each day during their period of fasting, after sunset – we were unexpectedly joined by a young Englishman who was supervising a World Bank financed cotton growing project just a little further up river, and whom we naturally invited to share our food.

I was, and still remain, highly suspicious of the 'help' which the banking system of the high-tech North extends to the poor South. The projects which they finance are usually those which will ultimately provide the high-tech North with the raw materials that its industries need. The poor South countries are plunged into debt which necessitates their having to grow cash crops in order to pay the interest on the national debt. Since the currencies of the poor South countries have been devalued on the high-tech North money exchanges, the cash crops are purchased for next to nothing, and in the meantime these countries no longer grow enough food crops to feed their people. In a good year, some of the money from the cash crops can be used to import food, but in a bad year, when the crops fail, the people starve.

Traditionally, the Muslims of the Sudan grew more grain than they needed, knowing that periodically there would be a drought. During the good years, the surplus grain was collected in the form of zakat – the means by which surplus wealth and a certain percentage of all crops and livestock are gathered each year and redistributed to the poor – and stored until it was needed, in the year of a drought, when it was shared out amongst those who otherwise would have starved. After a hundred years of colonialism and neo-colonialism, this economic base had been almost completely destroyed, to be replaced by slavery through debt in the good years and helpless dependence on overseas aid in the year of a drought.

Naturally our unexpected guest did not see things from this perspective, and thought that he was doing a good job in helping to develop the natural resources of the country and improve the economic status of the local population. It seemed odd to be speaking to another Englishman, in fluent English, for he was the first Englishman we had met since the one who had shared our simple meal on the ferry to Crete. Although we shared the same nationality, however, it became increasingly clear as our pre-dawn meal progressed that he was on a completely different wavelength to us, and that we were living in a very different world to the one to which he gave reality.

We were now in the last third of Ramadan, in which one tastes freedom from the Fire, and this was what we began to discuss, exploring the meaning of what it is to be in this state, and accordingly talking about the Garden. We had not been talking for very long, before our visitor made his contribution to the conversation. "I know a good joke about the Fire," he chipped in, with a look of glee on his face. "Everyone's there in Hell, standing up to their knees in shit. 'That's funny,' thinks one of them. 'This isn't too bad at all. It's a bit smelly, but at least it's not too hot.'" Our visitor paused dramatically, oblivious to the fact that we were not enjoying his joke in the least, and then continued. "Just then the boss comes in and says, 'Alright everyone! Your twenty minute break is up! Back on your hands again!'" He chuckled noisily while we kept quiet, for there was nothing to say that he would understand.

One of the meanings of freedom from the Fire, I reflected, is being free from ignorance of the fact that the Fire actually exists and the Garden actually exists. In this world, one's inward state is either that of someone in the Garden or of someone in the Fire, but in the next world, each one of us will either be in the Garden or in the Fire. Being ignorant of this is like being in the Fire.

We finished our meal together, avoiding needless argument by discussing what little we had in common, and then, when it was time to do wudu and prepare for subh and the day's fasting ahead, our guest bid us farewell and disappeared back into the darkness from which he had come.

❂   ❂   ❂

Once again it was the day of the jumua, and Abdal-Jalil had decided that after the jumua prayer we would continue our journey, and visit the first of the three Shaykhs whom Shaykh Al-Fattih had advised us to visit, a man called Shaykh Tayyab who lived not far away in a village called Tayyaba, on the other side of the Blue Nile.

Having done our ghusls well before the prayer, we made our way down to the mosque when we heard the adhan, listened to the khutba, did the prayer, and then followed Shaykh ar-Rayah – who had strode off immediately after the prayer since he was not interested in the speech which someone started to make – back to his simple zawiyya. We thanked Shaykh ar-Rayah for his hospitality as best we could, and then, leaving him stretched out on his bed under the tree doing dhikr and waiting for the time of asr to arrive, we made our way past the tall leafy trees to the bank of the Nile, just in time to catch the ferry over to the other side.

TAYYABA

Having safely crossed the river, we were given a lift to Tayyaba, where one of the fuqara of Shaykh Tayyab met and welcomed us. It was another hot day, and even the short journey from Abu Haraz had been enough to leave us tired and thirsty, although nothing like the dehydration and exhaustion which we had experienced during the first few days of Ramadan. How anyone could fast and do a day's work in this heat was still beyond me. We were shown to the travellers' rest room which was relatively cool after the direct heat of the sun, and told to relax and rest. We were welcome to stay as long as we wished, and insh'Allah we would meet Shaykh Tayyab after we had broken the fast after maghrib. Thankfully we lay back and relaxed on the cotton bedspreads, waiting for the sun to set.

Time passed, the sun set, the adhan was called and a small group of fuqara appeared and took us to a large room where we prayed maghrib and then tucked into a large bowl filled with steaming asida covered with thick meaty gravy. Asida, like the thin pancake-like bread we often had with our meals, is usually made from durra, the millet which forms the staple food of the Sudanese. Asida is like a thick pasty porridge which, when combined with the meaty gravy, is both filling and satisfying and nutritious. As soon as we had eaten and drunk our fill, we were taken to meet Shaykh Tayyab.

○   ○   ○

Shaykh Tayyab sat cross-legged on a mat on the ground, surrounded by his fuqara, like a king surrounded by his closest followers. Although the travellers' rest room, to which we had been shown, was part of a relatively modern two-storey building, Shaykh Tayyab's home was a simple thick mud-walled dwelling built in the traditional style, with a large shaded verandah, whose floor was carpeted with woven mats, at the front. It was on this verandah that he received us, giving us a firm greeting with a firm smile and a firm handshake. Shaykh Tayyab was a strong, handsome, well-built man who was clearly a born leader.

Having greeted us courteously, Shaykh Tayyab turned and said something in a low voice to one of his fuqara who went and returned, with six ice-cold cokes. Solemnly Shaykh Tayyab gave us two bottles each and told us to drink them, which we gladly did. They were deliciously cold and immediately put us at our ease, for we were all suffering a little from culture-shock, especially Mustafa who had become very silent for much of the time, and somehow that old familiar tingling taste that we had known since childhood reassured us and made us let go and relax. This simple action was a confirmation of Shaykh Tayyab's station, for the true awliya are not blind, and they are immediately aware of the need of anyone who enters their presence.

In the days that followed, I was to see how accurate this first impression was, for every day there was a constant stream of visitors passing in and out of his verandah, where he would receive them, either sitting cross-legged on the ground as he was now, or sometimes on a low bed. He would listen attentively to what each person had to say, and then would act accordingly: To some he would give a few words of advice; for others he would make a dua or write out a talisman, sometimes referring to the Qur'an which was always off the ground and close to hand; some he would tell to go over and sit in a corner where food would be brought to them; and others he would admonish firmly, perhaps giving them a gentle cuff over the ear. No one was turned away, and anyone could speak with him, young or old, man or woman. All kinds of people passed through that verandah, and it was clear that they all loved and respected this man who was so completely at their service, totally submitted to helping whoever came to him.

Having given us the medicine that we needed, and asked us the usual questions, such as where were we from, and where were we going, and who was our Shaykh, we sang a qasida called **Praise** from the Diwan of Shaykh Muhammad ibn al-Habib:

PRAISE

Praise is due to You, the possessor
of serenity, forgiveness and veiling.
My praise is part of Your blessing, O abundant Giver.

Praise is due to You, in number as great
as the drops of rain, and the grains of sand, and the pebbles,
and the plants of the earth and the fish of the sea.

Praise is due to You, in number as great
as the ants, and the jinn and men, and in quantity as great
as the sky, and the Throne, and the stars like scattered pearls.

In quantity as great as space itself,
and the Tablet of Forms, and the Footstool, and the moist earth,
and the number of all created beings on the Day of Gathering.

Praise is due to You, O my Lord,
as You deserve it,
for I cannot praise You fittingly to the full extent of time.

Praise is due to You, O endless Giver of gifts,
the One who grants opening and triumph
to the people of Allah.

Praise is due to You with every breath
with the body and the heart.
Look kindly on a slave who is perplexed by the command.

If my wrong actions weigh me down,
I still have a good opinion of You
that You will mend my broken spirit.

O Forgiving! Grant a turning away [from wrong action] to us
which will undo
what happened in our early years.

Increase us in blessing, light and unveiling,
and strengthen us in guidance,
with idhn and the secret.

Support us in our words and deeds,
and make our provision easy for us
– from where we know not!

Here we are standing at the door of favour,
waiting without hardship
for the Beloved to turn to us.

Swiftly, send us Your ease, O Answerer,
for You are the possessor
of generosity, liberality and goodness.

Your Bounty exists without our existence,
and Your Generosity pours down on us, undenied.

Give us success in the thankfulness which is our duty
and which itself calls for increase from You
without loss to us.

Free us from the prison of our bodies
and raise us up to the presence of the spirits
as a reward for our gratitude.

Let us see the meaning of the essence in every manifestation
in order to strengthen our witnessing
both in times of ease and trouble.

Annihilate us to ourselves and give us going-on in You always,
so that we may join the people who have inherited
the presence of the secret.

Your command to things is in the word 'Be – it is!'
So shape things for us
with firm intention and without deception.

Bless Ahmad,
the guide to the presence of purity,
with all the forms of perfection,

And his family and noble Companions,
and whoever prays for expansion of the breast
for the composer of these verses.

And, O Lord, through the compassionate guide, Muhammad,
grant us sciences that will benefit us
on the Day of Rising.

Strengthen us with lights at every instant,
and make us firm
at the sealing, the agony of death, and the grave.

(Diwan of Shaykh Muhammad ibn al-Habib)

We rounded off this beautiful qasida by singing a short blessing on the Prophet Muhammad, in the following form:

> May Allah bless him and his family and grant them peace,
> and his Companions and all the believing slaves of Allah.
> Amin. Amin. Amin.
> And peace be upon the Prophets and the Messengers.
> And peace be upon the Prophets and the Messengers.
> And peace be upon the Prophets and the Messengers,
> and on all the saliheen.
> And the last of our prayer is:
> Praise be to Allah, the Lord of the worlds.
> There is no great power and no strength but through Allah,
> the Mighty, the Great.
> My help is only with Allah.
> In Him I have put my trust.
> And to Him I turn in renewal.
> Praise belongs to Allah
> for the blessing of Islam,
> and it is blessing enough.
> Glory be to your Lord,
> the Lord of Might, above what they describe,
> and peace be upon the Messengers,
> and praise belongs to Allah,
> the Lord of the worlds.

And then it was time to pray isha and the tarawih prayers.

The word tarawih in Arabic means 'to become ruh', and this is the effect that these prayers have on you. The tarawih prayers consist usually of ten or twenty rakats and usually last somewhere between one and two hours. Each night of Ramadan, approximately a thirtieth part of the Qur'an is recited during the tarawih prayers, which means that by the end of Ramadan, anyone who has been present at these prayers every night will have heard the entire Qur'an being recited. Listening to the Qur'an like this is like bathing in light, and the effect of doing these prayers is to make your body seem non-existent, so that in effect all that 'remains' is your spirit, your ruh, which is pure light. Thanks to the tarawih prayer, you have 'become ruh'.

○ ○ ○

96   The Difficult Journey

We spent much of our time during these last few precious days of Ramadan doing dhikr, especially during the night, conscious of the fact that as soon as this blessed month was over, the going would be much tougher. The Prophet once said that when Ramadan comes, the gates of the Garden are opened, and the gates of the Fire are locked, and the shayatin are chained. During the rest of the year this is not the case, and indeed, I have always found that the first few days after Ramadan has finished are especially difficult, until one has readjusted to the rough and tumble of what is in fact a very different world.

On one occasion, on the 27th night of Ramadan, Shaykh Tayyab invited us to a small gathering of dhikr on his verandah after the tarawih prayers. Only the Shaykh and about five of his fuqara and the three of us were there. As soon as we were all seated comfortably, relaxed, like seaweed in still waters, and alert, like a cat waiting at a mousehole, the dhikr began. Soon I lost all track of time. The fuqara sang qasida after qasida, glorifying Allah and asking blessings on His Messenger, in the hauntingly beautiful African melodies that welled up deep from their hearts, the subtle rhythms being gently emphasised with the tambourine like drums that two of them held expertly in both hands, until I could no longer feel the hard mats beneath me or the stiffness in my joints, but only hear the sweet qasidas, not with my ears, it seemed, but with my heart, on which all my attention had been concentrated since the dhikr first began. Finally, perhaps two or three hours later, the sama came to an end, and Shaykh Tayyab indicated that we could go. Stiffly we rose to our feet, feeling light and bewildered. Shaykh Tayyab smiled on us, shook and kissed our hands as the Companions of the Prophet used to do, and bid us good night.

❂   ❂   ❂

Tayyaba, like its Shaykh, was a good place. It was a large and peaceful well integrated community whose members were like two hands washing each other, like the beams of a roof that support each other. There was no police force, nor any need for one, and no western styled school. All the children went to the maddrasah, where they received a traditional Muslim education along with a basic education in the knowledge which is necessary to deal with the world as it is today. Shaykh Tayyab was the undisputed leader of the community, and everyone whom we met and observed in his company loved and obeyed him. It was neither a rich nor a poor community, but clearly the canal system, which facilitated a steady water supply from the Nile, helped to ensure that the fruits of their labours in the nearby fields were plentiful.

As in so many of the villages in the Sudan which are centred round not only a good water supply, but also a good source of wisdom, two of the more noticeable buildings in the village were the tombs of Shaykh Tayyab's immediate predecessors, with their distinctive silver conical domes. Naturally we visited them, to make duas for their occupants, and noticed that there were a couple of men in heavy chains who spent much of their time clanking slowly about in the vicinity of the two tombs. On asking one of the fuqara who they were, we were told that they were suffering from one form of madness or another, and had been brought to Tayyaba – as apparently mad people often were – in order to benefit from the baraka of the awliya who were buried there, and hopefully even to recover. They were in chains so that they could not be violent, either to themselves or to anyone else.

This solution for dealing with the insane seemed far gentler and more humane to me than many of the western cures, and far more preferable to being locked up in an asylum and being heavily drugged or subjected to electric shock treatment. It was also good to know that the wise people in the Sudan were able to recognise when a person had been possessed by one of the jinn, and had the necessary Qur'anic sciences to cast it out, rather than ignorantly subjecting the possessed person's body and mind to all types of experimental and equally useless treatments.

We spent the last days of Ramadan in Tayyaba doing dhikr, reciting the Qur'an and singing the Diwan, relishing these last few days of freedom from the Fire. By now the robes which we had donned in Alexandria were very much the worse for wear, and the robes which had been made for us in Cairo were no longer new. Shortly before the day of the Id, Shaykh Tayyab summoned us to his verandah and had us measured up for a new robe each. Abdal-Jalil and Mustafa both chose white cotton, while I chose dark green cotton, much to Shaykh Tayyab's amusement and delight, since this was the colour worn by the fuqara of a particular Shaykh who were very poor, only possessing the clothes they were wearing and a brique in which to carry water for using in the toilet and for wudu.

As it happened the robes were ready for us on the night that the new moon of Shawwal was sighted, signalling that it was the end of Ramadan and that the next day was the day of the Id. Gratefully we accepted his generous gift to us, and with excitement and sadness prepared as best we could for the next day. Suddenly Ramadan had come to an end once again. We had come a long way since that first hot day when we boarded the ferry at Aswan, and we felt completely different, refreshed and renewed by the deep far-reaching effects of Ramadan.

Early the next morning, after we had prayed subh, we all did our ghusls, donned our lovely new flowing robes and freshly washed turbans, and waited for events to unfold. We had not yet paid our zakat al-fitr, which I was accustomed to paying in the form of grain or dates, but had been told that it had become customary to pay it in the form of its equivalent value in money. As it happened, we had exactly the right amount of money left on us to pay the zakat al-fitr for the three of us, and now we simply awaited the opportunity to hand it over to Shaykh Tayyab.

Soon after sunrise, two of the fuqara came to collect us, giving us some dates and milk to eat and drink so that we could formally end our fast, and then taking us outside, where there were hundreds of people everywhere, all dressed in brilliant white. Apparently everyone from the surrounding countryside came to Tayyaba for the Id prayer, so it was quite an event. A few days earlier, there had been several large camels tethered nearby, who were destined to be eaten at the Id feast. They had all disappeared now, presumably into the cooking pots.

The sun was not very high in the sky when Shaykh Tayyab appeared, dressed in shining white and surrounded by several fuqara beating large drums. For a moment he paused by us, and gave us a large smile as I handed over our zakat al-fitr with a firm "Bismillah!" Then, like a ship passing through the ocean, he sailed through the crowds, as the tempo of the drumming increased, and out onto a large open field on the edge of the village. Everyone followed and lined up behind him in straight rows, the women behind the men. The drumming stopped and gradually everyone began to fall silent. There must have been several thousand people there. It was breathtaking, and yet again I sensed that we were being given a taste of what life must have been like in the time of the Khulafa Rashidun, the first four rightly guided rulers of the Muslim community after the Prophet Muhammad had died, may the blessings and peace of Allah be on him and them.

The large crowd was now totally silent, row upon row of human beings, all facing Makka, waiting for the prayer to begin. The silence was broken by a loud firm "Allahu Akbar" from the Shaykh as he began the Id prayer, followed by the remaining takbirs and his strong firm recitation of Qur'an. It was an extraordinary experience to be doing the prayer with so many people, especially when we went into sajda, our foreheads resting lightly on the hard dry soil. How different it was to the wild adulation which I had witnessed at the Bath open air rock festival some eight years earlier, which was the only other comparable event in which I had been a part of a large gathering of people who had all come together for the same purpose.

Once the prayer was completed, Shaykh Tayyab gave a short khutbah, and then we all returned to the village, and the feasting began: freshly cooked camel and fresh bread, followed by simple sweetmeats and sweet tea. It really was a festival, and I marvelled at how so many people could be fed at the same time. Everyone was shining, fresh, recharged and rejuvenated by the month's fasting, sad to see the last of Ramadan but glad to be celebrating the Id.

Naturally, everyone wanted to greet Shaykh Tayyab, and in due course our turn came to approach the crowded verandah where he sat cross-legged on his low bed, surrounded by people. We intended to visit the two other Shaykhs whom Shaykh Al-Fattih had advised us to see on the two following days of the Id, and so, having been given something more to eat in one corner of the verandah, we asked the Shaykh's permission to leave. At first he did not want to let us go, but finally he relented, on the condition that we sing one more qasida from the Diwan before departing. Our visit to Tayyaba ended as it had begun, and we sang the qasida called **Praise** with joy.

Shaykh Tayyab embraced each one of us firmly with a large smile, pressing a twenty pound note into Abdal-Jalil's hand. "For your journey," he said, and having made dua for us, he smiled, looked directly at us, and nodded. We were free to go, and so we left his presence, sad to be leaving and glad to be on our way once more.

WAD MADANI

Although we had said our farewells to Shaykh Tayyab, we did not actually leave Tayyaba until early the next morning, after subh and breakfast. One of the fuqara kindly led us to the taxi truck stop for Wad Madani, and there we waited for about half an hour, while other would-be travellers also turned up.

It was clear that Ramadan was over and the shayatin had been let loose and were back at work again, for as soon as a lone taxi truck rolled up in a cloud of dust, most of the people there started fighting over the seats. We refused to let ourselves become drawn into this conflict, and as a result, although we had been the first there, we were still standing by the roadside when the crowded truck drove off again. A few minutes later, another taxi truck arrived which we had no difficulty in boarding. About three miles on down the road, we passed the taxi which we had been prevented from boarding. It had broken down and the engine was on fire. It was the first naked flame I had seen in a month. Ma sha'Allah.

Having reached Wad Madani, we transferred to another taxi which took us to the village in which Shaykh Jaiyli's zawiyya was situated. We made our way towards where it must be, guided by three silver missile-like domes which stood silently ready for countdown and take-off, and having arrived, we were immediately ushered into a large cool room of waiting people, and taken forward to the Shaykh who sat cross-legged on the ground at the far end of it with his eyes lowered, receiving a constant stream of visitors.

Shaykh Jaiyli was a young Shaykh, still in his thirties, it seemed from his appearance. He greeted us with a smile and asked one of his fuqara to take us into a back room where we were given some tea and something to eat. As always in the first few days after Ramadan, it felt very strange to be eating during the daytime, and each mouthful seemed like a special gift. After about half an hour, Shaykh Jaiyli joined us and greeted us once again. We were delighted to find that he spoke perfect English.

"I went through the entire western educational system," he explained. "After I had been awarded my PhD, I realised that I still didn't know anything. So I went to my father and said, 'Now, please teach me real knowledge.' He did, knowledge of Allah and His Messenger, may the blessings and peace of Allah be on him, and now I am here, doing what he used to do! However my time at university was not wasted. When young university students come to me, I know what is going on inside their heads." He smiled. "There was a time when I wanted to go out into the mountains and live in some remote place where I could just do lots of dhikr and devote all my time to Allah, but I realised that this was very selfish, and that I would be of much greater service helping people here, so here I am!"

Having told us his story, and given us sound advice in the process, Shaykh Jaiyli excused himself and returned to the room in which he received all his visitors. It was so refreshing to see a wise man being treated with such respect and trust. It was a sight which I have seldom seen outside the Muslim world.

That evening, Shaykh Jaiyli held a gathering of dhikr especially for us. One of the singers was totally drunk with light and soon had everyone smiling with the qasidas that he sang, including us, even though our Arabic was not good enough to catch their meaning. We also sang two or three qasidas from the Diwan of Shaykh Muhammad ibn al-Habib, and after a prolonged hadra and a feast, and greetings and farewells all round, retired thankfully to the beds which had been provided for us and went to sleep, knowing that we must set out for Al-Marraheh, where Shaykh Salih lived, early the next morning.

AL-MARRAHEH

Al-Marraheh is situated on the banks of the Nile about twenty miles beyond Omdurman. We had to return to Omdurman in order to catch a taxi lorry to Al-Marraheh, which we did without too much delay or difficulty. At the huge Omdurman bus and taxi lorry depot, however, our troubles began. Amidst conflicting directions and countless flies and great heat, we tried to make the journey before the day was over, thankful that we could at least quench our thirst whenever we felt like it now that we were no longer fasting. Although we had arrived back in Omdurman before dhur, we did not find ourselves on the right taxi lorry until after maghrib. It is sometimes said that the greater a wali, the more difficult the journey is to his door.

It was dark and late by the time that we jolted into Al-Marraheh, dismounted stiffly from the taxi lorry and found our way to the zawiyya of Shaykh Salih which was situated close by Shaykh Tayyib's tomb, the wali on whom, we had been told at Abu Haraz, no fly had ever been seen to settle. Nearly everyone there was fast asleep, including Shaykh Salih, wrapped up in either blankets or burnooses on the clean white sand. There had been a very large gathering of dhikr that day, and now that most of the visitors had left, the Shaykh and his fuqara were resting. The new moon had already set, and there was no electricity in Al-Marraheh, so the darkness was only diminished by the starlight, the curved pointed dome of Shaykh Tayyib's tomb looming up above us like a dark shadow against the sky. It was all rather an anticlimax, and we could not help feeling that we had missed the boat.

Fortunately some of the fuqara were awake and they made us welcome as best they could. A Tilley lamp was produced, and within minutes there were hordes of flying insects that fluttered about the hissing glowing light and all around us. We were hot and tired and dusty and sweaty and hungry and thirsty after our frustrating day, and could not help feeling bothered and ill at ease, as we sat with some of the fuqara, trying to communicate in our stilted Arabic and keep the fluttering insects at bay.

Within twenty minutes, food was placed before us, including sponge pudding and custard for our second course. After having savoured this unexpected delicacy with relish, and drunk our fill of hot sweet milky tea, we felt relaxed and at peace, and no longer ruffled and irritated. At this point one of the fuqara woke Shaykh Salih up, and having done wudu, he joined and greeted us without any display of annoyance at having had his rest disturbed. He was clearly a man of the instant, tuned into and accepting whatever the present moment required of him, and very humble because of his awe of Allah, and not at all proud because of all the knowledge that had been given to him.

Shaykh Salih was a giant of a man, both in his outward stature and in the extent of his wisdom. It was as if he were the sole survivor from another age, in which people had pursued knowledge with the same determination and will that a tyrant seeks power. He seemed to know all about all the Prophets from Adam to Muhammad, may the blessings and peace of Allah be on all of them, including the fact that Adam was about twenty feet tall, a fact which means that perhaps all those fairy tales about giants in days long gone are not so far-fetched after all. "Ask me whatever you want," he said kindly, his face calmly eager with anticipation, for he was clearly a man who liked to share his knowledge.

"Tell us something about Sayyedina Isa that we do not already know," asked Abdal-Jalil.

"Did you know," replied Shaykh Salih, "that the pregnancy of Maryam only lasted a few hours, and not nine months as it usually does?"

I certainly had not known this, and I had no reason to doubt the Shaykh's words. They only served to increase my own certainty that the description of the nativity of Jesus in the Bible is greatly embellished and largely inaccurate. The Qur'an describes the conception and birth of Jesus in these words:

> And make mention of Mary in the Book,
> when she had withdrawn from her people
> to a chamber looking East,
> and had chosen seclusion from them.

Then We sent Our spirit [the Angel Gabriel]
to her and it assumed for her
the likeness of a perfect man.
She said, 'Surely I seek refuge in the Merciful One
from you if you are God-fearing.'
He said, 'Surely I am only a messenger of your Lord,
that I may bestow on you a pure son.'
She said, 'How can I have a son,
when no man has touched me,
and when I have not been unchaste?'
He said, 'Like this: your Lord says, "It is easy for Me.
And We shall make him a sign for mankind
and a mercy from Us,
and it is a thing ordained."'

And she conceived him,
and she withdrew with him to a far place.
And the pangs of childbirth drove her
to the trunk of the palm tree.
She said, 'O would that I had died before this
and become nothing, forgotten.'
Then it was said to her from below her,
'Do not grieve!
Your Lord has placed a rivulet beneath you,
and shake the trunk of the palm tree towards you.
You will cause ripe dates to fall on you.
So eat and drink and be consoled.
And if you meet any man, say,
"I have vowed a fast to the Merciful One,
and may not speak to any person on this day."'

Then she brought him to her own folk, carrying him.
They said, 'O Mary, you have come with something amazing!
O sister of Aaron, your father was not a wicked man,
and your mother was not unchaste.'
Then she pointed to him.
They said, 'How can we talk to one who is in the cradle,
a baby boy?'
He said, 'Surely I am the slave of Allah.
He has given me the Book and has made me a Prophet,
and has made me blessed wherever I may be,

and has enjoined on me prayer and almsgiving
for as long as I live,
and obedience towards her who bore me,
and He has not made me arrogant, unblessed.
And peace on me the day I was born and the day I die
and the day I shall be raised alive.'

Such was Jesus son of Mary.
[This is] a statement of the Truth about which they doubt.
It does not befit Allah that He should take to Himself a son.
Glory be to Him!
When He decrees a thing He only says to it 'Be' and it is.
And surely Allah is my Lord and your Lord.
So worship Him.
This is the straight path.

(Qur'an: 19.16-36)

I had always wondered why, in this account, Mary had been questioned by her folk about her actions after the birth of Jesus and not before, since in a normal pregnancy it would have become apparent that she was pregnant some time before the baby was born. Up until hearing Shaykh Salih's words, I had always assumed that Mary must have withdrawn into seclusion from her people before she became visibly pregnant, but if, as Shaykh Salih said, her pregnancy was only a few hours in length, by the command of Allah, then it would explain how she only became visibly pregnant after she was alone.

No wonder, I reflected, I had always found the Christian festivals so intellectually unsatisfactory and so spiritually unsustaining when I was being brought up as a Christian during my childhood. The biblical account of the birth of Jesus was inaccurate and celebrated at the time of the winter solstice because no one knew on what day he had actually been born; Jesus had celebrated the sabbath on the Saturday, but we had done so on the Sunday in compliance with the Emperor Constantine's decree; and to cap it all, the festival of the alleged crucifixion of Jesus which was celebrated with chocolate fertility symbols at the time of the spring equinox was based on an event which had never actually taken place:

> And they did not kill him or crucify him,
> but it appeared so to them.
> And surely those who disagree about it
> are in doubt about it.
> They have no knowledge about it
> except that they follow speculation.
> And they did not kill him for certain.
> But Allah took him up to Himself.
> And Allah was ever Mighty, Wise.
> There is not one of the People of the Book
> [the Jews and the Christians]
> but will believe in him before his death.
> And on the Day of Standing
> he will be a witness against them.
>
> (Qur'an: 4.157-159)

Added to all this, we had been taught that Jesus was both a man and God at the same time, so that I had never been quite sure who I was worshipping or to whom I was praying, or even to whom Jesus was praying, since if Jesus was God he would hardly be praying to himself, and if he was not God then why were we being taught that he was? No wonder I had been so confused and ultimately forced by my intellect to abandon the Church altogether!

A few words from Shaykh Salih had helped me to assess and evaluate and focus more clearly on all that I had learned about the Prophet Jesus from the Qur'an and the recorded sayings of the Prophet Muhammad, may the blessings and peace of Allah be on both of them. This often happens with a wali. A few words from a wali can remove veils which hid knowledge about whose existence you never even knew.

By now it was growing late. After briefly visiting the tomb of Shaykh Tayyib whom we greeted and for whom we made dua, we were shown to our sleeping place, and were soon sound asleep. The Id of Ramadan was well and truly over, and insh'Allah we would be in Makka for the next Id, the Id of the Hajj! It was now less than ten weeks away.

○   ○   ○

We awoke the next morning to see clearly what kind of a place we were in. Al-Marraheh was a small peaceful village, nestling by a broad curve in the Nile, apparently miles from anywhere else. After breakfast we were taken to a rocky outcrop that overlooks both the village and the river. We were shown the narrow entrance to an underground cave in which Shaykh Tayyib had withdrawn to do sustained dhikr in seclusion. Near the entrance, on a ledge that looks out over the Nile, an indentation in the rock which is said to be one of his footprints was pointed out to us. Climbing to the very top of the outcrop, we were shown the remains of about five small circular khalwas, with walls made of stacked stones and minus their roofs, in which the murids of past Shaykhs had withdrawn to do sustained dhikr, sometimes for as long as forty days.

It was here that the Mahdi had learned from his second Shaykh, after memorising the entire Qur'an by heart under the guidance of his first Shaykh in a small maddrasah north of Atbarah. Apparently he had then taken the hand of a third Shaykh, because he considered that his second Shaykh was being too friendly with the British. It was his third Shaykh who had instructed him when to start his successful jihad against General Gordon and the British Army.

Having learned a little more about the past, we clambered down the rocks and made our way back to the zawiyya. Now that Ramadan was over, a certain stage in our journey had come to its natural close. We had boarded the ferry at Aswan not knowing what the Sudan would be like. Now, a month of light years later, we were feeling completely at home in our new environment, or rather Abdal-Jalil and I were, but not Mustafa. Mustafa appeared to be suffering from some form of concentrated culture-shock. During our time in the Sudan, he had become increasingly withdrawn and unresponsive, eating and speaking less and less. We had done what we could to make things easy for him, but with little success, until we had been reduced to hoping that it was just a passing phase which would soon be over. Most of the Sudanese fuqara whom we consulted thought that he had simply become so absorbed in the contemplation of Allah that he had virtually withdrawn from the world of the senses. Whatever the reason for his deep silence and loss of appetite, we were becoming increasingly concerned about his well-being, and the possibility that he might have to return to England was now becoming a probability.

After we had stayed for a couple of days in Al-Marraheh, Abdal-Jalil decided on the following course of action: He thought that Mustafa should spend the next week at Shaykh Al-Fattih's zawiyya in Omdurman, since this was familiar territory and it might help him to recover from whatever was troubling him. In the meanwhile, he wanted me to visit Shaykh Jayli, the Shaykh of our friend Abdal-Malik, who was at Kaddabas. And he, Abdal-Jalil, would stay at Al-Marraheh and learn what he could from Shaykh Salih. Accordingly, Mustafa and I should leave for Omdurman the next morning. Having left him at the zawiyya, I could continue on my way to Kaddabas; and we could all meet again at Shaykh Al-Fattih Qarib'Allah's zawiyya in a week's time, insh'Allah.

Everything unfolded as planned. Having said our goodbyes, Mustafa and I boarded a taxi lorry back to Omdurman, and within a few hours we were back at the zawiyya where we were warmly welcomed once again. Having explained our plans and hopes, I left Mustafa in the capable hands of Shaykh Al-Fattih and his fuqara, and went round to Abdal-Malik's house in order to obtain the directions to Kaddabas which he had promised to give us when he time came to visit Shaykh Jayli. It felt strange to be suddenly on my own, and I missed the company of both Abdal-Jalil and Mustafa. We had shared a great deal during the last three months or so, both rough and smooth and difficult and easy, and I had become accustomed to their constant companionship, especially since we all got on well with each other. Nevertheless, I was looking forward to my little journey to Kaddabas, and knocked at the door of Abdal-Malik's house in good spirits.

KADDABAS

Abdal-Malik opened the door himself and welcomed me with a broad unhurried good-natured smile, which widened even more once he had learned the purpose of my visit. He advised me to wait until the next morning when I could catch the early train, and in the meantime, welcomed me to stay at his house and rest until it was time to go. Having spent the rest of the day and the evening in his company, and having had a good night's sleep, we set out for the train station the next morning after breakfast. On the way, Abdal-Malik gave me the necessary directions, and on reaching the station, he bought me a return ticket, found me a good seat on the right train, and bid me farewell. A few minutes later, the train was heading north, back the way we had come only a month ago.

It was a slow train, stopping at every little station along the way, and now that Ramadan was over, the small markets which filled most of the platform at each halt were doing brisk business. At each station it seemed as if virtually all the passengers had disembarked to hurry over and buy dates and cakes and fruit and tea or coffee or a cold drink from one of the numerous thriving stalls. Each station was a colourful moving pattern of people, dark skin against white cloth, with the women looking like butterflies in their brightly patterned clothing, and everyone in a hurry to complete their transactions before the train moved on.

The old man opposite me, however, never moved. He just waited. And sure enough, once the rush to disembark was over, some of the vendors would clamber up into the train and swiftly make their way through the carriages, calling out their wares as they went. Every so often, the old man would lift his finger and buy whatever he wanted, smiling contentedly all the while. His every movement was filled with a complete lack of effort, and everything he needed seemed to come to him without any struggle. After a while, I noticed that he had a beautiful silver ring on one finger, with an inscription in Arabic engraved on it. I asked him what it said, and with a broad smile he held it up for me to see. It read: Fa-Sabrun Jamilun, part of an ayah from the Qur'an which means:

So patience is beautiful.

(Qur'an: 12.18)

Slowly the train trundled northwards, and patiently I waited as the day unfolded. Eventually we reached Atbarah, where we halted for some time, before continuing the slow journey northwards once again. Following Abdal-Malik's instructions, I eventually dismounted at a small station and walked through the powerful mid-afternoon heat to the banks of the Nile. A battered pontoon ferry was making slow progress across the broad sweep of the river, and I could see from the direction in which it had to point that the current under the apparently smooth waters must be a strong one. At last the ferry reached the bank, and all its passengers, including a robed and turbaned man on a large camel, slowly disembarked via the steel ramp which had been allowed to clang down onto the muddy bank. Soon the ferry was off again, as it crossed the mighty river yet again, and half an hour later I was on the other side of the Nile, walking south, with the wide waters of the river on my left, and the ocean of the desert stretching out to the horizon on my right.

I walked briskly, glad to be stretching my legs after the long journey, but soon becoming very hot in the searing afternoon sun. By the time I reached Kaddabas, I was covered in sweat and my mouth was dry. I was taken straight to Shaykh Jayli, who was lying on his side, surrounded by fuqara and swathed in white robes, so that he looked like a great white smiling sea-lion. He greeted me warmly and told one of his fuqara to take me to my room to rest and have a drink. Insh'Allah we would meet again tomorrow.

It was good to quench my thirst and stretch out on a clean bed in the cool shade of the guest room, but I was still full of energy, and once I had cooled down, I ventured outside to take a closer look at my surroundings. The faqir who had shown me to my room was outside, and informed me that there was a Tijani Shaykh nearby who taught the Qur'an at the maddrasah where the Mahdi had once memorised the entire Qur'an by heart. Perhaps, he asked, I would like to visit him. Naturally, I said 'Yes'.

✿ ✿ ✿

The maddrasah turned out to be about half a mile away across the desert, and although it was now late afternoon, I was hot and thirsty once more by the time we drew near to the small cluster of buildings that surrounded the mosque at Ghurbush. As we approached, a lone figure emerged from one of the buildings and came over to greet us. It was the Tijani Shaykh, a quiet dignified man, who sat us down on a straw mat in the shade of one of the buildings. Having greeted us and made us comfortable, he disappeared and then reappeared almost immediately with a tray of tall glasses containing fresh ice-cold lime juice. I was not at all sure how he had managed this, since there were no power lines to be seen and the place appeared to be without electricity. Thankfully we sat and sipped at our refreshing drinks. Between us and the mosque was a huge pile of small stones. Every time someone has completed learning the whole of the Qur'an by heart at this maddrasah, I was informed, a stone is added to that pile. There must have been thousands of stones in the pile, including, presumably, one for the Mahdi who had previously studied there about a century and a half before.

Shortly before maghrib, a band of about twenty fuqara suddenly appeared out of the desert. We all did wudu, the adhan was given, and then we did the prayer out on the sandy courtyard beneath the darkening sky. It was a lovely way to start the new day – for the Muslims' day begins at sunset and not at sunrise. This is because we follow a lunar calendar, which is about eleven days shorter than the solar calendar, and the new moon that heralds the start of a new lunar month is only visible for a short time directly after the sun has set.

After we had done the prayer, we had a small gathering of dhikr, reciting the Qur'an and singing several qasidas for about an hour, before stopping to drink sweet hot milky tea served in beautiful bone china teacups, accompanied by fresh light sponge cake. Again, I wondered how this had been accomplished in such rough and simple conditions. There was still no sign of electricity, and yet the tea and cake tasted better than anything I had experienced in any London patisserie. Having eaten and drunk our fill, I sang the qasida called **Praise** from the Diwan of Shaykh Muhammad ibn al-Habib, and then it was time to pray isha. Once the prayer was over, the band of fuqara bade us farewell and disappeared back into the desert until all that we could hear from them was the sound of the qasida that they had started singing, growing gradually fainter as the darkness swallowed them up. My companion and I thanked the Tijani Shaykh, a beautifully humble man, who wore no outward indication of his tremendous inward knowledges other than his impeccable behaviour, and then made our way back to the zawiyya at Kaddabas beneath a myriad of stars and a moon that was already over a week old. Ramadan was over and the Hajj was just around the corner!

❂ ❂ ❂

I awoke the next morning feeling rested and refreshed, but being rather dusty and travel-stained, I asked if it would be possible to have a good wash. I was given two buckets of water and shown to a nearby simple small wash house which, like all the buildings here, was made of thick mud and straw walls with a thick mud roof. By now I had become accustomed to making a little water go a long way by not wasting it unnecessarily. Using the first bucket of water, I soaped and rinsed my body from head to toe, and with the second bucket, I did a ghusl. Then, feeling wonderfully fresh and clean, and having put on a clean robe and turban which soon absorbed the water on my body, I was taken to meet Shaykh Jayli.

Shaykh Jayli was very old and had great baraka. He was one of those Shaykhs whose presence is such that you feel your inward state change noticeably and immediately the moment you draw near, before a word has been spoken or a glance exchanged. I approached with respect to shake and kiss his hand. Although, because of my poor Arabic, there was little that I could say or understand, I knew that there was great benefit in this meeting, for the state of a true Shaykh transforms the hearts of those who are near him, and this energy exchange is usually far more beneficial than any insight that can be achieved on a verbal, informational level. Very little was said. Shaykh Jayli asked me a little about myself and my Shaykh and then requested me to sing a qasida from the Diwan of Shaykh Muhammad ibn al-Habib, which I did:

COUNSEL

Peace be upon the brotherhood in every place,
a peace that embraces all
in every assembly.

I wish to give good counsel to all,
hoping for the attainment
of desire, might, victory and strength.

My first counsel to the one who has dedicated himself
to fear of Allah is that he accompany those
who are free in making-happen and in casting-out.

For this is the basis of wealth
if you are intelligent.
Rely on it and stick to the shari'ah.

All those who have obtained knowledge and dominion
have only obtained it
by accompanying a humble man,

By whom I mean the Shaykh
whose light has overflowed,
and who has brought secrets and wealth with him.

If you desire lights and the opening of inner sight,
then copy him in exaltation of Allah
and turn from conflict.

And persevere in dhikr taught with idhn
and neglect it neither
in the state of distress nor of success.

Enrich the awakenings that come from the dhikr
by keeping to the shari'ah,
and quickly tell your Shaykh all that happens to you.

So the negation of choice, and then all will,
is the purest of springs,
if you are able to hear.

These are the stations of certainty:
You start out with turning away [from wrong action],
doing-without, and then fear which brings restraint.

Hope, gratitude, then patience and trust,
then satisfaction
and the love that joins them all.

Its causes are the pure contemplation of what we have,
and of the perfection of the attributes,
then contemplation of the dazzling light –

By it, I mean the Messenger Muhammad,
may blessings be upon him
in quantity as great as all that is even or odd,

And on his family and companions
and every gnostic calling to the path of Allah
in every assembly.

(Diwan of Shaykh Muhammad ibn al-Habib)

After I had completed the qasida with a blessing on the Prophet Muhammad, may the blessings and peace of Allah be on him, Shaykh Jayli turned to one of his fuqara and said something to him in a low voice. There was a gasp of surprise. "Fifty!" I heard him say, but whatever it was, he left to do the Shaykh's bidding.

The faqir returned almost immediately, with an envelope in his hand, which he gave to the Shaykh, who in turn gave it to me. "This is fifty pounds," he said. "This is to help you on your way to the Hajj." And he beamed at me as if the matter was already completed, as if I had already been to Makka and done the Hajj. I was as surprised as the faqir had been. I did not know what to say, and there was nothing to say, other than to thank him for his generosity. The generosity of Allah has no bounds, and He gives to whom He pleases, and as the Prophet Muhammad once said, Allah does not cease to provide for you from where you do not expect.

○ ○ ○

Having wished everyone farewell, I retraced my steps along the banks of the Nile, recrossed the river on the ferry, and was given a lift to Atbarah, where I stayed with a descendant of the Mahdi until it was time to catch the train. After about three hours' rest, I was taken to the station by my host, a man called Abdal-Aziz, who gave me a beautiful deep red prayer mat before bidding me 'As-salaamu-alaikum' and disappearing into the crowd.

The journey back to Omdurman was peaceful and uneventful, and that evening I was back at Shaykh Al-Fattih Qarib'Allah's zawiyya, pleasantly surprised to find that Abdal-Jalil was already there. Mustafa's condition had not improved after his return to Omdurman, and if anything, he had grown thinner and more withdrawn. It was now clear that he would have to return to England, without going on the Hajj, although we were not at all sure just how this would happen. Insh'Allah we would find a way to find him an air ticket during the next few days. In the meantime, Abdal-Jalil and I had decided to travel westwards, insh'Allah, to the Jebel Murra, the Mountains of Time, the jewel of the Sudan, which Ibrahim had pointed out to us on the map in his atlas all those light years ago in Athens. If we had time, we would then loop down to the south, to Waw and then Juba, before coming back down the Nile to Omdurman. Since it was our intention not to return to Omdurman until just before the time of the Hajj, we decided that it would be wise to obtain our Hajj visas from the Saudi Arabian Embassy before setting out on our western journey, and accordingly we agreed that I should go to the Embassy the next day, while Abdal-Jalil stayed at the zawiyya with Mustafa. I went to sleep that night filled with anticipation and good expectations.

OMDURMAN

We awoke to the sound of the dawn adhan, and after doing the prayer and enjoying our breakfast of hot sweet milky tea and biscuits, I set out for the Embassy, which turned out to be some two hours' walk away. The entrance to the Embassy was surrounded by a large crowd of people, presumably hoping to obtain Hajj or work visas, and since there was not even a semblance of a queue, it was a long time before I finally found myself in front of the small grille which was set in the wall next to the locked gate. I explained our plan to a tired looking official who replied, very apologetically, that they had not yet started issuing Hajj visas, and that I would have to return in a month's time. After the long walk and the long wait in the heat of the sun, I was feeling hot and bothered as it was, and this response was too much for me: "But we plan to travel in three days time, insh'Allah," I said in exasperation. "We will not be back until just before the time of the Hajj. We cannot just hang around here for a month, and in a month's time we may be hundreds of miles away from here. You must help us. We are Muslims. We are your brothers. Please give us our Hajj visas now. Surely it can't be that difficult!"

The official looked at me apologetically, as if he was just as tired of modern bureaucracy as I was, and excused himself. He returned after five minutes. "The Ambassador would like to see you, but he is very busy today. Please would you come here tomorrow morning, and he will see you at ten o' clock."

I was not sure whether or not this was a genuine response, or just a way of getting rid of me, but I had no choice other than to agree to do as I was asked. Although I realised that the way the world was now organised necessitated passports and passport controls, I could not help wishing that I was living in the pre-colonial era, when a Muslim could travel freely through the Muslim lands from Morocco to Malaysia, using the Qur'an as his passport and the shahada as his visa. Since it was no longer possible to travel like this, simply because the Muslim lands were now being governed in accordance with western control methods, I was always slightly suspicious of the Muslims who were content to perpetuate these alien systems, even though they did not derive from the Qur'an or the Sunnah of the Prophet Muhammad. However it never did any good to draw this to their attention, and now, as in the past, I was obliged to submit to the way things were, simply because I was in no position to change them. I swallowed my impatience and agreed to return the next day.

❂   ❂   ❂

I was at the Saudi Arabian Embassy promptly at ten o' clock the next morning, expecting an impossible tussle with bureaucracy, but determined to do all that I could to obtain our visas, and trusting that, having come so far, Allah would give them to us. A pleasant surprise awaited me. I was allowed in through the gates, and shown directly to the Ambassador who was the epitome of helpfulness and politeness. "Look," he said in perfect English, "I'm very sorry, but we really are not ready to start issuing Hajj visas yet. It's not that we are trying to be difficult or anything like that. I understand your position. Please go on your journey, and I promise you, that when you return we will give you your visas, even if it is just before the Hajj is due to commence. Please believe me, and please accept this small gift as a token of our sincerity." So saying, he handed me an envelope containing a hundred pounds.

At first I was speechless with surprise at the way in which our meeting had turned out. Once I had found my tongue, I thanked him profusely. I had always assumed that diplomats were bureaucrats whose main purpose in life was to make life difficult and stop things happening, but here was a man of action and generosity, may Allah reward him. Wishing him all the best, and with smiles all round, I bid him farewell and returned joyfully to the zawiyya.

Suddenly our situation had clarified and crystallised, and we were in a position to do what we wanted. The hundred pounds was just sufficient to buy Mustafa a cheapo cheapo ticket back to Heathrow. By now he hardly spoke a word to anyone, even to Abdal-Jalil and myself, and really had to be coaxed to eat even a few mouthfuls of food. No one here was able to help him, and we hoped that the fuqara back in England would be able to do better, especially once he was back in familiar surroundings. It was a great pity that he could not continue the difficult journey with us, but

Omdurman 121

there was no other alternative other than to put him on a 'plane back to England. Insh'Allah one day he would be able to go on the Hajj – as indeed he did!

Within twenty-four hours, the air ticket had been bought, Mustafa's few possessions had been packed, and we were at Khartoum airport. I accompanied Mustafa through the customs, since he now often did not respond to direct questions and did not seem to be fully aware of everything that was going on around him. His visa for the Sudan was now one day overdue, for we had not bothered to extend it once it was clear that he would be returning to England. The customs official began to make a fuss, but stamped his passport and waved us on, once I had explained that Mustafa was ill and must return on that flight. I waited with Mustafa in the departure lounge until the call for his flight came over the public address system, and asked a fellow passenger on the flight to look after him, before wishing a very puzzled Mustafa 'As-salaamu-alaikum' and a safe journey.

Having rejoined Abdal-Jalil, we were just in time to see Mustafa board the aircraft, and minutes later the 'plane had taken off safely and was out of sight. We took a taxi directly to the main Post Office and sent a telegram to Ibrahim in London, asking him to meet Mustafa on his arrival. Then, having done all that we could to help our travelling companion, we returned to the zawiyya, packed our bags and went straight to bed after we had prayed isha. Tomorrow, insh'Allah, we would set out on the next stage of our journey, to the Jebel Murra!

The next morning we were summoned to have breakfast with Shaykh Al-Fattih Qarib'Allah, who, as always welcomed us and fed us, his finely-featured face lighting up when we told him that we would be travelling west, insh'Allah, but expressing great puzzlement when we added that we might then head south. "Why do you want to go to Waw and Juba?" he asked, as if we were stupid. "There aren't any Muslims down there!" And he then proceeded to give us the names of two walis, one of whom lived in El Obeid and the other of whom lived just outside it, whom he recommended we should visit. Our appetising breakfast came to its end, and once again our generous host bade us farewell, making sure that it was well understood that we should come and stay as his guests at the zawiyya once we had returned to Omdurman and before we left for Makka. May Allah give Shaykh Al-Fattih light and peace in his grave. So much good came to us through him!

Having said our farewells to Shaykh Al-Fattih and his sons and those of his fuqara who were present, we set out on our western journey, travelling light and feeling light. In a way, our time during Ramadan had been very concentrated and sometimes demanding, and now we were free to live at a more relaxed pace, travelling how and where we wished, with no pressures to constrain us. Although the baraka of Ramadan is a wonderful experience, it was nice to be able to eat and drink whenever we felt hungry or thirsty, and although the benefits of doing dhikr are innumerable and unquantifiable, it was good to be easing off from the high intensity of dhikr which had been sustained during the month of fasting. As Shaykh Abdal-Qadir once said, 'Not too much and not too little makes you supple and not brittle!'

As we sped along the western road in a taxi truck, with the sun on our weathered faces and the wind flapping our robes, I mellowed into the sounds of the Sudanese pop music that blared out from a fellow passenger's ghetto blaster. With its intricate and insistent drumming rhythms and plaintive organ music and singing, it sounded like what it must be like to fly through the desert on a galloping camel. Right now it felt very good to be alive. We were young and healthy and on the move, on the way to Makka, insh'Allah, via the Mountains of Time!

○ ○ ○

Our first objective was to visit two Shaykhs who did not live all that far away from Omdurman, Khalifa Yusuf who lived at Omduwamban, and Shaykh Nur who lived in a small village about half a mile further on down the road. After about a couple of hours on the road, we were dropped off at Omduwamban, and after asking some people for directions, soon found ourselves sitting on a shady verandah, waiting for Khalifa Yusuf to appear.

Khalifa Yusuf was in charge of one of the several traditional Qur'an schools that are dotted about the Sudan. Despite the growing demand for a western style education, it is still customary for young children to be sent to these schools and not to leave until they have learned the whole of the Qur'an by heart, a process which can take between one and five years, depending on each individual child's aptitude. Having learnt the Qur'an by heart at an early age, they spend the rest of their lives discovering its limitless meanings and keeping it alive by reciting it continuously. The Prophet Muhammad said, may the blessings and peace of Allah be on him, that the best of people are those who learn and teach the Qur'an. Many of those who have learnt the Qur'an by heart become Imams and teachers, and thus it is preserved, not only on paper but also in the hearts of people.

Khalifa Yusuf was clearly a man who was much in demand, and yet he still found time to come and graciously welcome us, sitting very still, cross-legged on a bed which was on the verandah, and surveying existence like a mighty eagle high on its mountain, a king completely abased before his Creator, listening with close attention as we sang a qasida for him from the Diwan of Shaykh Muhammad ibn al-Habib. After talking with us for several minutes, he graciously excused himself, saying that we were welcome to stay the night, and disappeared through a large archway, his white djelaba hanging aristocratically from his tall thin body as he moved graciously out of sight.

Within twenty minutes, a lovely meal of very bland food was placed before us by one of his fuqara. "This will do you good if you have an upset stomach," he said. – This was exactly what Abdal-Jalil was suffering from at the time. After we had finished eating, and prayed maghrib, we were taken on a guided tour of the Qur'an school, which was spread out over a large area. There was a very large sandy courtyard where much of the teaching took place, and in the middle of which was a huge fire. In the pre-electricity days, this had been the students' main source of light and warmth during the night, and although there was now electric light, it was still kept burning. We were shown the simple flat wooden boards on which passages from the Qur'an were written in charcoal-based ink. Once one passage had been memorised, it could easily be washed off, and the next passage inscribed in its place. We were also shown the simple dormitories where the students slept. Since it was still the hottest time of the year, many of the students had carried their simple wooden framed beds outside and placed them under one of the numerous shady trees. Here it was cooler, and you could fall asleep with the night breeze caressing your face, which, after we had prayed isha, was exactly what Abdal-Jalil and I did, lulled asleep by the incessant hum of the Qur'an which had filled the air ever since we had entered the grounds of the Qur'an school – not issuing from tape recorders and public address systems as we had experienced in the streets of Cairo, but from the hearts of live people. It was like being in the middle of a human beehive.

As I slipped gently into sleep, I reflected on the beauty of the place. It was good to know that such valuable teaching was still very much alive, and that it had not been completely eradicated by the Empire builders, who at one time had attempted to close down all the maddrasahs in the country – not only in the Sudan but also in all the Muslim lands that had been occupied – in a vain attempt to 'educate' the Muslims out of Islam.

◦ ◦ ◦

After praying subh in the Qur'an school's crowded mosque the next morning, and sharing breakfast with some of Khalifa Yusuf's fuqara, we took our leave as the students prepared for another day's memorising of the Qur'an. Although I envied them, I also knew deep in my heart that I did not have the same capacity to learn as them, and that my destiny lay elsewhere. We made our way down the road through the early morning sunshine, everything still fresh and new and cool, and after a while we arrived at Shaykh Nur's zawiyya.

The contrast to the Qur'an school just up the road was very marked. There was a small mosque, a few huts, a patch of grass, a handful of fuqara, some ducks and chickens, Shaykh Nur in a very simple djelaba and turban, and that was it. It was an empty yet peaceful place.

Within about an hour of having arrived, a simple and yet sumptuous feast had been prepared, and everyone who was there had food to eat, with the leftovers going to the ducks and chickens. The pace of life here was peaceful and unhurried. After praying dhur in the simple mosque, we rested in the shade during the heat of the afternoon, prayed asr and rested some more, prayed maghrib and had a lively gathering of dhikr, ate supper and drank tea, prayed isha, and then to bed, sleeping on rough wooden framed beds out on the patch of grass beneath the heavens, until the dawn adhan and a beating drum told us that it was time to do wudu and pray subh.

After a simple breakfast of bread and tea, we thanked Shaykh Nur and his fuqara for their hospitality and retraced our steps back to the Omduwamban bus and taxi truck depot. Soon we were back in Omdurman and at the train station, where we were just in time to board the train that was travelling south to Kusti. From there we would head west, insh'Allah. At last our western journey had really begun!

KUSTI

Although I had the fifty pounds which Shaykh Jayli had given to me, and although Abdal-Jalil still had most of the twenty pounds which Shaykh Salih had given him, we had decided to be thrifty, and had bought fourth class tickets in the crowded wooden slatted seats section of the train. The compartment was very hot and full of poor people, and I felt especially sorry for the mothers with babies and small children. The seats were hard and uncomfortable, and became harder and more uncomfortable as the journey continued. For a while we gazed out of the open windows at the slowly changing landscape, as the ancient steam engine slowly pulled its great load of numerous carriages slowly southwards, never far from the Blue Nile, past Jebel Awliya and towards the Sannar Dam.

After a while, our stomachs told us it was time to eat, and we walked up the length of the train until we reached the dining car, which was only a couple of carriages away from the engine. In our present state of wealth, the food seemed relatively inexpensive, and we settled down to a good meal, joined by a beggar for whom we bought the same as ourselves. He subsequently appeared on two other occasions during our journey, once about two hundred miles further west, and then subsequently back at the zawiyya in Omdurman, and on each occasion we gave him something, knowing that, at least to some extent, our future welfare depended on being generous to those whose need was greater than our own. For all we knew, he might be Al-Khidr, the Prophet who is said always to be alive, and who comes to people disguised as a beggar to test their generosity and willingness to help the poor and the bereft.

When we had finished eating, the beggar left us, and we decided to stay where we were, since the seats were padded and the dining car relatively empty and spacious. The train was very slow. There had been heavy rains a few days earlier and at times it was necessary for someone to walk ahead of the train to make sure that the lines were still safe and that not too much sand had been washed away from underneath the sleepers. Once the heat of the afternoon had lessened, we followed the example of many of our fellow travellers and climbed out and up onto the roof of our carriage which swayed gently with the motion of the train as we crawled through the ever changing desert terrain. Small lengths of sugar cane were cheap and plentiful, and I soon found myself peeling off the outer casing of a piece of sugar cane with my teeth and chewing on the freshly exposed sweet juicy pith, spitting out the remains once all the sweetness and moisture had been sucked out, just as I had as a small boy in central Africa. It really did feel as if we were on a great adventure now, and it was good to be alive.

Whenever the time for the prayer arrived, the train would slowly grind to a halt, wherever we happened to be, and all the passengers would stream out of the carriages to relieve themselves discreetly, squatting with their backs to the train and their long robes veiling them, before doing the prayer either singly or in small groups. The sand was full of thorns, and once your sandals were off to do the prayer, you had to be very careful where feet, hands, knees and head came to rest. There was plenty of time, however, and no rush, and when the train finally began to move on once again, it did so slowly that everyone had more than enough time to clamber back onto the train. It was all so very relaxed and easygoing, and so different to the rapid highly regulated train travel of Europe, where the demands of efficiency and punctuality make it unthinkable that public transport should halt so that people can pray.

Here, although progress was slow, there were no particular deadlines to be met, other than to do each prayer in its time, and one could simply relax and watch the world go by, to the accompaniment of the stirring Sudanese pop music that was always playing there somewhere in the background, rollicking along with its distinctive organ sounds and the driving rhythm of the drums that only the Africans have, in whichever part of the continent you happen to be, with their haunting yearning singing that fills the heart with longing even though you can only catch the odd word here and there. Wherever you go in the world, people always sing the same song, always sing about love, whether it is about love for this or that thing or person, or about love for Love itself.

❂   ❂   ❂

At the Sannar Dam we turned westwards, heading for the setting sun, surrounded by the starkness of the desert until another band of green appeared before us, heralding the White Nile long before we reached it, its banks covered with thick jungle. Shortly after maghrib, we slowly rolled to a halt at Kusti station, feeling like strangers in a strange land once more, for it was very different to the Sudan we had come to know and love further north.

We dismounted, stiff from our day's travel and unsure about what to do next. Up to now we had always had the address of someone or other, and usually a Shaykh at that, whom we knew would welcome and look after us. Here, we were completely on our own. We had hardly finished slapping the dust from our robes, when a man came up to us.

"Do you have somewhere to stay tonight?" he asked.

"No," we replied.

"Then please come and stay at my house tonight. You are most welcome."

Not for the first time during my travels in the Muslim lands, I marvelled at such straightforward hospitality. How different this man's attitude was to the majority of people in the 'civilised' world, including myself, where we are taught to steer clear of strangers and where hospitality has become largely a question of business once it moves outside the realm of immediate family and close friends.

Our host guided us through the darkness to his house, welcomed us, fed us, gave us beds on which to sleep, and, next morning after breakfast, made sure that we were back at the station in good time to catch the train that was going to El Obeid.

Although we planned to spend some time in El Obeid, Abdal-Jalil had been told that there was a wali living at a place called Kaduqli which was up in the Jebel Nuba, and accordingly we decided to go there first. This meant that we would have to leave the train at a place called Ar-Rahad, the nearest place on the railway line to Kaduqli.

AR-RAHAD

We arrived at Ar-Rahad in the early afternoon. It was a bright friendly sunny town, and we decided that the first priority was to find something to eat. During Ramadan I had never felt hungry, but, as always, as soon as the month of fasting was over, the pangs of hunger reappeared. During the morning, a man wearing dark glasses had passed by us on the train, and Abdal-Jalil had impulsively said, "I can't stand people who wear dark glasses indoors!" Since then, two men wearing dark glasses had bought us iced drinks along the way, and now we had not walked very far through the dusty streets of Ar-Rahad before yet another man wearing dark glasses greeted us and offered to buy us a meal. Smiling broadly at each other, we gratefully accepted his invitation.

Having enjoyed our meal of meat stew and bread, we thanked our host and made our way towards the taxi truck depot, stopping on the way to buy two brightly coloured and beautifully woven palm leaf fibre mats. We now had something to lie on whenever we needed to rest. On reaching the depot, we were informed that we would have to wait until the next morning for a lorry going to Kaduqli. We were in no great hurry and, having bought some peanuts and dried dates which were as hard and as sweet as butterscotch, we rolled out our mats in the shade of a nearby tree, deciding to spend the night there.

Shortly before maghrib, a young friendly man approached us and asked us where we were sleeping that night. When he heard our reply, he exclaimed magnanimously, "You can't stay here! Come and stay at my house!" as if his was the biggest mansion in town. Gratefully we accepted Adam's offer – for that was his name – and followed him back to his home. Adam's house was a small circular thatched hut which was barely large enough to accommodate the one large wooden framed bed that stood grandly inside it. Adam apologised for the fact that his wife was away visiting relations which meant that he could not feed us properly, but this was no problem, and after praying maghrib and isha, we sat round the small fire he had made outside the hut, sipping hot sweet tea and munching away at the dates and nuts which we had purchased earlier. When it was time to go to sleep, we turned down Adam's suggestion that all three of us should somehow cram ourselves inside the hut, and rolled out our mats alongside the fire, saying that we would far rather prefer to sleep under the open sky than be squashed up inside his house.

❁ ❁ ❁

The next morning we thanked Adam, who had shared all that he possessed with us, for his hospitality, and returned to the taxi truck depot. We did not have long to wait before our lorry arrived, and soon we were bumping out of town and into the desert on the powerful Mercedes truck, perched precariously on all the merchandise that had been loaded onto it, along with about ten other people. We could have paid extra for the privilege of sitting up front in the cab with the driver, but the prospect of sitting out in the open air had appealed to us, and it was not until we had been jolted about in the back of the lorry for some time, with no secure seating and the fine powdery dust thrown up by the back wheels billowing around us and choking us, that we began to realise the advantages of being in the cab.

After a while, however, we left the desert terrain behind us, and began to climb up into the less dusty foothills of the Jebel Nuba. The road was still very bumpy, and the lorry seemed to lurch and buck about in every conceivable direction without quite turning over, but I could feel a lovely feeling of excitement and freedom within, as if we were on some adventurous expedition into unknown territory where no human being had been before. This was much more exciting than travelling first class in a European intercity express! The air was clear, the scenery was breathtaking, and we were alive!

As the sun climbed higher in the vast blue sky, we began to feel the strength of its heat, and, imitating the Tuareg, Abdal-Jalil and I unwrapped and rewrapped our turbans so that our necks and heads were completely covered except for our eyes. Not only were our skins protected from the sun, but also the cloth over our noses acted as a filter for the air we breathed, for every so often the lorry's wheels would still kick up clouds of dust into our faces as it lurched down into a dried up water course and then strained up the other side.

By now the hills were clothed in various forms of vegetation, and even trees, and after a while we emerged onto a relatively flat plateau covered in thick elephant grass. Half way across this plateau, we were amazed to see a whole community of nomads coming towards us, all their belongings strapped to the backs of huge oxen, the women bare-breasted and the men carrying spears. The truck drew over to one side to let them pass, and silently they passed us, without a word of greeting or thanks being spoken by anyone, until the last of them disappeared from sight round a bend in the track and into the elephant grass. They belonged to a different world to us, living as their ancestors had lived, and I was grateful that for those few brief minutes we had been fortunate enough to catch a glimpse of how they lived their lives.

The Mercedes lorry drew out back onto the dirt track and we continued on our way, eventually emerging out of the elephant grass and up into another series of larger foothills. After a while, we reached a refreshment stop, a large thatched hut under a large leafy tree, where we bought the inevitable bowl of foules mesdames, bread, guavas and hot sweet milky tea. It was one of the best meals of our entire journey.

Having satisfied our hunger and thirst, we did wudu and prayed dhur and asr, and then we were off again, climbing higher and higher into the Jebel Nuba, until finally, just before sunset, we rolled into Kaduqli, nestling in the depths of the middle of nowhere. We had only just clambered down from our perch on top of the lorry's cargo, when the adhan was called in the nearby mosque, and, having dusted ourselves down and done wudu, we were just in time to catch the prayer.

Having prayed a further two rakats for isha, for naturally we were doing travelling prayers, we made our way to the nearby outdoor cafe and ordered two badly needed ice cold cokes, for we were now feeling quite tired and thirsty after the day's travel. We had hardly lifted the bottles to our lips, when a policeman came up to us and brusquely asked us for our passports. After all the hospitality that we had received during the past few months, his sudden rudeness shocked us, but naturally we did as he asked. The policeman flicked briefly and officiously through our passports, and then looked sternly at us. "You have no permit to be here," he said. "You are breaking the law. Who are you and what are you doing here?" Patiently we explained the reason for our visit, but he did not seem to believe us.

"You must come to the police station for questioning immediately," he said threateningly.

"Certainly not!" replied an outraged Abdal-Jalil. "We haven't done anything wrong. We aren't causing any trouble. We have only come here to visit a wali, and insh'Allah we will be leaving tomorrow. Right now we are tired and thirsty and you are preventing us from enjoying our drinks. This is no way to treat fellow Muslims!"

The policeman clearly had no desire to discuss the matter further, and tried to catch hold of us both simultaneously, with the result that he caught neither. Successfully keeping the table between him and us, we hurriedly downed our cokes, and then, seeing reinforcements approaching, we retreated swiftly to the lorry and clambered back on board, as a large crowd gathered to watch the fun. It had all happened so quickly that no one really knew exactly what to do next. After repeatedly ordering us to come down, without success, the policeman told the driver to take the lorry down to the police station, where, now that we were completely surrounded by police, we eventually agreed to descend and submit to their interrogation.

Since our intentions were good and we had nothing to hide, there was not really very much to say, and I was just telling the Chief of Police yet again that this was no way to treat Muslims and that he would have to answer to Allah for his actions on the Last Day, when the adhan for isha came floating into the office. "Look," said Abdal-Jalil in exasperation, "that is the adhan for isha. We will do the prayer and then leave. We have no desire to stay any longer in such an unfriendly place. Are you going to stop us, or are you going to let us go?"

Fortunately, the Chief of Police realised that we were sincere and harmless and that the whole confrontation had been totally unnecessary. "You may go," he said, and, having prayed isha for a second time, we clambered stiffly aboard a truck laden with watermelons which happened to be leaving for Ar-Rahad, and bumped off into the night, still feeling indignant and mystified at the treatment which we had just received.

○ ○ ○

Later on in our western journey, I was told that the way we had been treated at Kaduqli was the way that the British Administration had treated the Sudanese when it was in power there. The police force at Kaduqli had merely been imitating the behaviour it had learned from the Sudan's former rulers, and as a result we had been given a taste of what it must have been like for the Sudanese to be governed by the British.

○ ○ ○

The journey back to Ar-Rahad could not have been more different to the journey to Kaduqli. I felt tired and dispirited as we bumped through the night, which was pitch black. It was impossible to sit up on the mound of large smooth watermelons that filled the truck, and although we tried to relax in a more or less horizontal position, it seemed that there were always at least two or three, and often more, unyielding watermelons pressing uncomfortably into us.

Eventually we bumped into Ar-Rahad in the early hours of the morning, tired, hungry, thirsty, and aching all over. We made our way to the station, unrolled our mats and just lay there, glad to be completely horizontal and motionless at last. Eventually the sun rose once again, and at last we ascertained that there would be a train that day, but not until after asr. We spent the day resting and eating and drinking, until at last our train arrived. Since it was a relatively short journey, and since the previous day's travelling had been tough, we had decided to travel first class, a decision which we soon regretted, for although the seats were covered in plush red velvet and there was air conditioning and we had a compartment to ourselves, it was dead. There was no life going on around us, no fellow travellers to chat to, or share your food with, no hustle and bustle. You could not even lean out of the sealed window and feel the wind on your face. It was a prison, and we were glad to escape from it as soon as the train rolled into El Obeid.

EL OBEID

It was already dark when we reached El Obeid, but we knew where we were going, since Shaykh Al-Fattih had advised us to search out Shaykh Al-Amin, who lived near the tomb of Wali Ismail, on our arrival. After visiting him we were to visit Shaykh Abdur-Rahim who lived at Zariba, another large Qur'an school situated about forty miles out of El Obeid in the middle of the desert.

Although it is a sunnah not to arrive unannounced or uninvited at someone's house after maghrib, we were very tired and simply found our way to the tomb of Wali Ismail and from there to the front door of Shaykh Al-Amin without pausing to reflect whether or not we would be causing any great inconvenience by turning up so unexpectedly. We need not have worried. Shaykh Al-Amin greeted us like long lost relatives with a shining smiling face, and ushered us into his simple house with words of greeting and not a single question.

Within minutes food was placed before us, and as we ate, another visitor arrived, a tall well-built man with a flashing smile who spoke very good English. His name was Abdal-Qadir, and apparently he knew both Shaykh Al-Amin and Shaykh Abdur-Rahim very well. He joked and chatted away with us for about an hour, and by the time he rose to leave, it was agreed that he would show us around El Obeid the next day and then take us out to Zariba whenever it was convenient. Cheerfully he bid us good night, beaming all over with anticipation and joy, and disappeared back into the night.

Shaykh Al-Amin showed us to a room with two beds, with mattresses and clean sheets, and having showed us the shower room and toilet, bid us good night. Abdal-Jalil had first go in the shower, and then, although I was very tired, I washed all my dirty clothes in the shower, then my body, and then, having prayed maghrib and isha, I finally sank into bed and fell fast asleep, grateful for the cool clean sheets and glad that all my clothes were freshly washed. How different this night was to the one that had preceded it.

○ ○ ○

We awoke the next morning well after sunrise, having slept right through the dawn call to prayer. Having done wudu, we each did two rakats to make up for the prayer that we had missed, and then emerged into the sunlight of a brand new day, feeling clean and refreshed and rested. I was in good health, al-hamdulillahi wa shukrulillah, but Abdal-Jalil was still having trouble with his stomach. After all the processed food to which we had become accustomed in the West, the rough and ready food that we had been eating for the past two months especially was still a trifle harsh for our previously pampered innards, and it was probably only because I had been travelling for most of my life that my digestive system had adapted more readily to the change in diet than his.

We found ourselves in a large enclosed compound, bordered by one storey buildings on three sides and a high wall with a door in it on the fourth. As is often the case when you arrive somewhere at night, the place looked completely different in the day to what I had imagined it would look like in the darkness. Shaykh Al-Amin soon appeared, his face still shining and smiling, and soon we were confronted by a huge breakfast which included one very sweet dish which left us both feeling a bit queasy.

As we ate, we watched in amazement as the menagerie which surrounded Shaykh Al-Amin revealed itself. As well as the usual chickens and cats that were free to roam as they wished, there were also several rabbits scurrying about, a goat, and a dog and a monkey, all moving about the compound of their own accord. The dog and the monkey especially made us laugh, for the monkey would dance about in front of the dog, goading and taunting him until the dog finally lost its cool and leapt at him. With a neat side-step and a jump, the monkey would suddenly be sitting astride the dog's shoulders, mischievously tugging at its ears and grinning all over his monkey face, before playfully leaping off and starting the game all over again.

We were still watching the dog and the monkey, and still laughing whenever the monkey dodged the dog and leapt on his shoulders, when Abdal-Qadir appeared through the door in the wall, grinning broadly and welcoming us warmly. After chatting with Shaykh Al-Amin for a while, we took our leave and began our look around El Obeid, commencing with a visit to the tomb of Wali Ismail. After this we were taken to Abdal-Qadir's office. He was in charge of petrol distribution in this region, and just needed to do a little paper work before he could legitimately take the day off. This was soon completed, and as we drove through the streets of El Obeid, which turned out to be a large town perhaps as large as Omdurman, Abdal-Qadir insisted that we should come and stay as his guests for the remainder of our stay in El Obeid. Having agreed to do so, we returned to Shaykh Al-Amin's compound to collect our luggage, thanking him especially for having given us such a welcome. "I love you for Allah!" he replied, his whole face shining and smiling.

❂ ❂ ❂

Abdal-Qadir's house was a large one, built in the same compound pattern as Shaykh Al-Amin's abode, so as to ensure privacy for the men and the women when it was needed, without causing isolation. His courtyard was filled with flowers and bougainvillea, and he had twelve children. All the boys shared one bedroom, and all the girls shared another. He also had two slaves from southern Sudan whom he treated with kindness and respect, only giving them work of which they were capable, and in return providing them with the same shelter, food and clothing as the rest of his family.

Abdal-Qadir was a powerful powerfully built man who exercised his authority and influence in a balanced and judicious manner. Clearly his position in the community was an important one, for without petrol, many vehicles and ventures would literally grind to a halt, and yet he was not at all arrogant and treated everyone with respect. He was a servant to all, and therefore their master, not a tyrant, and although he was very much involved in the nitty gritty of everyday affairs at a significant level in his community, he was also a man who constantly remembered Allah, not only at the time of the prayer, but also during the times between each of the five daily prayers. Abdal-Qadir was a lover of Allah and His Messenger and His awliya, and he mentioned Allah frequently and loved dhikr.

We had moved into Abdal-Qadir's house on the Wednesday, and that evening he suggested that we should go to Zariba the next day, since there would be a very large gathering of dhikr there on the Thursday evening, it being laylat-al-jumua. Accordingly we went to bed straight after isha, and early the next morning, after subh and breakfast, we set off into the desert in Abdal-Qadir's sturdy Range Rover. As always, I marvelled thankfully at the way in which events had unfolded in accordance with our intentions. Clearly Zariba was a remote place that was difficult to reach, and yet Allah had provided us with the best of guides and means of transport to get there, without our having had to lift a finger.

✿ ✿ ✿

The journey turned out to be a slow one, for as soon as we had left El Obeid behind us, the road to Zariba was no more than two parallel sandy ruts that stretched out ahead of us through the powdery deep orange-red sand of the desert. The only sign of life other than ourselves were the thorny acacia trees and tough gum-arabic trees that were dotted about the barren landscape in profusion. On several occasions the Range Rover became bogged down in the sand, whenever we began to move too fast or too slow, and then it was necessary to shovel out the sand from around the back wheels and place long steel runners under and in front of them, so that they had something to grip onto when the vehicle started up again. The day grew hotter and hotter as we crawled through the desert at not much more than a fast walking pace, and it was with relief that we finally glimpsed the trees and houses of Zariba in the distance. Finally we drew up outside Shaykh Abdur-Rahim's house, hot and thirsty and covered in dust, and glad that we had arrived.

ZARIBA

As we dismounted stiffly from the dusty Range Rover and stretched our legs, a tall handsome man dressed entirely in voluminous white robes and a flowing turban appeared as if from nowhere and embraced each one of us with a welcoming smile. I felt as if I would drown in the hug and be swallowed up in the folds of clean white cloth that covered this extraordinary being who hardly seemed to have a body, but rather a fine energy field that was given form by the robes and meaning by the face that smiled out at us from beneath the turban. It was Shaykh Abdur-Rahim, and he was clearly a man of Allah.

We were shown into his large cool house and immediately served with refreshingly cool drinks. He and Abdal-Qadir were clearly on very good terms, and the two chatted and laughed away together while Abdal-Jalil and I recovered from the journey. After Abdal-Qadir had explained who we were and what we were doing, we were taken on a tour of Zariba, which was very beautiful in its simplicity.

At the Qur'an school's centre was a vast courtyard of clean sand, from which all the desert thorns had been meticulously and painstakingly removed by hand. The entire courtyard was lined by shady green trees, on the other side of which were the learning and living quarters of all the Qur'an students, of whom there were several hundred. At one end of the courtyard was a very large mosque which was in the process of being extended and doubled in size. I realised now why Shaykh Abdur-Rahim had smiled earlier on when I had said that I did not like the new reinforced concrete mosques that were being built in the Sudan, but rather preferred the old traditional mud-walled mosques and especially the small road-side mosques that were often no more than simple shelters made with upright poles and thatched roofs. Clearly this was all very well where there were small numbers of people involved, but with a community the size of Zariba's, modern building methods did have a distinct advantage.

Near the mosque was the place for the large fire which, as at Omduwamban, had been the only main source of light at night before the arrival of electricity. Here, as at Omduwamban, it was still kept burning, even though they now had their own generator and good electric lighting at night. Again, as at Omduwamban, the air was full of the sound of Qur'an being recited, like the hum of bees, and as we strolled round the school, every so often we caught a glimpse of a class in full swing, all the students sitting cross-legged on the floor and busily reciting the Qur'an with their Qur'an boards in their hands, while their teacher quietly moved from student to student, making sure that each individual was getting it exactly right.

At the other end of the courtyard, near Shaykh Abdur-Rahim's house, was a small circular wall with a diameter of about twenty yards. I was told by one of the Shaykh's fuqara that sometimes Shaykh Abdur-Rahim used to walk round and round the inside of the wall for hours and hours late at night doing dhikr, like some giant human dynamo. Shaykh Abdur-Rahim was a very finely balanced being who could be both serious and light-hearted without going too far to either extreme. He was very playful and always joking, as if to compensate for the harshness of the thorny desert that stretched away uncompromisingly to the horizon in every direction, but also, as I saw clearly at maghrib when he led the prayer in a mosque packed with hundreds of men, he was the leader of the community here at Zariba, and its guide – its living heart – and its business each day was dhikru'llah and the learning of the Qur'an by heart, a trust which, as the Qur'an itself states, even the mountains refused, because of its gravity and weight.

There were no distractions here at Zariba, no games to play, or music to listen to, or films to watch, or novels to read; no daily newspapers or favourite programmes on the television; no sidewalk cafes or shops in which to pass the time of day; not even a small friendly neighbourhood supermarket. If you were not at Zariba for Allah, there was no way you could stay at Zariba for very long.

After we had prayed maghrib, Shaykh Abdur-Rahim's strong sweet clear voice carrying distinctly to every corner of the large mosque without the assistance of a microphone or public address system, we were welcomed back to his house where a sumptuous feast served on huge circular metal trays was placed before us. They contained far more than the dozen or so people present could possibly eat, including several roasted pigeons and chickens, as well as rice and bread and a vegetable stew, but I knew that none of it would be wasted, and was careful to eat the small morsels of food that had fallen off the trays onto the mat on which we were seated cross-legged. Shaykh Abdur-Rahim smiled at me in approval. "Your wrong-actions will be forgiven even before those morsels of food have reached your stomach," he said.

We had just finished eating from a tray loaded with green yet sweet juicy oranges and dripping pieces of red watermelon, and were sipping at the customary glasses of sweet hot milky tea, when the adhan for isha was called. By the time we had finished our tea and done wudu and walked across the huge courtyard to the mosque, the people there had clearly been waiting for several minutes. The mosque was absolutely full with men dressed in white robes and turbans, and there was that lovely peaceful silence that only surrounds people who are waiting patiently to do the prayer. It was a beautiful sight, although I could not help feeling a little guilty for having been partly the cause for the delay. Space was made for us in the front row, and again Shaykh Abdur-Rahim's beautiful voice filled the mosque and pierced our hearts as he recited the Qur'an in a firm straight forward recitation.

After isha, everyone did their sunnah prayers and then made their way out of the mosque and into the courtyard, filling it with white, as the stars and moon shone down on us from a huge unclouded empty sky. Then the gathering of dhikr began. There must have been about six hundred men out there, sitting on the sand of the courtyard that was still warm from the heat of the sun, in a large circle, singing qasida after qasida, all of which they appeared to know by heart. After what seemed like two or three hours, we all rose to our feet, and the hadra began. I had always been taught by my own Shaykh never to do a standing-up hadra after eating a meal, but as I had not eaten a great deal at supper, and as some time had elapsed since our meal, it felt alright to go ahead and do it.

"Hayy Hayy-Hayy, Hayy Hayy-Hayy, Hayy Hayy-Hayy, Hayy Hayy-Hayy, Hayy Hayy-Hayy," the Name of Allah Al-Hayyu, the

144 The Difficult Journey

Living, the One Who is Alive in each instant, the One Who is Breath, the One Who fills every living thing with Breath, the One Who gives Life, was being invoked repeatedly over and over again, in a steady intoxicating rhythm, and I joined in with concentration and force, my body and mind completely relaxed yet alert, as I surrendered to the dhikr, recalling momentarily the following ayat of Qur'an:

> Surely in the creation of the heavens and the earth
> and in the difference between night and day
> are signs for those who have understanding,
> those who remember Allah
> standing, sitting and reclining,
> and reflect on the creation of the heavens and the earth:
> "O our Lord, You did not create this in vain,
> Glory be to You,
> So protect us from the punishment of the Fire."
>
> (Qur'an: 3.190-191)

As the invocation increased in intensity and steadied, Shaykh Abdur-Rahim moved into the middle of the large circle of men who stood side by side with their hands lightly clasped, swaying gently in time with the dhikr. He was followed by about five singers, including Abdal-Qadir who was singing his heart out, and three men with tambourines who accentuated the rhythm of the invocation with their lithe drumming fingers. The qasida that the singers were singing soared out above the rhythmical invocation that surrounded them, and although the form and rhythm of the hadra was slightly different to the large hadras which I had experienced in Morocco and England, the overall effect and texture was very much the same.

Shaykh Abdur-Rahim and his dynamic entourage began to circle round the inner periphery of the circle of dhikr, giving each man a fresh charge of energy as they passed him by, the drumming and the singing and the invocation all combining beautifully in an unrestrained and yet perfectly measured glorification of our Creator whose clarity and purity and vibrancy could not be denied for an instant by anyone whose heart was open. Round and round they circled in the moonlight, like a large white galleon inside a harbour with all its white sails unfurled before the wind, above us the vastness of the sky illuminated by the moon and the stars, and around us the darkness of the desert, with the large fire flickering away over by the mosque, and the air around us and in our lungs alive with the steady rhythmical invocation of Allah the Living, "Hayy Hayy-Hayy, Hayy Hayy-Hayy, Hayy Hayy-Hayy, Hayy Hayy-Hayy, Hayy Hayy-Hayy, Hayy Hayy-Hayy," which seemed as if it would go on for ever.

It was both beautiful and majestic and when the hadra finally grew faster and faster in tempo and then came to an end, we felt as light and as clean as the air which filled our lungs. After some recitation of Qur'an, the gathering of dhikr was over, and everyone retired to their beds or mats to sleep. As Abu Yazid once said, "O Allah, You have to feed me and I have to praise You!"

Abdal-Qadir, Abdal-Jalil and I were given comfortable beds to sleep on in Shaykh Abdur-Rahim's house, and we wasted little time in getting into bed. I fell immediately into the deep dreamless sleep that often follows an evening's gathering of dhikr, and did not awake until the sound of the adhan for subh brought me back to my senses, still feeling light and transparent and refreshed, as if my body was my ruh, rather than its temporary dwelling.

We stayed for the jumua, everyone dressed in dazzling white and filling the mosque to capacity, and then, after thanking Shaykh Abdur-Rahim for his great generosity and being embraced by him just as when we had first arrived, we clambered back into the Range Rover for the journey back to El Obeid, now completely refreshed and revitalised, with our difficult journey to Kaduqli now already no more than a memory.

In a way, I envied the small boys and young men who were busy memorising more Qur'an even as we drove away. They would all have access to wisdom in a way and to a degree that would always be beyond my grasp and outside my experience, and yet, at the same time, I was grateful for the life that I had had up to now, and did not wish that it had been any different. Looking back at it in this remote part of the world, I was well aware that it had been amazing, and right now it did not look as if it was going to become any less interesting.

EL OBEID

We arrived back in El Obeid in good time, the return journey seeming much shorter than the outward journey, as is often the case, and after showering and eating an early supper, two of Abdal-Qadir's elder sons announced that they were going to the cinema. Would we like to come too? – Of course we would!

The cinema was really no more than a large oval area surrounded by a high wall and filled with chairs. It had no roof, other than the vast dome of the heavens. At one end was the entrance, above which was a small balcony with the most expensive seats and the projection room, and at the other end was the screen which was just a white-washed square on the wall. When we arrived there was a large crowd outside the cinema, including some twenty to thirty beggars, some of whom were selling Benson and Hedges cigarettes, either in packets of ten or singly. Abdal-Qadir's two sons treated us to seats on the balcony, and having bought cold cokes and freshly roasted peanuts in twisted cones of cheap paper, we watched the cinema rapidly fill up before the show began.

The programme commenced with western-style adverts which had been shot in European and American cities. They seemed alien and out of place in the present raw desert setting, and it was almost like a visual invasion from another very different world, selling products which were unnecessary and unneeded by the people who were watching. Perhaps the most ironic advert was the one for Benson and Hedges, depicting a young innovative executive on the move in a smart suit and tie with his carefree liberated lady in tow, drawing confidently on their superior cigarettes with complete reassurance as they whirled through the revolving doors of some five star hotel and came to rest in the plush lobby. The reality of the beggars in rags outside the cinema, holding out packets of Benson and Hedges in the hope of earning a few pennies, contrasted starkly with this romanticised illusion of the freedom that comes with being a successful consumer.

Neither of us knew what film it was that we were going to see. It turned out to be **Godfather 2**. Neither of us had seen **Godfather**

1, and, as with the adverts, it seemed very incongruous to be watching this film under a starry African sky, especially so soon after our visit to Zariba. Nevertheless, it was interesting to see a portrayal of a world which we had not seen for what seemed ages, and the nature of the brotherhood of the Mafia contrasted vividly with the brotherhood of the Muslims which had been displayed to us during the past months again and again. As the Prophet Muhammad once said, the best aspect of Islam is to greet those you know and those you do not know and to feed the guest.

The next day was a Saturday, yawm al-sabd as it is called in Arabic, which means the day of the sabbath. All the original followers of Moses and Jesus, peace be on them, celebrated the sabbath on the Saturday, until the Emperor Constantine changed it to the Sun day to make it coincide with the weekly festival of the Roman sun god, in one of his various attempts to synthesise early Christianity with the traditional customs of the Romans. Abdal-Qadir had to return to his office, since the Muslim 'weekend' takes place on the Thursday and Friday of each week, and accordingly Abdal-Jalil and I spent the day resting, for we planned to continue our travels the next day.

That evening the three of us went round to visit Shaykh Al-Amin, may Allah have mercy on him, in order to say goodbye and thankyou. One of the sciences with which he was familiar was the use of Qur'anic ayat as medicine and the preparation of Qur'anic talismans to ward off harm. Abdal-Jalil, who was still troubled by an upset stomach, asked him for a cure, and I, for some unknown reason, asked for a cure to combat the ill-effects of cold, sensing that it would be needed at some time in the future. Shaykh Al-Amin prepared the cures for us, writing them out on pieces of paper which were then folded into neat triangles. These had to be burnt and the smoke breathed in to be effective. Abdal-Jalil took his medicine on the spot, while I stored my paper triangles safely away for future use.

After we had eaten supper and sung several qasidas from the Diwan of Shaykh Muhammad ibn al-Habib, we were taken to a gathering of dhikr with Shaykh Ahmad and his fuqara. This particular group followed the way of doing-without in the world, and their only possessions were the clothes they were wearing and a tin brique to carry water so that they could wash their private parts after using the toilet and do wudu before the prayer. They were all very poor outwardly, and inwardly rich in their contentment with and knowledge of Allah. They were all dressed in dark green robes, the same colour as the robe which Shaykh Tayyab had had made for me just before the Id at the end of Ramadan, and since I was wearing it at the time, they all greeted and treated me as one of themselves.

Their dhikr was very ecstatic, and after singing a few qasidas as they stood in a large circle, several of the fuqara literally took off into the middle of the circle, dancing, diving, cartwheeling and somersaulting high into the air, like a circus of acrobats performing for Allah, for their was certainly no human audience before whom they were playing. This behaviour was in marked contrast to the teaching which I had received from my own Shaykh, which was to be inwardly drunk while remaining outwardly sober, and he had always been quick to curtail any outward display of inward intoxication that the dhikr might have caused. Nevertheless it was interesting to witness this small band of fuqara dancing and singing for Allah. They were not doing anyone any harm, and there was no doubting their sincerity and spontaneity, for they certainly were not concerned with attracting other people's attention or putting on an act.

At the height of the dhikr, Abdal-Jalil and I were asked to sing a qasida, which we did:

ANNIHILATION IN ALLAH

O seeker of annihilation in Allah,
say all the time: 'Allah – Allah'

And withdraw into Him from other-than-him
and with your heart – see Allah.

Gather your concerns in Him and He will be enough
in place of other-than Allah.

Be a pure slave to Him
and you will be free from other-than-Allah.

Submit yourself to Him and be humble
and you will win a secret from Allah.

Invoke Him with gravity and sincerity
in the presence of the slaves of Allah.

Conceal it when He is manifested to you
with lights from the essence of Allah.

With us, other is impossible,
for existence belongs to Allah.

Constantly cut through your illusion
with a pure tawhid to Allah.

So the oneness of action appears
at the beginning of dhikr of Allah.

And the oneness of attribute
comes from love of Allah.

And the oneness of His essence
gives going-on with Allah.

Joy to the one who walks
on the path of dhikr of Allah,

Believing in a living Shaykh
who is a gnostic of Allah.

He holds constantly to His love
and sells his self to Allah.

He rises in the night to recite His word,
longing for Allah.

And so gets what he seeks
of the power of knowledge in Allah.

Our gifts are from a Prophet
who is the master of the creatures of Allah.

May the purest of blessings be upon him
in quantity as great as the knowledge of Allah,

And on his family and companions
and everyone who calls to Allah.

This very powerful qasida from the Diwan of Shaykh Muhammad ibn al-Habib seemed to have a sobering effect on the gathering, partly because of its meaning and partly because its rhythm was different to the other qasidas which the fuqara had been singing, but once it was completed, the fuqara continued with the qasidas with which they were familiar, and after a long and rather uncontained hadra, the gathering of dhikr came to an end.

After the dhikr was over, we were invited back to Shaykh Ahmad's simple wooden pole walled, grass thatch roofed, zawiyya, to share in a simple meal of doughnut-like buns and sweet milky coffee. Shaykh Ahmad, who appeared to be very young and radiant, presented us with a small bottle of pure sandalwood oil, beaming all over his face, and we used it constantly thereafter as a most refreshing olfactory tonic which helped us to both feel and smell good. Ever since then, I have never caught the scent of sandalwood without remembering the Sudan, and especially Shaykh Ahmad and his flying fuqara!

●   ●   ●

The next morning, we were up at dawn, and after doing the prayer and eating breakfast with Abdal-Qadir, we bid him the most grateful of farewells and returned to the train station, carrying the best of memories of our stay in El Obeid and Zariba with us. Our hosts had welcomed us and honoured us, and we had all had a good time as a result. They had been glad to have an opportunity to be generous, and fortunately for them, they still lived life at a pace at which it was possible to welcome and entertain unexpected guests, without being pushed for time and regarding them as an unwanted imposition.

During our stay in El Obeid, we had asked Abdal-Qadir about the Jebel Murra and whether or not it was worth our while to visit them. He had told us that they were indeed well worth visiting, and that we could have a good healthy rest there, especially if we went to a place called Nyertati, where it was very green and beautiful, and where there was fresh fruit in abundance. Apparently there was a huge mountain nearby, called Daribe, which was an

152 The Difficult Journey

extinct volcano in which there were two lakes, one of which contained sweet drinkable water, and the other of which was fed by a hot-spring whose water was bitter and unpalatable.

Delighted with Abdal-Qadir's description of the Mountains of Time, we had decided to continue our journey westwards by taking the train to Nyala, and then continuing on to Nyertati by lorry. There were no trains from El Obeid to Nyala, and accordingly it was necessary to first return to Ar-Rahad, through which the train to Nyala passed.

Carefully avoiding the first class, and not wanting to travel fourth class again, we decided to try out the third class compartments, and having bought our tickets we boarded the train. The seats were simple, but padded, and soon we were off on our way back to Ar-Rahad, content and relaxed, as we gazed out at the desert that stretched away in every direction. It was good to be alive.

NYALA

We arrived at Ar-Rahad in the late morning, sunny and welcoming as before, and discovered that we had several hours to wait before the train for Nyala was due. We passed the time wandering about the market place, stopping to pray dhur and asr just after mid-day, and on coming across some leather workers we had two small leather bags made for us, to carry our possessions more easily. These amounted, for my part, to two robes, two sets of baggy Sudanese underwear, two turbans, some soap, shampoo, toothpaste and a toothbrush, and of course my woven mat which I carried separately, rolled up and slung over my back like a quiver. It was good to be travelling so light, and not to be weighed down by excess baggage.

Having completed our business in the market, we returned to the station and rolled out our mats under a shady tree where we rested until the train arrived. Since the journey to Nyala was expected to take about eighteen hours, we had booked a couple of bunks in a second class compartment, but when we finally boarded the crowded train which was packed full of people, it was to find our compartment already fully occupied, as was the rest of the train. We resigned ourselves to a long and uncomfortable journey, sometimes lying in the corridor, and spending much of the time up on the roof of one of the carriages. From time to time we would spot a little floor space on which to curl up and snooze intermittently, but there was a constant flow of passengers on the move, and so it was impossible to sleep for any decent length of time. Soon we were hot and dusty and tired, and although we downed many a cold coke, bought from one of the vendors who tirelessly threaded their way up and down the length of the train carrying their wares in large buckets packed with chunks of melting ice, it would only take about five minutes before we were feeling hot and thirsty again.

Shortly before maghrib, the train came to rest at a busy junction town, and thankfully we descended from the train to stretch our legs and do the prayer. Afterwards, while we were waiting for the train to move on, my eye caught sight of a mighty tussle going on by one of the railway lines. Two dung beetles were fighting furiously over a small piece of dried dung, surrounded, ironically, by enough large clods of dung to last them both for months. How like the world this was, I thought with a wry smile.

A few minutes later, soon after I had remounted the train, I was suddenly aware of a quiet scrabbling near my right breast pocket in which all my paper money was stored. I looked down to see two fingers trying to find a way in through its narrow entrance. They belonged to a man who apparently had his back to me, but whose arms were tightly crossed so that the thieving fingers of his right hand could pass under his left armpit and into my breast pocket. I drew back sharply, both startled and amazed, and pointed at him with my right index finger. "Just watch it," I said, "or else!" and I made a chopping gesture over his wrist. Giving me a shifty look, he swung down from the train and disappeared into the growing dusk. I found myself shaking slightly, for this was the first time in my life that I had ever had anyone try to rob me in this way. I shook my head in pity. If he had just come up to me and asked for some money, I probably would have given it to him.

The train continued with its journey soon afterwards, and somehow we sat or stood it out, just waiting for it to end. It was a difficult journey, but eventually it came to an end as all journeys do, and soon after sunrise the next morning we found ourselves in the wild west of the Sudan, in Nyala, feeling a little like two would-be cowboys from the east coast newly arrived in town.

There were no gunfights or bank hold-ups in progress, and no saloons, but we pulled up a chair at a sidewalk cafe and downed a fresh guava juice on the spot, followed by freshly made coffee, served in dinky little red earthenware containers which had a type of stringy moss stuffed down their spouts to act as a filter, and tahnia – or halwa as it is called elsewhere – a warming snack made principally from crushed sesame seeds and honey which has one of the sweetest tastes on earth. The whole place had the feel of a wild frontier town, and even the people were different, more naturally spontaneous and less consciously refined than the people we had met further east. Most of the men were still dressed in the distinctive white djelaba and huge coiled turban of the Sudan, but we noticed several tribesmen from further south who were extremely tall and thin, with startlingly bright orange hair, indicating the existence of the very different worlds that lay to the south.

Suitably refreshed, we looked around the large market place to see what was on offer, and then set about locating a man called Abdal-Jabbar, whose address had been given to us by Abdal-Qadir in El Obeid. Everyone whom we asked for directions was very helpful, and soon we were knocking at the door of the man for whom we had been looking.

Abdal-Jabbar turned out to be a portly merchant with a large family and a large house on the outskirts of town. The tasbih in his right hand was constantly moving in time to his lips which, when he was not actually talking to anyone, were continually engaged in silent dhikr. Clearly he was one of those men whom the Qur'an describes as:

> **Men whom neither merchandise nor trading divert**
> **from remembrance of Allah**
> **and establishing the prayer**
> **and paying the zakat,**
> **who fear a Day when hearts and eyes shall be overturned,**
> **so that Allah may reward them for the best of what they did,**
> **and give them increase from His bounty.**
> **And Allah provides for whomever He wishes without any**
> **reckoning.**
>
> (Qur'an: 24.37-38)

Naturally, Abdal-Jabbar seemed a little surprised to find us at his door, but, after reading the note which Abdal-Qadir had written to him, he welcomed us in and sat us down in his large shady garden. We were tired after our long journey and in need of a good sleep, and accordingly we spent the whole day resting, before being treated to a large simple supper of grilled goat, bread and fruit.

Abdal-Jabbar insisted that we must first obtain a permit from the local authority to travel to Nyertati before continuing our journey, and, having learned from our experience at Kaduqli, we acquiesced and accompanied him to the offices of the Chief of Police the next morning. The man in charge was friendly and helpful, and after grandly pinging the large bell on his desk to summon a minion to bring us all some tea, and a little smalltalk, he stamped our visas with the necessary permission and sent us on our way.

Abdal-Jabbar, whose tasbih had not stopped moving through his fingers throughout the entire morning, appeared to be relieved and glad that it had worked out alright. He drove us into the centre of town and dropped us off at the taxi truck depot with a smile and a wave, before disappearing off down the road, his lips still moving in silent dhikr.

It did not take us long to locate a lorry bound for Nyertati, and although it already seemed to be overloaded, somehow there was just enough room to squeeze us both in amongst the other passengers who were perched on top of the great load of goods that filled the back of the lorry. In no time at all we were off once more, heading towards the setting sun and out into the desert, making for the dark line that was just visible on the very edge of the far horizon, making for the Jebel Murra, the Mountains of Time, with faint childhood memories of Rider Haggard's books and King Solomon's Mines edging into my awareness, blending in with the rush of the wind and the sound of the driving Sudanese music which played excitingly in the background, as we sped through the dazzling sunlight with a trail of dust billowing out behind us.

There was no doubt about it, we were on the move, and right then, in that moment, there was no other place that I wished to be, not even Makka, nor Madina, nor 'home' which I had already left years ago anyway. As the saying goes, home is where you happen to be for the day; home is where you hang your turban; home is where the heart is.

JEBEL MURRA

By late afternoon we had reached the foothills of the Jebel Murra, and Daribe, the extinct volcano, was now clearly visible, looming out high above the other mountains that surrounded it. From where we were, it did not look particularly high or far away. "Insh'Allah we'll climb that," said Abdal-Jalil.

The road to Nyertati was in much better shape than the one to Kaduqli, but it was still a bumpy one, and as it began to climb and twist and turn, the lorry shook us about in every direction, so that, wedged as I was between two people and a sharp-cornered tea-chest, all I could do was to grunt 'Allah!' with each bump and jolt. There was a brief respite when the lorry stopped for people to buy fresh milk from a very old woman who was pasturing a few cows by the roadside, but soon we were off again, still climbing steadily, with more and more vegetation appearing on the hill-sides and the growing dusk turning almost imperceptibly into the darkness of night. As the stars began to appear and twinkle, the dark mass of Daribe loomed ever nearer, daring us to come and have a closer look. "Yes," I said, "insh'Allah we'll climb that."

After driving through the night for a couple of hours or so, we came to a halt at a small road-side caravanserai, with walls made from poles driven into the ground and a roof thatched with long grass. It was quite a large shelter, and inside there was a welcoming fire that hardly gave off any smoke. The night air was cold at this altitude, and Abdal-Jalil and I were glad to huddle round the fire for warmth with everyone else, sipping hot sweet milky tea and feasting on what had now become our confirmed staple diet, foules mesdames, spiced with ground cumin, olive oil and tahini, and bread.

Eventually we learned that we would be staying the night here, and continuing our journey in the morning. After praying maghrib and isha, we rolled out our mats as near to the fire as was possible without being greedy or discourteous, and slept as best we could, although it was too cold, in our thin cotton djelabas, to relax fully and sleep deeply.

◎ ◎ ◎

We awoke to the sweet sound of the adhan, a daily experience which I still miss and long for when I am not in Muslim territory, and having done the dawn prayer and shared breakfast with our fellow travellers, we continued our journey up into the Mountains of Time with the sky gradually lighting up behind us until, suddenly, we were bathed in sunshine.

It was a brand new day, the air was clear and fresh, and the sides of the mountains were covered in trees and vegetation from which a thousand birds sang their praises of the Creator. The day was full of promise and it was so good to be alive, here and now, more than a million light years away from the gloomy, noisy, stifling factory at which we had worked in Athens, and which was probably, at this very moment, still churning out bottle after bottle of synthetically flavoured water for the consumption of Athens' thirsty tourists, while there, and elsewhere, millions of white collar workers would either just be in the middle of, or starting or finishing, another routine day at the office. What an amazing world it is, so many different worlds and lives in every moment, forever changing in every instant, and never the same again!

We reached Nyertati that morning, and after finding something to eat and drink in the market place, including the luscious fruit that Abdal-Qadir had promised us, we decided to avoid any conflict by going to the police before they came to us. We tracked down the police station, which was about twenty minutes' walk away from the centre of the small village, and met the Chief of Police who did not seem in the least bit surprised or interested in seeing us. Having briefly checked our passports, he said that we were welcome in Nyertati, and asked a bystander to show us to the rest-house, which turned out to be what must have once been the District Commissioner's house during the British Colonial era in the Sudan.

There was the neatly thatched roof, the white-washed walls, the spacious verandah with the red-polished concrete floor and the remains of what must have once been a very beautiful lawn and garden. It was like suddenly being transported back to the world of my childhood, for this was the kind of house in the kind of place in which we had lived for much of the time, and for a brief moment I was a child again, playing in the garden that was full of bird song and waiting for the call that lunch was ready, or sitting unnoticed on the verandah while my parents and a few other grown-ups sipped at their sundowners and talked about things that I did not understand while I tuned in to the sounds of the crickets and the frogs and the throbbing of the drums that came singing out from the dark African bush where you could not walk at night in case the hyenas or the lions or a night-adder got you.

That world was now long gone, and the sight of this empty house, which looked as if no-one had ever lived in it again after the last white bwana had left for good, brought the point home to me very forcibly that life is very transient and short and nothing lasts for very long. I was momentarily stunned. People come and go so swiftly.

○ ○ ○

Our guide left us to it, and having taken stock of our surroundings, we decided that the first priority was to wash, both our bodies and our clothes. Just a little way down the hillside and along was a river, which I reckoned must be free from bilharzia, since we were pretty high up in the mountains and the water appeared to be flowing quite swiftly. We followed a small path that seemed to lead in its direction, meeting a host of laughing nubile schoolgirls all dressed in white along the way, and on reaching the river we followed it along a while until we reached a large pool that seemed to be out of sight of any of the other dwellings that dotted the hillside.

Using my childhood test for bilharzia, I let a large bit of spit drop from my mouth into the water. If it stayed together, the water was alright. If it dispersed, the water had bilharzia. Of course I was no longer certain whether or not this was a valid way of testing for bilharzia, but at any rate the spit stayed obligingly together, and furthermore, on feeling the temperature of the water, I was pretty sure that it was far too cold for any bilharzia parasites to survive in it.

Without further ado we plunged into the pool's cool depths, and soon we were sunning ourselves on the rocks while we waited for our freshly washed robes and turbans to dry in the sun, feeling gloriously clean and healthy with our skin tingling from the combined effect of the cold water and the hot sun.

Eventually, after praying dhur and asr on a large flat rock at the rippling water's edge, we returned to the rest-house, driven by the pangs of hunger and thirst, and having stored our few belongings in what must have been the sitting room, we returned to the market-place where we bought tea, sugar, powdered milk, dates, bread, fruit, a tin with a handle in which to boil water, a box of matches, and two small enamelled tin bowls from which we could either drink or eat. On our return, we built a small fire on the very edge of what had once been the front lawn, and brewed up some hobo tea to have with our dates and bread. It was the first meal that we had prepared for ourselves since coming to the Sudan. As we sat there cross-legged on the grass, sipping and chewing with relish, I could not help smiling as I recalled some of the more cultured teas that I had enjoyed as a child out on our bush-station front lawns, tea served in china cups along with home-made chocolate cake baked especially for me by my loving mother. Whatever the outward form, I certainly enjoyed my afternoon tea!

The sun slowly sank until it was out of sight, and as soon as it was clearly dusk, we prayed maghrib and isha out on the remains of the front lawn, probably something that the last white men here had never done, before turning in for a good long sleep. However, the house had that deserted feeling that deserted houses usually have, full of past events and old ghosts, and beneath our thin mats, the concrete floor was cold and hard. Neither of us slept particularly well that night.

○ ○ ○

The next morning, we brewed up outside on the lawn, with the dew still glistening on the long blades of grass that had never heard the sound of a lawnmower, and ate a simple breakfast of fruit and bread and dates. As we gazed out at the hills and mountains that surrounded us in the cool of the early morning, we decided that this might as well be the day that we went and climbed Daribe, insh'Allah. It did not seem to be too far away, and insh'Allah we could be there and back in the same day, stopping off, perhaps, just long enough to have a hot bath in the hot spring up there, for neither of us had washed with heated water since leaving England all those months ago.

We stored most of our few possessions in the house, certain that they would be safe there for the day, just taking our small leather bags with what was left of the food we had bought the previous afternoon and our two little bowls to make it easier to catch the water from the mountain streams that we were bound to pass. As an afterthought, I popped the box of matches into my robe pocket, something that I had always done as a young boy when going out for the day in the African bush. You just never knew when they might come in handy. And then, travelling extra light, we chose a path that was going in the general direction of Daribe, and started to walk.

DARIBE

To begin with, the path was broad and well-trodden, flanked by terraces of durra and small orchards of fruit trees, with small neat villages dotted about the beautifully green mountain sides. It was warm but not hot and we walked swiftly without feeling tired or uncomfortable. We climbed steadily up into the mountains without appearing to come any nearer to our goal, and gradually the terrain became more rugged and less cultivated, while the path became less well-defined.

After a couple of hours or so, we met a group of men along the way who came from one of the neighbouring villages. Having found out where we were going, one of them offered to guide us there in return for a couple of pounds, but we declined his offer, since the path we were on seemed to be leading us straight there. While we were discussing the matter with him, two of his companions had disappeared off the path into a nearby durra patch. After a few minutes they returned, their pockets filled with small tomatoes and their hands full of durra, which they proceeded to rub expertly between their palms, to remove the husks, before offering us the raw millet to eat. Politely we accepted this light snack, before bidding them goodbye and continuing on our way.

Soon after this, the going began to become much more difficult. The terrain was growing rougher and rougher, and there was no longer one clear path, but many paths which seemed to be leading in one direction but then ended up going in another. Often the likely looking path we had chosen simply petered out, or ended in dense bush or an impassable ravine, and we began to wish we had accepted our would-be guide's offer. We kept going, however, determined to arrive and certain that we would if we did not give up. The more we walked, the further away Daribe appeared to be, and often we would arrive at the top of a rise, thinking that only the final ascent now remained, only to find another series of foothills and ravines rising up between us and our objective.

It was by now clear that we would certainly not be back at Nyertati for maghrib, and indeed I was beginning to wonder whether we would even reach the top of Daribe by then. We stopped to pray dhur and asr and to eat our food by a small rushing mountain stream, and were soon joined by two monkeys who watched instant flight. At this point, we were not quite sure exactly where we were, or even of the way back to Nyertati, but decided not to be beaten by the mountain. Insh'Allah we would continue heading up towards the mighty peak, and hopefully find shelter in one of the villages which we kept on coming across from time to time, once it began to grow dark.

On we went, trying this way and then that way, caught up in this natural maze of hills and ravines, and beginning to feel both tired and hungry, for we had been walking almost continuously all day on only a couple of light meals of bread, dates and fruit. Suddenly, the light began to fade rapidly. It was maghrib, and there was not a village in sight. We found water, did wudu and did the prayer. I had always found that if you do the prayer promptly as soon as its time is due, good things happen after it, a phenomenon which is especially noticeable if you happen to be in a bit of a fix at the time.

This occasion was no exception, for as soon as we had finished the prayer, a man materialised out of the dusk and, using sign language, signalled us to follow him. As the Prophet Muhammad once said, Allah does not cease to provide for you from where you do not expect, and as Allah says in the Qur'an:

> So remember Me – I will remember you.
> And thank Me and do not reject Me.
> O you who trust, seek help with patience and the prayer.
> Surely Allah is with the patient.
>
> (Qur'an: 2.152-153)

We followed our unexpected guide through the gathering darkness, and after about twenty minutes' walk, we arrived at a small village which was no more than a small huddle of thatched huts, and were shown to the remains of what must have once been a very simple mosque. It appeared that we had gone beyond the borders of Muslim territory in this part of the Sudan, and were now with a small community living in fitra – simple harmony with nature – but which did not live and worship Allah in accordance with the pattern of life and worship that had been embodied by His last Messenger and his community. Certainly we could not understand what our friendly guide said to us, and he did not appear to understand any of our limited Arabic.

There were no lights or fires anywhere, and no signs of life. It looked as if everyone had already turned in for the night. Our guide signalled that he was going to turn in too. We signalled that we were hungry. He smiled understandingly and signalled us to wait before disappearing into the darkness, while we tried to keep warm in the cold night air. A few minutes later he returned with a squawking chicken dangling and flapping from one of his hands. He signalled that he wanted two pounds for it. We signalled OK and gave him the money, whereupon he attempted to hand it over to us there and then. We signalled that he should cook it. He shrugged his shoulders, but thankfully agreed to do so, which was just as well, for having had a sheltered upbringing, and in our present state of fatigue, even this simple task seemed to be beyond our capacity.

Our host disappeared once more, chicken still in hand, and reappeared with a large metal wok, a bucket of water and presumably his son who was carrying some firewood. Swiftly he made a fire at the edge of the remains of the mosque which only had a few upright poles left for its walls and virtually no thatch for its roof. While some water was being heated in the wok, he killed the chicken by cutting its throat and then proceeded to pluck it, dipping it from time to time in the warm water, and depositing the newly plucked feathers straight onto the fire. Quietly I said 'Bismillah', just in case he had not, determined to eat some very badly needed protein.

Within ten minutes the chicken was completely plucked, the wok had been rinsed out briefly with some water from the bucket, and the bird was sizzling away over the flames. Nothing was wasted, and all the innards of the bird were cooked at the edge of the wok as well as its flesh. The innards were soon ready, and these our host and his son devoured with evident enjoyment. Soon after, the meat was ready, and our host offered us the entire contents of the wok, utterly astonished when we invited him and his son to join in our simple feast. They would only take a couple of small mouthfuls, but no more. We, on the other hand, tucked in hungrily and ate most of it, tough but tasty, saving only a couple of wings for the next day. Leaving us to it, our hosts disappeared into the night, while we tried to make ourselves comfortable on the hard ground in our thin robes. It was very cold by now, and the fire had died right down, but we were so tired that we fell asleep anyway.

❂ ❂ ❂

We awoke at first light the next morning, stiff and cold and cramped, and having prayed subh, using tayyamum, we dozed fitfully until the sun rose and some people appeared. Soon we were surrounded by all the villagers, men women and children, who must have thought we were beings from another planet, but who were nevertheless very friendly towards us. A huge bowl of steaming asida, the thick sticky smooth porridge which is made from durra, was brought, along with hot sweet green tea, and we all tucked in, smiling away and making appreciative sounds, but still confined to very simple communication through sign language.

We managed to make it clear that we wished to climb to the top of Daribe, and when one of the men offered to guide us there for a couple of pounds, we did not repeat our error of the day before, but accepted his offer immediately. Soon we were on our way again, for neither of us had eaten very much, still thinking that we would be at the top in no time, especially now that we had a guide.

Our guide clearly knew this part of the country like the back of his hand, and changed direction at the various cross-paths without hesitating or faltering in his stride. He was young and strong and fit, and his lungs were used to the altitude, and having started at a cracking pace, which even the long-legged Abdal-Jalil had difficulty in sustaining, he did not slow down, even when we emerged from the last of the flanking foothills and began the final and very long and winding ascent. Four hours after setting out, we were still on the move, climbing still higher and higher, and suddenly I felt very out of breath, with my heart pounding away and a feeling of faintness in my head. I just had to stop and rest, and so we did, stretched full out in the bracken, for we were now well above the tree line, and with my lungs still gasping for breath. I think Abdal-Jalil was also glad to stop and have a breather, although he was a fast mover himself, and indeed throughout the entire journey I had often had difficulty in keeping up with him once he was striding out at full stretch.

As we tried to regain our breath and some energy to continue, we looked out back over the way we had come and all around us. It was a beautiful view, like all mountain peak views, with the Jebel Murra stretching out around us in every direction under a clear blue sky, and with only the rim of Daribe still looming above us. I am surprised that there are not more people who say, in answer to the age-old question of 'Why did you climb the mountain?', "Because we wanted to see the view!"

Meanwhile, our guide, who had probably spent his whole life surrounded by such beauty and majesty, was eager to continue, but I was still simply unable to rise to my feet, and after a few minutes more, he indicated that he was not willing to wait any longer and had to be on his way. He signalled that we were now very near to our objective, and pointed out the path ahead that we should take. We thanked him, paid him the sum we had agreed, and watched him take off along the path once again. Within minutes, he was out of sight round the next bend. Together Abdal-Jalil and I ate the last of last night's chicken and then fell fast asleep, completely exhausted.

❂   ❂   ❂

When we awoke, it was well into the mid-afternoon, and already there was a chilliness in the wind, for we must have been about ten thousand feet above sea level. Over to the west, we could see where the mountains began to flatten out again into the desert. The view certainly was very breathtaking for we were very high up now. We both felt much stronger now, although we were very thirsty, for it had been several hours since we had last drunk from a mountain spring and there was no water this high up. Hopefully we would find water inside the crater, and clearly the only way to go now was up.

With renewed vigour we set off again along the path, and, to our surprise, within about forty minutes we were on the lip of the crater, looking down at the two lakes that lay serenely below us in the quiet sandy bottom of the crater which was lightly sprinkled with grass and a few trees and what looked like a herd of wild horses or donkeys. With only the sound of the wind around us, we gazed at the circular rim of the extinct volcano which was now clearly visible for the first time, the dividing line between two worlds, the one that lay within it, and the one that lay beyond it. Everything was pure and still and dreamlike. We looked in awe and amazement. The whole journey had been worth it, just to reach this moment in time at this place in the Mountains of Time.

It was breathtaking, like a kind of Shangri-La, a different world, and we exchanged a glance of recognition, knowing that there was not really anything that either of us could say, because to see is beyond speech.

"This is where I'll spend the Third World War!" I said spontaneously, for this was the nearest I dare come to trying to express the absolute peace and security and freedom from any form of pollution that this amazing vista evoked within my heart. We exchanged smiles, paused a moment longer to drink it all in, so that perhaps the memory might last for ever, and then began the dangerous descent down the steep crumbling inner wall of the crater that had been eroded and scarred by the elements for centuries.

It took another hour and a half or so to clamber down the steep treacherous sides of the crater, but at last we had reached its flat grassy sandy floor, and, burning with our exertions and the thirst that had kept us going, we walked slowly across this beautifully level surface towards the lake which looked as if it was the one you could drink from, since its shores were clear and lined with healthy looking vegetation and trees, whereas the shores of the other one were encrusted with what looked like white mineral deposits.

The sun was still just shining down onto us when we reached the waters of the lake and discovered that they were sweet and cool. Pulling off our turbans and robes, we waded out into the still water in our floppy Sudanese underwear, with the fine mud squeezing up between our toes until we were in deep enough to keel over and sink and float in its glorious wetness, sipping the water lazily through half-opened lips and soaking the water up into our dried out bodies through every pore of our skins, like two dried up sponges that have suddenly been dropped into the ocean after a life-time on a dried-up shore where it never rains. It was sheer bliss.

At last, suitably refreshed, we exchanged our dry robes for our wet underwear, which we laid out in the last of the sun to dry. Then, having done wudu, we prayed dhur and asr out there on the high valley floor, with a cool breeze and the late afternoon sun drying our hair, and hardly a sound to be heard, not even a bird, other than a firm "Allahu Akbar" each time we changed position in the prayer. Someone once said that the creation is a veil over its Creator, so if you find the veil beautiful, just imagine how beautiful the One Who is veiled by it is.

Feeling revitalised and strong again, we strolled over to the other lake which was about half a mile away, hoping to find that its waters were warm, only to find that they were just as cool as the waters in which we had just been floating. Clearly the hot spring which fed this lake was not nearby. Nor was there any time to look for it, for dusk was approaching and now that we were in shadow it was much cooler. It was essential to collect some firewood while we could still see what we were doing.

We retraced our steps back to the sweet water lake, collecting pieces of firewood as we went, put our virtually dry underwear back on under our robes, and when it was time, I gave a loud adhan that echoed out into the silence and beyond into empty space. Having prayed maghrib and isha, we drank our fill at the lake, filled our little bowls with water, and made our way through the growing darkness to the spot where we had been gathering the firewood together, still awed by the beauty and the majesty and the silence and the stillness of this world within a world, the dark encircling rim of the crater that surrounded us on every side outlined against a sky that was just beginning to fill with stars.

As I lit the fire I was glad that we had brought the matches. Now that the sun had set it was definitely cold and no doubt it would become very cold in the small hours of the morning. The fire soon burst into flame, but the fuel was very dry and burnt rapidly. Within an hour we were groping about in the darkness, trying to find more fuel, and it did not take us long to realise that it was going to be a very cold night and that a few sticks and our thin cotton robes were not going to be nearly enough to keep us warm.

Fortunately, I had noticed a very large tree trunk lying on its side when it had still been light, and after about twenty minutes search in the darkness we managed to locate it. There was no moon to help us, for it was around the end of the lunar month – which meant that there were only about five weeks left before the rites of the Hajj began in Makka – and although there was a myriad of stars above us that reminded me of the nights we had spent at Humaysara by Shaykh Shadhili's tomb, it was still very dark down in the depths of the extinct volcano's crater. Despite our inability to see anything very clearly, we managed to find enough kindling to start a fire along the whole length of the dead tree trunk, and in no time at all we had a huge bonfire that seemed to light up half the valley. Soon we were warm once again, and after sipping some of the precious water which we had been carrying about with us in our little bowls, we stretched out, one on either side of the blazing fire, exhausted and hungry, but beautifully warm, and fell fast asleep. Just before I went under, I remember vividly recalling a sentence from one of Shaykh Abdal-Qadir al-Murabit's books called **The Way of Muhammad:** "The way lies across the mountains of madness – and they have to be crossed."

❂   ❂   ❂

We awoke the next morning before sunrise, stiff and hungry, but still very much alive. The entire tree trunk had completely disappeared, transformed into a long thin pile of still smoking ashes and embers. Abdal-Jalil's robe had a couple of small round burn holes from where he had rolled too close to the fire. The water in our drinking bowls was covered in a thin layer of ice. It had been a very cold night indeed, and if it had not been for the dead tree trunk, al-hamdulillahi wa shukrulillah, we probably would have ended up suffering badly from exposure to such cold.

Having quenched our thirst with the iced water, we made our way to the lake in the growing light, did wudu and prayed subh, and then decided what to do next. The prospect of returning all the way that we had come was simply too much for us, and accordingly the only other alternative was to go on, over the top and down the other side. We had noticed that there appeared to be a gap in the wall over on the far side of the crater and decided to go and investigate it a little more closely. Since we were already beginning to feel a little weak from hunger, there seemed no point in spending any more time searching for our elusive hot spring. That hot bath would have to wait until another day.

There was indeed an opening through the crater wall at that point, out of which a river gushed and tumbled steeply down through one ravine after another, and although we could not be sure whether or not it was possible, we decided to follow the river down the side of Daribe, in the hope that we would eventually come across a village lower down where we could eat and rest, before walking round the base of the mountain back to Nyertati.

Having drunk our fill from the cold clear water, we commenced our steep descent, sometimes climbing down through the boulders through which the river tumbled and splashed in a series of rushing waterfalls, and sometimes taking to the steep sides of the ravines that bordered it, hanging on to the trees and bushes that grew thickly around it. Fortunately there did not seem to be any snakes about, or if there were, then our noisy approach must have driven them into hiding.

It was a dangerous climb down, and we both had to be very careful not to slip or fall. A twisted ankle or even a broken arm would not really help matters at all. The loose earth was what had once been ash and lava, and it crumbled easily in the hand or under foot once any weight was put on it. At one point, where the river cascaded down into a sheer hundred foot waterfall, we had to branch up and then round and down the steep ravine edge, and at this stage suddenly I found myself climbing up an almost vertical cliff face, about two hundred feet above the river, with Abdal-Jalil just ahead of me saying, "I can't help you here, you'll have to do it by yourself," trembling with weakness and fear and praying that the tufts of grass would not come away in my hands, as I repeated 'Hasbuna'llahu wa ni'm'al-wakil' – 'Allah is enough for us and the best Guardian' with every breath, probably more out of hope than certainty, until finally I pulled myself over the lip of the cliff edge to relative safety with a great gasp of relief. We had come close to death there, and we wanted very much to stay alive.

"If we ever get back to Omdurman," I said, and right then it seemed a very long way away, "I'll buy you a cold coke at the Khartoum Hilton!" We both laughed at the very idea of it, and then continued threading our way down the edge of the ravine, trying to concentrate on our every move. Slowly, step by step, we lost height, and by mid-day the worst was over. It was now possible to walk along by the edge of the river, and in places a path was discernible through the thick grass and clumps of trees that had appeared in greater profusion than before along its banks. Although we had not eaten for over twenty-four hours, during which we had expended a considerable amount of energy, and felt light and weak, at least we were not thirsty, and we continued on our way, certain that we were bound to meet someone sooner or later.

At last we spotted a herd of sheep round a bend in the river, and then three young children sheltering in the shade of a tree. We must have looked a sorry sight, as well as probably being the first white people they had ever seen, for as soon as they saw us stumbling towards them and waving at them to attract their attention, they immediately took off with loud piercing cries of alarm, speeding up the mountainside with amazing alacrity, until they disappeared out of sight in a matter of minutes. It was not quite the reception we had been expecting, but we decided to pause a while and pray dhur and asr, for the children may well have gone to fetch one of their parents.

After we had done the prayer, we lay back in the shade, feeling exhausted and weak and empty of energy. No one appeared from the direction in which the children had disappeared, and by now we were feeling so weak from hunger that we seriously started to discuss the possibility of catching one of the sheep, killing it with Abdal-Jalil's small Sudanese knife and cooking it on the spot. If no-one appeared in the meantime, we could always leave some money under a stone by the skin in payment.

We had virtually decided to do just that, when we suddenly heard what can only be described as an African yodel from further down river, followed by a fainter more distant yodel that must have been uttered in reply. The two yodels continued back and forth between each other in a long range conversation, the louder of the two appearing to be coming closer towards us, and after about five minutes we spotted an African woman driving some cattle along the opposite bank of the river in our direction.

We moved into the open and shouted and waived at her, like two shipwrecked sailors that have just sighted a passing ship. She soon spotted us and made her way down to the river's edge at a point where it was easy to cross over the large boulders around which the river danced and sang. When she was about twenty paces away from us, she sat down, cross-legged on the ground. We did likewise. There was a small silence as she looked enquiringly at us.

"As-salaamu-alaikum," we said.

"Wa alaikum as-salaam," she replied.

We breathed a silent sigh of relief. At least we were back among Muslims. There was not really much to say, especially since she only spoke her own mountain dialect. We pointed at our mouths and at our bellies, and she nodded, with a look of great compassion and understanding that could only have come from a person who had also experienced hunger and thirst and fatigue. Rising to her feet, she signalled us to follow her, which we did, across the river and back the way she had just come. After about twenty minutes, we came to a path that branched off away from the river, and this she signalled us to follow. We thanked her gratefully, and started off down the path while she went back to recover her cattle.

We walked for about forty minutes, wondering what was going to happen next, when, just as it was beginning to grow dark, we came across a simple cluster of three round stone-walled grass-thatched huts built next to half an acre or so of ripening durra. We entered the small compound which appeared to be deserted and called out in our hoarse voices, "Allahu Akbar! Allahu Akbar!"

At first there was no response, but then an old and weathered lady appeared from out of one of the huts and motioned to us to sit down and wait on the low stone wall that bordered the compound. She disappeared and then reappeared with some water for us to drink, just as an old and weathered man appeared out of the dusk. Having exchanged greetings, we did wudu and prayed maghrib together, Abdal-Jalil and I following on with two more rakats for isha. Then Abu Bakr, for that was our host's name, took us each kindly by an arm and guided us over into one of his simple huts, laying down a couple of straw mats on the sandy floor for us to sit on.

"Al-hamdulillahi wa shukrulillah," I said gratefully.

"Al-hamdulillahi wa shukrulillah," he replied with an understanding smile.

◉ ◉ ◉

Within minutes it was clear that Abu Bakr was the jewel of the Jewel of the Sudan whom we had wondered about all that time ago back in Ibrahim's small flat in Athens. He was completely at one with his surroundings, every action in harmony and never more or less than the moment required. Although we were now at a much lower altitude than the night before, it was still cold, and seeing that we were feeling it, Abu Bakr laid and lit a small fire in the middle of the hut which soon warmed up as a result. Having seen to our immediate comfort, Abu Bakr disappeared out of the low doorway, and after about twenty minutes returned with an enamel dish filled with steaming asida and a thick meaty gravy.

The simple meal went straight into the top ten most delicious meals of my life. With each tasty mouthful, we could feel warmth and strength returning to our tired limbs, and once again, life was possible after all. Again, I recalled some of my Shaykh's words, spoken some three years earlier in the zawiyya in London, where at the time it had seemed as if I was destined to stay for ever: "You will travel, everywhere. And one day you'll be happy just to be in a hut somewhere in Africa, with only a bowl of porridge to eat!" How true these words had turned out to be! Momentarily my eyes filled with tears of recognition as I tasted the reality of what once had only been imagined with deep longing.

After we had eaten our fill, there followed sweet, sweet green tea which completed our contentment completely. Never had such hardship been followed by such ease it seemed, it was so sweet and delicious. I did not know how to begin to say thankyou to this simple king of the mountains who did not question us or judge us, or ask for money despite his great poverty, but who just gave us what we needed, with all the generosity and grace and compassion of a truly noble human being, may Allah give him and his loved ones peace in their graves and palaces in the Garden.

After our feast was over, and having shown us how to arrange the wooden slats that kept out the cold across the doorway, our generous host bid us goodnight and returned to his wife. Minutes later we were fast asleep, and minutes later, or so it seemed, we were awake again in the first light of dawn, a little cold now that the fire was no longer alive, but rested. Abu Bakr appeared at the doorway soon after we had awoken, and after praying subh together, we had a simple breakfast of asida and tea, before being joined by Abu Bakr's son, who was called Sulayman, pulling a camel behind him.

Without further ado, the four of us set off on the next stage of our journey, following small winding paths through the dawn light, breathing in the clear air good and deep, shivering slightly and wishing that the sun would soon appear to warm us up once again. At first Sulayman was riding his camel, but as we began to climb up through the hills that bordered the narrow river valley, he was obliged to dismount and pull the protesting animal along behind him, snorting and grunting as only camels do.

After about an hour, with the sun just risen and lighting up the world, we arrived at a small market place, where we bought Abu Bakr and Sulayman and ourselves some dates. Then Abu Bakr pointed out the path that we were to follow next, signalling that we should just keep going along it for quite a way, but unable to convey where it would actually lead. Then, having ensured that we were on the right track, the jewel of the Jebel Murra and his son bid us a friendly farewell, his old and weathered face creasing into a deep smile, before disappearing back into their world for good, leaving us at a complete loss as to how we could ever thank them enough or repay them for their kindness, other than to ask Allah to give them everything that they needed in both this world and the next one.

Having drunk our fill of water at the market place, we set out on the path that Abu Bakr had indicated. We appeared to be on the flank of another mountain side that was on the opposite side of the river which we had followed down the side of Daribe, but the lie of the land favoured us, and we could see that the path gradually sloped round to our right. Having come right over the top of Daribe, we were now sweeping round its base in a very wide circle. If we just kept going, eventually we should hit the road that led back to Nyertati, just as we had hoped back there in the crater. As we walked swiftly along the path, trying to make as much ground as possible before it began to grow hot, and breathing only through our noses with our mouths tight shut so as to delay becoming thirsty, I looked back at the mighty peak of Daribe, recalling the beauty and the majesty of the secret world that nestled safely in its crater. Despite the hardship involved, our visit there had been worth all the trouble, especially now that we were safely back amongst other people.

As we walked, the terrain became less mountainous and more hilly, and we found ourselves back in the land of small villages and durra plantations. At one stage we passed by a series of ancient terraced walls built with dark volcanic bolders that had clearly survived from another age long past, and were strongly reminiscent of the far more famous ruins of Zimbabwe. Every so often, we would come across a mountain stream, dancing down the hillside and across our path, which meant that we never grew too thirsty, provided that we just kept on the move and did not rest until we came to the next stream.

The sun rose higher and higher in the ever blue sky, as the earth around us grew flatter and flatter, and gradually we began to feel more and more tired as the day wore on and the miles went by under our dusty sandals. Our muscles were no longer stiff after such sustained movement, but they were beginning to ache, and our faces were looking burnt and weather-worn after their long hours of exposure to the sun and the wind. Despite the heat of the day, we had both developed colds after the cold of the previous two nights, and it was with a certain degree of relief that, after passing through an increasing number of villages, we finally arrived at Kalukitti.

KALUKITTI

Kalukitti was a boarding school in what appeared to be the middle of nowhere. All the teachers spoke good English and welcomed us, politely amazed at the journey which we had just made, for it was hardly an escapade that they would have expected 'educated' people to attempt. We were given milk and biscuits to eat as soon as we had arrived, and later a meal after maghrib, before being shown to a room with two beds graced with mattresses and clean white sheets and blankets. After a quick cold shower each, we climbed into our beds, relaxed and ready for a good long sleep.

It felt strange to be indoors, and I felt constricted by the four solid walls and the ceiling above me, as I recalled the description of the feelings of Mowgli in Rudyard Kipling's **The Jungle Book** when he first left the wolf pack and went to live in the village. After having spent so much time under the vast vault of the heavens and on the wide earth that stretched out to the far and ever changing horizons of the world, the room seemed like a prison, and I found myself remembering how I had felt as a young boy at boarding school in Zimbabwe, surrounded by the vast exciting expanse of the African bushveld, but confined within the school system and forbidden to go 'out of bounds'.

Although I was grateful for the kindness and hospitality that the teachers had shown us, and knew that I was far too helpless to ever be a mountain man for any decent length of time, I did not share the same sentiments as Abdal-Jalil, who every so often during the past few days had been saying, like some latter-day Papillon, "If we ever get back to England one day, I'm going to find a nice comfortable flat with central heating and a thick carpet and lots of cushions and hot water and lots of food – and I'll never leave it!" I loved the change and excitement and unpredictability of the open road, and right then I never wanted to leave it, but to be ever on the move through life, for ever meeting new faces and passing through new places, gloriously alive and somehow for ever young!

❀   ❀   ❀

We awoke the next morning after a long and lovely sleep, but still feeling very drained of energy and tired after all the walking we had recently done, and decided to spend the day resting before proceeding any further with our journey. We sat in the shade and relaxed, while the daily life of the school went on around us, dozing off from time to time, and tucking gratefully into the food which our hosts provided for us after each prayer time.

By the end of the day we both felt much better, and I even had the energy to help one of the teachers with his advanced English correspondence course. Once again, I could not help noticing that those who had received a western styled education did not have the same perception of life and vitality as the older generation of people who had received a traditional Muslim maddrasah education and who, although they might not be au fait with or even aware of the existence of the latest technological developments further north in the world, or Darwinian evolutionary theory, or Jungian psychology, or the philosophy of Nietzsche and Heidegger, were nevertheless definitely far more aware of the true nature of existence and the human self.

This difference in quality of being was noticeable both amongst the adults and the children. The adults who had received the western information pack were usually full of questions that often obscured the answers they were either consciously or unconsciously seeking, and, for example, there was a marked and noticeable difference between the controlled thought-orientated energy of the pupils at Kalukitti and the contained yet shining radiance of the Qur'an students at Zariba. Ma sha'Allah. Allah gives knowledge to whomever He pleases as He pleases, and whatever we know, we only know a little.

○ ○ ○

After another good night's sleep, we were ready to continue our journey, and after a final meal at Kalukitti, one of the teachers very kindly saved us a long walk by driving us straight to the dirt road that led to Nyertati, dropping us off at the very same caravanserai at which we had slept the night after leaving Nyala on our way up into the Jebel Murra. It looked very different in the full light of day, but its hot sweet milky tea was still excellent.

Not long after we had said goodbye and thankyou to our benefactor, a lorry bound for Nyertati rolled up in a cloud of dust, and having paid the driver the fare, we clambered on board the back and were soon bumping along on our way through the bush to Nyertati for the second time in our lives. Daribe, as ever, loomed far above us, only now we looked at it with different eyes. We had been there! We had climbed it! We had been inside it! Alhamdulillahi wa shukrulillah!

NYERTATI

A few hours later, and we were back in Nyertati market place, our faces sunburnt and weatherbeaten, our robes and turbans covered in dust, and both of us with well-established colds. It seemed very odd to be sneezing away on such a hot day. We went over to a simple hut restaurant and bought two large bowls of the meat stew of the day. We were just about to start eating, when Abdal-Jalil suddenly rose to his feet. "Hang on a minute," he said, and strode off towards a man who was selling herbs and spices, returning shortly with a generous helping of powdered chilli pepper in a twist of paper which he sprinkled liberally over the contents of our two bowls. It was one of the hottest stews I had ever tasted, but by the time we had finished eating, we had also stopped sneezing.

Having eaten, we returned to the old District Commissioner's house. Our few belongings were still there, safe and untouched, and it was almost as if we had not been away. It was almost a week since we had set out for our day-trip to the hot-spring at Daribe. Although we had not had the hot bath we had been expecting, it sure had been quite a journey. Having had a good wash down in the river and put on clean clothes, we brewed up a good strong tea at the edge of the ex-lawn and looked at each other with fresh exultant smiles. "We'll never be able to tell anyone exactly what happened," I said with awe and excitement. "There's no way anyone could express exactly what's happened in words." – And I was right!

❀ ❀ ❀

After staying a couple of more days at Nyertati, resting from our unexpected adventure and enjoying the greenness and relative coolness of the mountains and the sweet juicy fruits that were not available in the desert, especially the mangos, we decided that it was high time to head back to Omdurman and, insh'Allah, Makka. The time of the Hajj was only about four weeks away, and although we had originally hoped to loop down south and east from Nyala to Waw and Juba before heading north through Malakal and Kusti and so back to Omdurman, we did not want to miss the boat by leaving things too late or being held up by bureaucracy, besides which, we had had enough adventuring for the time being, and now only wanted to fulfil what had been the underlying purpose of all our travels during the past months – which was to do the Hajj, insh'Allah!

❀ ❀ ❀

We caught a lorry going to Nyala very early one morning, bumping and jolting back all the way that we had come, with Daribe growing smaller and smaller in the distance and the vegetation becoming drier and drier and more sparse, until we were speeding through the heavy heat of the desert once again, with the Jebel Murra no more than a smudge on the horizon and the secret world in the crater of Daribe unknown to all except those who had been there.

We sped into Nyala at about noon, every mile that we had travelled a mile nearer Makka, and bought tickets on a lorry that was leaving for Omdurman later that afternoon, this time paying that little bit extra for the privilege of riding up front in the cab with the driver. With a few hours to spare, we wandered around this wild west town, downing a couple of tumblers of freshly squashed fruit juices at a sidewalk cafe, followed a little later by some fresh coffee and tahnia, just as we had done on our first arrival in Nyala. How often things end as they begin.

As we made our way through the crowded market place, looking longingly at the large plastic bottles full of thick wild honey from the Jebel Murra but deciding not to buy any, my eye caught sight of a large strong leather camel-bag, and since the bags which we had purchased in Ar-Rahad had proved to be too small and rather flimsy, I bought one on the spot. Soon all my possessions had been transferred into it, including a couple of kilos of dried dates and some bread for the journey ahead, and we drifted on through the busy market place, my new acquisition slung round my neck and over my back, with my mat rolled up and hanging from a shoulder under one arm. I really did feel like a soldier of fortune, and a very fortunate one at that!

❀ ❀ ❀

The time to head further east arrived, and eagerly we clambered aboard the large Mercedes lorry, relaxing into the luxuriously padded seats of the cab, and greeting our smiling driver, a tall powerful man called Bashir, which in Arabic means 'Bringer of Good News'. He turned out to be the most good-natured lorry driver that I have ever sat beside, nearly always smiling and hardly ever angry, even when, only an hour into the journey, the lorry sputtered to a halt with carburettor problems. Although the lorry's two mechanics soon freed the blockage, the same thing happened again a few miles further on, and only showing the slightest trace of exasperation, Bashir told them to dismantle the fuel tank and give it a thorough clean out. While this was being done, one of the passengers helped himself to a few groundnut bushes from a nearby field, pulling them out whole and then setting fire to the lot by the roadside. A few minutes later, everyone had freshly cooked peanuts, roasted in their own shells.

After about an hour, everything was as it should be, and we were on our way again. The two young mechanics, Umar and Adam, were aged about twelve and nine, and I marvelled at their very practical understanding of the internal combustion engine, an understanding which I have never yet mastered myself. Clearly neither of them had been given any formal school education, and yet they knew how to keep the large diesel engine of that lorry in good running order, and whenever I was nearby when the bonnet was up, I noticed that the engine was always in spotless condition, despite the dusty sandy road across the desert that we travelled.

For about the next week we progressed steadily eastwards, speeding along when the road was hard, and crawling along when it was no more than two shifting ruts leading through the shifting sands of the desert. Whenever we met another vehicle coming the other way, it was always Bashir who moved off the road to give way, even though this often meant that the heavy lorry became bogged down in the sand, and had to be laboriously dug out, so that the long metal take-off strips could be inserted well under the back wheels, to enable the lorry to churn its way back into the two parallel grooves that stretched out and disappeared into the desert ahead. May Allah bless Bashir. He always made way for people, and so Allah made the way clear for him.

184 The Difficult Journey

Although we were in the cab, sheltered from most of the hot sun and much of the dust that was constantly kicked up by the wheels, with support for our backs and cushions under our bottoms, it was still a bone-shaker of a journey, and after a while I fell into a kind of daze as the hours and the miles and the days and the changing scenery passed us by like a kind of long extended dream, sometimes reciting what little Qur'an I knew by heart, sometimes singing from the Diwan of Shaykh Muhammad ibn al-Habib, sometimes singing my favourite pop songs that had been long embedded in my heart, sometimes just singing whatever came to my lips, sometimes chatting with Abdal-Jalil or Bashir, and sometimes just sitting in silence, watching the world go by, or reflecting on what had happened along the way so far, not only on this journey but on my whole life's journey. Altogether it had been pretty amazing, as it was right now, despite the heat and the dust and the constant rattling and shaking, as we moved slowly across the desert and the sun moved slowly across the sky, followed a little later by the moon, that was growing just a little larger and staying up there just a little longer each night.

Occasionally, we would stop at lone caravanserais where we all bought and shared foules mesdames and bread and fruit if there was any and sweet milky coffee or tea, sometimes stopping to do the prayer if it was time to do the prayer, and sometimes stopping for the night if it was time to catch some sleep, rolling out our mats and sleeping soundly near the inevitable fire, with the smell of woodsmoke in the air and always the music of the Sudan playing somewhere around us, filling the heart with yearning and the desire to be on the move again, which, soon enough, we would be, rattling off once again into the early morning sun after praying subh late, just before the sun swam into sight, and eating yet another breakfast of foules mesdames and bread and hot sweet milky tea.

After about three days, we reached El Obeid, only stopping briefly this time to refuel and eat and drink that luxury called a cold coke and do the prayer, and then we were on our way again, the road gradually becoming more well-defined and firmer, and the miles speeding by more rapidly as the time went by, until, another couple of days later, we were on tarmac once again and on the joyful exciting home-run into Khartoum where finally this modern ship of the desert rolled to a halt, stopping near the edge of the main open market place, with tall buildings all around us, and hundreds of people coming and going. As we lowered ourselves gently out of the cab for the last time, it was bewildering to be surrounded by so much activity, after the emptiness and loneliness of the desert.

We shook hands with Bashir and Umar and Adam and the other passengers whom we had come to know a little at our caravanserai meals, united by the journey we had just made, the same journey that the Mahdi and his army had made a century earlier, only on foot, and bade each other farewell. It had been a lovely journey, and one that we would always remember.

Then, shouldering our few possessions, the only possessions we had in the whole wide world – and how rich I felt to be weighed down by so little – we walked over to where the small open-backed taxi vans stopped before leaving for Omdurman, and caught the next one going there, bumping along the familiar road that led past the point where the Blue Nile and the White Nile meet, the Khartoum Hilton glinting opulently nearby in the late afternoon sun and reminding me of the promise I had made to Abdal-Jalil by the steep cliff edge on the side of Daribe, and then past the Mahdi's tomb, its now familiar silver missile-shaped roof forever waiting to blast off into outer space, and so to the busy Omdurman market place which we had not seen for over a month. Another brief half a mile's walk down roads we now knew well, and at last we were at Shaykh Al-Fattih Qarib'Allah's zawiyya once again, tired and dusty but very well, just looking forward to our first shower in a week and a good long sleep, and being greeted first by the fuqara and then by Shaykh Al-Fattih himself, welcomed and feasted and treated like princes once again, and with the Hajj only just around the corner!

OMDURMAN

For three days we did nothing but rest. Now that we had come to a temporary rest, the cumulative effect of the last month's travels had caught up with us and we felt shaken and tired. We spent much of the time laid out on our backs completely relaxed, just letting our bodies recover from the hard travelling to which they had been subjected. Then, once we were on a more even keel, we began to make the necessary preparations for the Hajj.

To begin with, I went to the Saudi Arabian Embassy which was surrounded by even larger crowds of people than on my two previous visits. After waiting patiently for hours outside, wondering what would happen when I was inside, and making dua after dua asking Allah to give us whatever was needed to get us to Makka in time for the Hajj, and then to give us an acceptable Hajj, I finally gained admission into the building, and found that the Ambassador was true to his word. The same official with whom I had dealt before was there to help, looking even tireder now as the applications for Hajj visas reached their climax, and after filling in the usual forms, our two passports were stamped with the necessary visas.

There still remained the other requirements that were preconditions to the granting of the visas: We were meant to have return air-tickets and enough money to cover our expenses while in Saudi Arabia.

"How much money do you have?" asked the official.

"About fifteen Sudanese pounds between us," I replied.

"Do you have your return air-tickets?" he continued.

"Not yet," I answered. "Actually we intend to return to England overland via Istanbul, after visiting the Prophet in Madina, salla'llahu alayhi wa sallam, so we only need to buy a one-way ticket."

The official frowned, and I waited with my heart in my mouth, silently asking Allah for a way through. Surely we would not be turned back after having travelled this far? We might not be very rich, and we might not be very worthy, but our intention to do the Hajj was sincere.

The official hesitated and then made his decision, walking over to a small safe in the wall. He returned with some money which he put in an envelope, and also wrote something in Arabic on two slips of paper which he stamped and signed. Then he handed them and the envelope to me.

"Here is a hundred pounds to buy your tickets. You better hurry up, because the last 'plane will be leaving in a week or so. Normally you would have to show that you have at least two hundred pounds each to cover your expenses while you are on the Hajj. Since you can't, show these two slips of paper to the officials at Jeddah, and they will let you through, insh'Allah, and put you on the bus to Makka. Have a good journey, and may your Hajj be accepted!" He gave me an encouraging smile and shook my hand warmly.

Minutes later, I emerged from the coolness of the air-conditioned building back into the heat and the bright sunlight, slightly bewildered and very grateful and elated by the unexpected generosity that had been shown to us. We now had the means to reach Makka! All we had to do now was get there in time! Al-hamdulillahi wa shukrulillah! If all officials were as kind and as helpful as the man at the Saudi Arabian Embassy in Khartoum, travelling would be a great deal easier!

○ ○ ○

Early the next morning, Abdal-Jalil and I were in Khartoum to book our tickets. The official at the Embassy had been right. There were very few flights to Jeddah left, and most of them were fully booked. We were very fortunate indeed to find two seats on one of the last flights before the Hajj deadline, and we emerged from the travel agents with joy, holding the two precious tickets that meant that we should be landing in Jeddah three days before the rites of the Hajj began.

"Come on," I said. "Let's go and have that ice-cold coke at the Hilton that I promised you!" Half an hour later we were sipping at our very expensive ice-cold cokes in the up-market Khartoum Hilton, looking rather incongruous amongst the wealthy trendies, and even the waiters in their smart uniforms, for we appeared to be the only people in the hotel who were dressed in robes and turbans, which, although they had been freshly laundered and ironed by the washermen who worked incessantly in their little shelter on the corner near the zawiyya, still had a slightly battered thoroughly well-travelled look about them.

Since the whole place was air-conditioned, we found that the cokes only made us feel cold, rather than refreshing us, and accordingly we righted the balance by having a hot cappuccino and a sticky cake each. Having spent as much in half an hour as we had been spending in a week on the road, we retreated back to the world that we preferred and busied ourselves with our final preparations for the Hajj.

○   ○   ○

There was still about a week to go before we were due to take off, so we had plenty of time to buy the few items that we needed: Firstly, our ihrams, the two large pieces of seamless white towelling which we would be wearing during the rites of the Hajj, one piece wrapped around the waist and the other draped over the left shoulder, down under the right armpit, and then back over the left shoulder again. Since all one's clothing and footwear worn during the Hajj has to be free of any sewing or stitching – simplicity itself – we also bought a pair of plastic sandals each, which we began to wear immediately so that the skin on our feet would harden up in the right places. We intended to do the Hajj entirely on foot, and did not want to end up hobbling along with painful blisters half way through it.

We also purchased a brique each, cleverly fashioned from various tins and pieces of tin all soldered together, so that we could have our own water supply for the toilet and doing wudu when water was not plentiful, and, probably inspired by the tales about the Mahdi which we had heard along the way, and still filled with the pioneering spirit that had been given such a free reign during our western journey, we also bought a heavy Sudanese sword each.

190 The Difficult Journey

Abdal-Jalil's was a mighty one, about four feet in length, while mine was lighter and smaller and easier to handle, being only about two feet in length. We never used them, and I ended up throwing mine into the Thames one chilly winter's day a couple of years later – letting go of what had now become the past – but at the time, it was good to have them, and they helped to make us feel true warriors of Islam!

Back at the zawiyya, we spent our time studying the passages of the Qur'an and the Hadith that describe the rites of the Hajj, as well as reading other people's descriptions of the Hajj, which we had brought with us, so that we knew exactly what we had to do once we reached Makka. Naturally the daily pattern of life at the zawiyya continued on around us, and, as we had done before, we continued to join in the gatherings of dhikr that were frequently held there, as well as spending some time each day with Shaykh Al-Fattih. He had already been on the Hajj about forty times, but, because of the trouble he was having with his knees, had decided not to go this year. If our understanding of Arabic had been better, he probably could have given us a much more comprehensive and deeper understanding of the rites of the Hajj and their meaning, but as it was, we had to be content with just knowing the basics and benefiting from the baraka of sitting with him.

Only one other task remained: Before we had left England, Shaykh Abdal-Qadir al-Murabit had instructed us to visit the awliya and to sing the Diwan of Shaykh Muhammad ibn al-Habib wherever we went. This, to the best of our ability, we had done. Sayyedina Shaykh had also asked Abdal-Jalil to bring him back a hand-written Qur'an from the Sudan. This we still had to acquire.

During our first stay at Shaykh Al-Fattih's zawiyya, during Ramadan, one of the other Shaykhs whom we had visited had been Shaykh Hamza whose zawiyya was only about twenty minutes' walk away. He had several hand-written Qur'ans, and since we had not been able to acquire one during our subsequent travels, it now appeared that he was to be our last as well as our first resort.

Strangely enough, the matter had been clarified for us when we had been in the crater of Daribe. During that very cold night when we had slept alongside the blazing tree trunk, I had dreamt, just before dawn, that a figure wearing a white robe and turban and holding a tasbih had said to me, "Whatever you do, don't visit Shaykh Hamza again." On first awaking, I had not really had time to reflect on the dream, although there was something about it that had struck me as being rather strange, since we had been immediately concerned with our own personal survival. Later on in the day, during one of our rests half way down the side of Daribe, Abdal-Jalil had mentioned the fact that we still had to find a hand-written Qur'an from somewhere, and had said that he thought Shaykh Hamza was probably our best bet, whereupon, prompted by my recent dream, I had said that I thought we should not go to him. Naturally Abdal-Jalil had thought that my response was rather odd, and on re-running the dream through my mind, I had realised what had struck me as being rather strange about it: Although the figure in the dream had been dressed like a Muslim, there had been fire in his eyes. It must have been Shaytan trying to deflect us off course, a'udhu bi'llahi min ash-shaytani'r-rajim.

Accordingly, now that we were back in Omdurman, we went round to visit Shaykh Hamza one evening after maghrib, and told him what our Shaykh had requested. Shaykh Hamza paused.

"Hand-written Qur'ans are worth a lot of money," he said.

"We only have six pounds between us," replied Abdal-Jalil, "but you are welcome to all of it. Is that enough?"

Shaykh Hamza smiled. "Keep your money," he replied. "I was only testing your sincerity. You are welcome to have one of my hand-written Qur'ans. Please give it to your Shaykh with my greetings. Only a couple of weeks ago I had a dream in which I met Shaytan riding on a camel. 'Where are you off to now?' I asked him. He replied that he was going to England. 'Why there?' I asked. He replied, 'The people over there are intelligent, so I have more work over there than in places like here where the people are half asleep!'" Shaykh Hamza, who was a large man, laughed heartily. "A'udhu bi'llahi min ash-shaytani'r-rajim! Here, have this one. Bismillah!" and so saying, he handed Abdal-Jalil a beautifully hand-written Qur'an, wrapped neatly in a clean piece of cloth. Having thanked him very much, we returned to the zawiyya, relieved that we had found what we were looking for. Now we could leave the Sudan without any regrets!

❂   ❂   ❂

There remained only one more thing to do, and that was to have a haircut. Our hair had grown quite long, and we decided that it would be wise to have it cut short, since while you are in ihram it is not permissible to groom or comb or even remove any of your body hair. Clearly it would be easier to comply with this requirement if our hair was good and short, and accordingly we dropped in at a barber's shop near Omdurman market. The barber was not quite sure how to begin at first, since he was only used to cutting relatively short dark curly hair, but once we had made it clear that we wanted our hair cut very short, he went about his business with alacrity, and soon we were shorn of most of our locks.

Shortly after this, I met a muqaddem in the market place who invited me into his nearby home for a welcome drink of cold orange squash. He spoke good English, and after talking briefly about the Hajj, he began to talk about the future of the Sudan: "President Numeyri will not rule over the Sudan for many more years. Towards the end of his rule, he will come closer to Islam. Shortly before he is removed from power, the Mahdi will visit the Sudan."

The muqaddem was, of course, not referring to the Ahmad al-Mahdi who had fought General Gordon, but to the rightly-guided leader of the Muslims who will be called the Mahdi and whom the Prophet Muhammad said will appear near the end of time to fight the Dajjal – the Anti-Christ – and his followers until the return of Jesus who will kill the Dajjal and his followers by a miracle and then re-establish harmony and justice amongst the peoples of this earth, ruling in accordance with the final revelation of the Qur'an and, after his natural death, being buried next to the Prophet Muhammad in Madina, may the blessings and peace of Allah be on them both.

It seemed that the muqaddem was indicating that it might not be very much longer before these prophecies were fulfilled, and certainly this was not the first occasion on which I had been informed that both the Dajjal and the Mahdi are alive and on the face of the earth. The subsequent passage of time has proved the muqaddem's words about President Numeyri to be accurate, but as for his words about the Mahdi, Allah knows best.

Certainly the muqaddem was a man of integrity and sincerity, and when he began to talk about what happens when you embrace Islam, his words rang true: "To really understand, you have to make a journey, from your mind to your heart, and when you have made that journey you find that they are not separate, they are one, and then you understand, and then you understand what Islam is about."

The muqaddem knew Shaykh Al-Fattih Qarib'Allah well, and indeed the next evening, which was a Thursday night, he came to the gathering of dhikr which was being held in the mosque at Shaykh Al-Fattih's zawiyya. During the meal, after the hadra was over, he invited Abdal-Jalil and I to visit the tomb of Shaykh Muhammad an-Nil, who had been one of the Shaykhs in the line of transmission of knowledge and wisdom between the Prophet Muhammad and his own Shaykh, the next day, after the jumua. This we agreed to do, and, sixteen hours later, we were there, at the tomb of Shaykh Muhammad an-Nil.

There was a large crowd of people there, many of them dancing and clapping their hands and singing the Shaykh's name repeatedly, and the general impression that I received was one of disorder and a lack of true spiritual courtesy. We threaded our way through the crowds until we were in the small building that covers the Shaykh's tomb and greeted him, before making dua to Allah, asking that he be given baraka and light and peace in his grave. By now it was well after asr, and since it has been transmitted through the Prophet Muhammad that there is a special time on the day of the jumua, between asr and maghrib, when whatever you ask for will be given to you, I spent some time making dua, asking Allah for all that I wanted, including a safe journey to Makka, and an acceptable Hajj, and a safe return to England. I also asked for a wonderful life, and an easy death, and peace in the grave, and no fear on the Last Day, and a swift entrance into the Garden, both for myself and for everyone that I loved and for everyone that I met. Finally, I asked to be given what all the true awliya are given, the highest deepest knowledge that there is, gnosis of Allah.

We had just left the tomb when the adhan for maghrib rang out over the dusty crowded patch of land that surrounded it, and quickly finding somewhere to do wudu, we were in time to join the prayer line. After the prayer was over, we were invited to join a circle of dhikr, which we did, but not for long. It was ragged and unco-ordinated, and the hadra was more like an ignorant tribal dance – accompanied by clapping and shouting and prancing about – than the serious concentrated invocation of Allah done standing that I knew and loved. Exchanging understanding glances, Abdal-Jalil and I withdrew from the circle, and disappeared quietly into the night. We had no need of this kind of gathering.

Perhaps our perceptions that evening were coloured by our general state and condition. Perhaps we were just tired from our travels, or perhaps we had just had enough of visiting the awliya, whether in their bodies or in their graves. After all the meetings we had had along the way, I knew for certain that the only Shaykh with whom I really wanted to be was my own Shaykh. Although one should not really be concerned with comparing different Shaykhs, for it is like comparing different mirrors – whatever their outward form, they are bound to give you basically the same reflection – I had met no one who was as balanced or as knowledgeable or as wise or as correctly behaved as Shaykh Abdal-Qadir al-Murabit. I realised just how pure an Islam it was that he embodied and transmitted, and just how accurate and perceptive and truthful his words were. I could not have wished for a better guide and teacher.

The beauty of it all is that every sincere follower of a Shaykh is certain that his or her Shaykh is the best Shaykh in the world – and they are all right, for every one is given the Shaykh that they deserve, in accordance with their own sincerity and strength of resolution, the Shaykh who is best suited to guide them along the path that leads to knowledge and wisdom.

One visits many Shaykhs for the baraka and for spiritual gifts and knowledges, but one only takes one Shaykh as one's spiritual healer and guide along the path that leads to self-knowledge and gnosis of Allah. Loyalty to one's Shaykh and trust in him is part of sincerity. One of the gifts of our journey so far had been the realisation and confirmation of this basic truth. I had always trusted Shaykh Abdal-Qadir from the first moment that we had met, but it was good to realise more fully just how good and reliable a guide he was, and to know with greater certainty that I had no desire or need to look for any other Shaykh.

Perhaps also, I realised that soon, insh'Allah, we would be visiting the tomb of the man through whom all the awliya receive their knowledge and wisdom, and without whom there would not have been any Shaykhs to visit or any Hajj to do, the Prophet Muhammad, may the blessings and peace of Allah be on him and on his family and on his companions and on all those who follow him with sincerity in what they are able until the Last Day. Even the greatest Shaykh is only a drop compared to the ocean of the Prophet Muhammad, and the realisation that we would be visiting the Last Messenger's tomb in Madina once the Hajj had been completed, insh'Allah, put everything into perspective.

Furthermore, beyond all these considerations was the fact that in a only a few more days we would be in Makka, insh'Allah, immersing ourselves deep in the worship of the One who is the Source of all the Prophets and all the awliya and indeed of everyone and everything in creation. This prospect put everything even more into proportion, as our attention was directed away from the realities of the creation towards the Reality of the Creator, and the inescapable realisation of the meaning of the words that, whatever appears to exist, Allah is the First and the Last and the Outwardly Manifest and the Inwardly Hidden. As Allah says in the Qur'an:

Allah has created you and what you do.

(Qur'an: 37.96)

KHARTOUM

Suddenly, swiftly, at the speed of light, time had flashed by. We were at Khartoum Airport, waiting for our flight to be called. Our last days in Omdurman were already in the past.

We had said farewell to Shaykh Al-Fattih Qarib'Allah, through whom so much good had come our way, and to his sons and fuqara, sad to be leaving and glad to be on the move once again. Just as we were boarding the taxi that was to take us to the airport, Shaykh Al-Fattih had pressed forty pounds into Abdal-Jalil's hands, with a broad smile. "For the Hajj!" he had said encouragingly, a giant of a human being even though his body was frail and weak.

Then the taxi had whisked us off to the airport in good time, where it seemed that all the 'planes and all the people there were bound for Jeddah. Some of the pilgrims had already changed into their ihram, although Khartoum was not the point at which it was customary to do so. In fact this was a point that bothered me a little, for although I was aware that those approaching Makka from the west should change into ihram at a place called Al-Juhfah, a place which was north of Jeddah, it rather looked as if we were going to have to change into ihram in Jeddah itself. I just hoped that this would be acceptable.

We sat patiently in the airport building, sipping cool drinks from time to time, for we had a good three or four hours to wait before our 'plane was due to take off, watching all the other people in the building who, probably without exception, were thinking about the Hajj in one way or another. How different this was to the scene that had greeted us at Gatwick airport, and how different we were to the two people who, along with Mustafa al-Alawi, had waited for our flight to Athens, not knowing quite what to expect in the months ahead, but determined to do it somehow, whatever it was, and above all to do the Hajj.

A thousand images of our travels between the two airports, and everything that had taken place along the way, flashed through my mind, especially once we had set foot on the shores of Africa, merging into a mental collage of memories that was breathtaking. It had been truly wonderful. Never knowing what would happen next, or whether we would ever make it, the adventure had unfolded, permeated with baraka and rahma, until finally, here we were, safe and sound, just waiting to make that short hop over to the Arabian peninsula! I felt as if I was the most fortunate man in the world!

We just had time to pray maghrib and isha in the small airport mosque and then it was time to be off. Our flight was called, we boarded the plane, and soon we were off into the darkening sky, speeding towards Jeddah, fit, healthy, acclimatised to the heat and the culture that prevailed in this part of the world, and hoping against hope that, having come this far, we would be enabled to go all the way. We were completely ready in every way to do the Hajj, and we could not have imagined a better preparation. As one of our hosts at Abu Haraz had observed, the Sudanese have a saying: "When Allah created the Sudan, He smiled!" It just has to be true!

JEDDAH

We touched down at Jeddah in the warm humid night, just one more 'plane load of pilgrims among hundreds of thousands, and made our way into the airport building, where the inevitable customs formalities awaited us. Abdal-Jalil's lengthy sword was soon discovered during the baggage search, and we were detained for a short time in a small room, sipping at the sweet pale Saudi tea without milk from the miniature glass mugs which we had been given, while an official politely explained that they would retain the sword at Jeddah until it was time for Abdal-Jalil to leave the country, when he could pick it up again. We were taken to the large room where all confiscated weapons were deposited, and Abdal-Jalil's mighty sword joined the fearsome array of almost every kind of weapon imaginable, ranging from knives and clubs and swords to pistols and even machine guns. My sword, rolled up in a robe at the bottom of my camel-bag had remained undetected, and since I had no intention of using it on the Hajj, I did not declare it. I did not intend to return to England via Jeddah, and accordingly to surrender it now would be to lose it.

We rejoined the queue for passport control, and as we waited, I recalled the story I had heard of one old man who had travelled to Saudi Arabia to do the Hajj without a passport. He was stopped at the border and asked for his passport.

"Passport?" he said. "What's a passport?"

"Your passport! Your book!" replied the customs officer.

"Ah my book? – Here's my book!" said the old man, pulling out his Qur'an, whereupon he was allowed across the border!

Eventually it was our turn to have our passports examined, and they were stamped without any more delay. We emerged from the building to find ourselves in 'pilgrim city', a large complex containing simple open-plan shelters, shops, restaurants and a mosque with nearby toilet and shower facilities, where pilgrims could stop and rest temporarily before being finally cleared to continue on their way to Makka. By now it was too late at night to go through the remaining formalities, so we changed the forty Sudanese pounds that Shaykh Al-Fattih had given to us into Saudi rials, bought ourselves a simple meal of foules mesdames and bread, and after a good hot glass of Lipton's tea, we rolled out our mats on the beautifully cool concrete floor of one of the temporary shelters and went to sleep, hoping for the best.

The next morning, after praying subh and having breakfast, we presented ourselves for processing, surrounded by a sea of pilgrims who were arriving from just about everywhere else in the world. It was an extraordinary and colourful sight, for there were so many outwardly different kinds of people moving in every direction, whose inward intentions and final goal were all fundamentally the same. At the edge of 'pilgrim city' was a vast coach park, and as we waited to be processed, we could see that there was a constant flow of coaches, leaving full and returning empty, as they ferried load after load of pilgrims to Makka.

For the first time, I considered how difficult it must be to organise all the facilities needed to deal with the sudden influx of pilgrims that occurs each year without fail. As a result of modern communication and travel technology, it was now possible for people to travel to Makka in far greater numbers than in the past. Whereas, at the time of the Prophet Muhammad's pilgrimage – for he only did the Hajj once in his life – the pilgrims could be counted in tens of thousands, now they were counted in hundreds of thousands, and it had been estimated that this year there would be a million and a half people doing the Hajj. People had been coming to Makka on pilgrimage ever since the time of the Prophet Abraham, and the people of Makka had always traditionally shown hospitality to them since those times, but now it was necessary to provide that hospitality on a far greater scale than ever before.

Saudi Arabia's new-found oil wealth had made it possible to build the airports and the roads and the living facilities needed to cater for such large numbers of temporary visitors, but it still must be very difficult to run all these facilities efficiently, especially when many of the pilgrims arriving in Saudi Arabia each year would be unable to speak very much Arabic. I did not envy the task of the

Saudi Arabian administrators in the least, although clearly it was a great honour to be the host to so many 'guests of Allah', those who travel fi sabili'llah, in the way of Allah, seeking only the pleasure of Allah and the vision of Allah, for the Prophet Muhammad once said that the people in the Garden will see Allah as clearly as we see the full moon in this world, and it is this vision of Allah for which the hearts of all true believers yearn, whether they know it or not.

At last it was our turn to be processed, and, to our dismay, we found that our way was blocked. The tired official shook his head. We did not have return air tickets, and we did not have enough money, and therefore we could go no further. Again and again I drew the official's attention to the two slips of paper which the helpful official at the Saudi Arabian Embassy in Khartoum had written out and officially stamped in order to clear the way for us, but the tired official just shook his head. These bits of paper might mean something in Khartoum, but they were not valid here. Again and again I explained how we had been travelling for the last four and a half months on our way to Makka to do the Hajj. Surely he would not just stop us like this after we had come so far. We were Muslims. We were his brothers. He had to help us! The tired official just shook his head. We did not have return air tickets and we did not have enough money.

"Then what do you expect us to do?" asked Abdal-Jalil, trying not to become angered by this unfriendly bureaucracy.

"Come back tomorrow," was the reply.

Baffled and shaken, but determined to cut through the red tape and official policy somehow, and still expecting and relying on Allah to get us to Makka in time to do the Hajj, we returned to our temporary shelter in 'pilgrim city' and waited for tomorrow to come. Surely Allah was not going to stop us now!

'Pilgrim city' was an extraordinary place to be in, with only another two days to go before the Hajj began, and although we were anxious to be on our way, it was good to have time to become accustomed to being in the midst of so many people, a constant ebb and flow of humanity that was forever changing as more and more pilgrims arrived, dressed in all manner of colours and styles of clothing on arrival, but all dressed the same on departure, the men simply wearing two large pieces of white cloth and the women wearing simple white ankle-length dresses and white head scarves. This was the real united nation, I reflected, people from everywhere and every walk of life in the world gathered together, all united by the same prophetic teaching, despite their having come from so many different countries with their different climates and their different customs and cultures, and all recognisably following the same way of life, based on the worship of Allah and the example of the Prophet Muhammad and his family and companions, may the blessings and peace of Allah be on them.

In the midst of this constantly moving sea of people, Abdal-Jalil and I immediately recognised four familiar faces, those of Mansura, Sabah, Rukaya and Rashida, four of the ladies from our community in England who had just flown in direct from Heathrow to Jeddah. Apparently they too were having some difficulty in being granted clearance to continue their journey to Makka. Native English Muslims were still few and far between at that time, and accordingly were often subjected to more stringent tests in order to prove that they were indeed true Muslims and not just people masquerading as Muslims, for, as is well known, only Muslims are permitted to enter the protected cities of Makka and Madina.

In the light of this meeting, I was glad that we had been delayed, since it enabled us to catch up on the main news from England, and the ladies to pass on a message to us from Shaykh Abdal-Qadir. Three of the men from our community in England, Muhammad Abdal-Bari, Uthman and Muhammad Qasim, had arrived a few days earlier and were already in Makka, staying as the guests of Abdal-Hamid who was a friend of ours living in Makka. We were to join them there at Abdal-Hamid's mother's house, whose address Mansura now gave to us. Muhammad Abdal-Bari was to be the Amir of our group during the time of the Hajj.

Once our immediate situation had been clarified, we were of course eager to find out how Mustafa al-Alawi was doing. Naturally we had often thought of him during our western journey to the Jebel Murra, but had had no way of finding out what had become of him. Apparently he had arrived back safely but bemused from Khartoum, and was now slowly but surely recovering from his state of silence and withdrawal. We were both relieved to hear that our telegram had been received and Mustafa met on arrival at Heathrow, and glad to know that he was on the mend.

Having exchanged our news with the four ladies, they disappeared back into the sea of pilgrims, determined to obtain their official clearance through to Makka, while I reflected on the perfection with which Allah arranges events. We think we know what is happening for much of the time, but every so often we are reminded that we are only an infinitesimal part of a much larger scheme of things. As Shaykh Ahmad ibn Ata'illah once said, when an ignorant man awakes in the morning, he says to himself, 'I wonder what I will do today,' and when a wise man awakes in the morning, he says to himself, 'I wonder what Allah will do with me today.' Thanks to our being delayed, we now knew where to go when we reached Makka, and insh'Allah we would now receive the opening we were expecting.

● ● ●

Later on that afternoon, we met the ladies again, now dressed in their ihrams and just about to depart for Makka. Apparently the go-ahead had been given to them by one of the top officials who was called Abdal-Wahhab, which in Arabic literally means 'the slave of the One Who Bestows'. We bid them farewell and have a good Hajj, for they were staying elsewhere in Makka and would be doing the Hajj separately, and then decided to go and find Abdal-Wahhab ourselves. There was a danger that the tired official whom we had seen earlier that morning would just keep on shaking his head and saying 'Come back tomorrow', until it was too late to do the Hajj, and accordingly we tracked down Abdal-Wahhab's office with renewed determination and hope.

We were shown into a small waiting room that was full of people also waiting to see Abdal-Wahhab, and it was not until the end of the afternoon that we found ourselves seated in his office. Tea was brought for us, as we patiently repeated all that we had said to the tired official that morning, and patiently Abdal-Wahhab listened to us, examining our passports, and the slips of paper from the Khartoum Embassy, and the letter which had been written for us by Shaykh Abdal-Haleem, the head of the Al-Azhar University in Cairo, requesting all Muslim authorities to grant us safe passage. Having listened to all that we had to say, and having examined all our documentation, Abdal-Wahhab looked at us and smiled at us and asked us to come back the next morning. It had been a long day for him. It was getting late. It was time to close the office for the day. We had been hoping for a swift decision, but had no choice other than to say that we would be at his office as soon as it was open the next morning.

❁ ❁ ❁

We were back in the waiting room early the next morning, and after another long wait were shown into Abdal-Wahhab's office once again. Again we repeated what we had said the day before and again Abdal-Wahhab listened to us and examined our bits of paper. Once again we were asked to go and wait in the waiting room, and once again we resumed our seats.

By now we were both beginning to feel slightly apprehensive, for there was a very real possibility that we would be prevented from going any further. According to the current rules, we were not eligible to do the Hajj because we were not rich enough. These requirements did not derive directly from the Qur'an or the Hadith, but from relatively recently created man-made laws, and yet if the officials chose to apply them strictly, there would be very little we could do about it. It was true that the Qur'an says, with reference to going on the Hajj, **"So make provision for yourselves"**, but the very next phrase makes it clear that:

the best provision is taqwa.

(Qur'an: 2.197)

To have taqwa is to be careful about what you do, out of awe and fear and love of Allah, and accordingly it is dependant on having knowledge and sincerity. Neither Abdal-Jalil nor myself were particularly knowledgeable, but we did try to act on what little we knew with sincerity, and to that extent we had our share of the best provision. We knew enough to know, however, that whether or not we would be given permission to enter Makka did not depend on how much taqwa we had, nor even on how much money we had. It depended solely on the overwhelming generosity of Allah. We sat there in silence in the small waiting room outside Abdal-Wahhab's office for hours, utterly helpless and at the mercy of Allah, as I quietly made dua after dua, repeatedly calling on Allah to give us the clearance that we needed to go to Makka, repeating one of His most beautiful names over and over again: Ya Wahhab! Ya Wahhab! Ya Wahhab!

Shortly before the office was due to close, having spent the whole day there, other than a couple of brief breaks to go to the toilet and to pray dhur and asr, we were summoned back into Abdal-Wahhab's office for the third time. Abdal-Wahhab rose to his feet and handed us back our passports without any word of explanation, but with a big smile: "You are free to go to Makka now," he said. "Catch whatever bus you wish after you have changed into your ihram. We have assigned you a mutawwif, whose name has been stamped on your Hajj visa. You will be shown where to go once you have arrived in Makka. May your Hajj be acceptable!"

I was so relieved I almost cried.

MAKKA

Relieved and trembling, we returned to the temporary shelter where our belongings were, and unpacked our ihrams. All that we needed to do now was to have a ghusl and put on our ihrams and then we could be off. Clearly it was not going to be possible to put on our ihrams at Al-Juhfah, but insh'Allah it would be acceptable to put them on where we were.

The practice of putting on ihram at particular places, depending on the direction from which a pilgrim was approaching Makka, had been established in the very early days of Islam, when all the pilgrims came from the Arab tribes who lived either in or around Makka, and who accordingly approached the city along established caravan routes. In the present age of air and sea travel, it appeared to make sense to put on ihram as soon as and wherever one reached the borders of the Haram, the area of sacred land that surrounds Makka, and which, as was relevant in our case, extends as far as Jeddah.

By now it was maghrib, and having prayed maghrib and isha, Abdal-Jalil and I made our final preparations for the Hajj. Having done my ghusl under a powerful cold shower, I put on my ihram and then did two rakats in the nearby mosque, followed by dua, asking Allah for a simple straight forward Hajj that was acceptable and full of understanding. From now on, until the rites of the Hajj were completed, I had to comply with the special obligations that apply to anyone who is in ihram. As regards myself, I could not groom myself in any way, such as by cutting or pulling out any of my hair, or even combing it, or trimming my nails or wearing perfume. As regards my environment, I could not kill any plant or insect or animal. As regards other people, I had to keep my temper and not waste time in idle conversation. Had I been married and my wife been with me, we would have had to refrain from making love as long as we were in ihram. In other words, everyone on the Hajj had to keep a low profile, so as to ensure that there was an absolute minimum of conflict and damage, and to enable each person not to be distracted by the actions of others or themselves from the remembrance of Allah.

One of the means by which each pilgrim's attention was directed to the remembrance of Allah while in ihram was the repetition of what is known as the talbiya, a particular form of dhikr which, if repeated constantly with awareness and understanding, makes you realise more fully that there is only Allah to worship and that He is our Lord and we are His slaves.

As soon as I had finished making my dua, I began to repeat the talbiya, which I had already memorised while we had been in the Sudan:

**Labayk, Labayk, Allahumma Labayk.
La sharika lak, Labayk.
Inna'l-hamdu wa'n-ni'mata laka wa'l-mulk.
La sharika lak.**

Which means:

**I am totally at Your service, I am totally at Your service,
O Allah I am totally at Your service.
You have no partner, I am totally at Your service.
Surely the Praise and the Blessing are Yours and the Kingdom.
You have no partner.**

Repeating the talbiya out loud but not loudly, Abdal-Jalil and I made our way to the point from which all the coaches departed for Makka, and after about an hour's wait, we finally boarded a coach. As soon as it had filled up with pilgrims, we were off, rolling smoothly out of Jeddah and gliding through the night towards Makka along a smooth road.

After a while, the coach stopped briefly at the sign that said 'No non-Muslims permitted beyond this point' and our passports were checked once again. Soon we were off again, cruising quietly through the cold desert night, shivering slightly with fear or excitement or cold, or all three, and feeling both tired and wide awake at the same time, as, again and again, we repeated the talbiya:

**Labayk, Labayk, Allahumma Labayk.
La sharika lak, Labayk.
Inna'l-hamdu wa'n-ni'mata laka wa'l-mulk.
La sharika lak.**

✧ ✧ ✧

After what seemed an age, we glimpsed the lights of the city of Makka ahead of us, nestling down in a rocky valley that was surrounded by dark mountains, and at last we rolled into Makka, just as the adhan for subh was being called. The streets were full of people making their way to the huge mosque that stands at the heart of Makka, and all the shops and eating places were already open. There was a calmness and deep resonance about the place that made you realise this was no ordinary city. If there was any rush here, right now, then it was to get to the mosque in time to pray subh, rather than to have another busy day at work. I looked out of the window of the slowly moving coach at the people and streets of Makka in awe. It was beautiful in its majesty.

The coach rolled to a standstill, and we emerged into the half-light of dawn. It was the 8th of Dhu'l-Hijjah, the day on which the rites of the Hajj commence. We had arrived just in time! There are in fact three slightly different ways of doing the Hajj, depending on how soon before the 8th of Dhu'l-Hijjah you arrive in Makka. Abdal-Jalil and I had intended to do the simplest form of the Hajj, which is called Al-Hajj Al-Ifrad, right from the beginning of our long journey, and as it had turned out, this was the most suitable form to do in our particular circumstances.

Having left the bus, we decided that it would be best to find Abdal-Hamid's mother's house and make contact with Muhammad Abdal-Bari and the others before commencing the preliminary rights of the Hajj, and for this reason we did not immediately go straight to the huge mosque that surrounds the Ka'aba, the cube-shaped building that was originally built by the Prophet Ibrahim, and which all Muslims face whenever they do the prayer. Instead, we found a quiet corner where we prayed subh, and then had a much needed glass of hot sweet tea at one of the numerous cafes that adjoin the Haram, as the area occupied by the Ka'aba and the mosque that surrounds it is often called.

As the sky grew lighter and lighter, we could see around us more clearly, and we watched in amazement as an endless stream of people came and went. The air was radiant with light and vibrant with energy, glowing with baraka, and through it all passed hundreds of thousands of people. From where had they all come? Where did they all sleep? How were they all fed? It was a miracle!

Once the sun had risen, we started to look for the house of Abdal-Hamid's mother, and after asking several people along our way, which was full of pilgrims from many different countries mostly dressed in ihram and repeating the talbiya in firm strong voices, we finally found the house, which turned out to be only about fifteen minutes' walk away from the Haram. It was one of the traditional Makkan houses, with a wooden balcony and carved wooden shutters and a very solid studded wooden door.

We knocked at the door, and suddenly there was Abdal-Hamid, smiling broadly and welcoming us inside. We were shown in to a simple sitting-room, and there were the rest of the fuqara, Muhammad Abdal-Bari, Uthman and Muhammad Qasim, beaming away at us, as glad to see us as we were to see them. We exchanged hugs and handshakes and then news. The ladies had arrived safely and were staying with other friends as already arranged. Everyone in our community back in England was fine. Mustafa al-Alawi, as the ladies had already told us back in Jeddah, was also making a good recovery. Everything was fine, alhamdulillahi wa shukrulillah!

Within minutes, Abdal-Hamid's mother and sister had prepared a simple meal for us all, and as we ate hungrily, we caught up on all the news and told the others a little about our travels in the Sudan. In the course of the conversation, Muhammad Abdal-Bari began to tell me that Shaykh Abdal-Qadir had told him to arrange a marriage for me, with the help of Shaykh Al-Bukhari in Madina, but I cut him short. "Let us discuss this after the Hajj," I said. "A man in ihram should neither marry, nor become engaged to be married, nor arrange a marriage!" Although I did want a wife, I turned away from even the thought of marriage for the time being. All I wanted to do right now, especially after having travelled so far and for so long, was to do the Hajj. There were only a few hours left in which Abdal-Jalil and I could do the preliminary rites of the Hajj, and then it would be time to leave Makka and head for Mina, a small valley that lies about five miles to the east of Makka.

Accordingly as soon as we had finished the meal, we all did wudu and then headed for the Haram. It was agreed that once we were there, we would all do what we either had or wanted to do, and then meet up again after a few hours in a certain part of the mosque, directly opposite the golden water outlet which projects slightly out over one side of the flat roof of the Ka'aba. As we approached the Haram, the streets became more and more crowded. There was so much activity that I just had to lower my eyes and concentrate on my heart, repeating the talbiya constantly, as we approached the high walls and even higher minarets that surround the Haram, making for one of the huge arched entrances that lead into the mosque from every side. As we drew nearer, I felt very small and insignificant and alone. Every individual here was surrounded by thousands upon thousands of other individuals, and yet each one of us was as alone as we will be once we are in our graves. It was not a lonely feeling that I felt, but rather the realisation that I was alone.

There is only Allah.

THE HARAM

We entered the Haram through the entrance known as Al-Bab As-Salaam, which in Arabic means 'the gate of peace', and into the midst of the huge crowds of people that filled the mosque. It was an extraordinary and awe-inspiring sight. Never had I seen so many people gathered together in one place, and they were all there for the same reason, for Allah. Wherever you looked, there were people dressed in white. Some were standing, or bowing, or prostrating or sitting, as they did voluntary prayers; some were sitting quietly, doing dhikr or reciting the Qur'an; but the vast majority were moving in a huge anti-clockwise circle. And at the very centre of all this movement, towering above everyone, at the still point of the turning world, stood the Ka'aba in all its magnificence and glory.

"Subhana'llah!" I breathed, as my gaze fell on the Ka'aba for the very first time in my life. It seemed to hang in the air, like a very clear mirage, stately and serene, still and immense, draped in a black finely embroidered covering that had golden calligraphy running round it near its top edge, with its bottom edge furled and tied up, so that it was out of the reach of even the tallest man that might try to reach up and touch it. Around this point moved the vast swirl of thousands upon thousands of pilgrims, all immersed in the remembrance of Allah, all forming a human whirlpool that turned and turned without a moment's pause. It was amazing, and for a few moments we gazed at this ever-changing kaleidoscope of people, not just because the Prophet Muhammad once said that to look at the Ka'aba is to worship Allah, but simply because it was such a beautifully majestic sight to behold.

Then, walking carefully across the huge carpeted area of the mosque that was sheltered by an apparently never-ending series of domed ceilings which were supported by arched columns of fine marble and adorned with large hanging chandeliers, we edged towards the main current of the human whirlpool that swept slowly and inexorably across the open unroofed area that stretches out beneath the open sky, between the covered part of the mosque and the Ka'aba itself. As we moved out into the open, I could see that the covered area of the mosque was sometimes two and even three storeys high, and that there were people circumnambulating the Ka'aba even on those levels and at that distance. We all stepped out into the main current, and soon became separated by the constant flow of people.

❂   ❂   ❂

It was at this point, as I prepared myself to do the first preliminary rite of the Hajj which is to circle the Ka'aba seven times, that I recalled the advice of an old man from Sierra Leone whom I had met at the East London Mosque one evening, shortly before Abdal-Jalil and Mustafa and I had set out on our journey. He had greeted me by name, chuckling softly and covering me with the special perfume that is usually put on the famous Black Stone which is set into one corner of the Ka'aba at about chest level, and which is the customary starting and finishing point for each circuit – or tawaf as they are called of the Ka'aba.

"Never lose your temper or fight anyone while you are in ihram," he had said cheerfully but seriously, "or your Hajj will not be accepted. You will see people fighting each other to reach the Black Stone. Do not behave like them. I know a much easier way of reaching it!" He had laughed in great amusement at the ignorance of the people whom he had told me not to imitate. "All you have to do," he had continued, "is just approach the Black Stone as close as you can without having to push or shove. Then do nothing more, other than asking Allah to take you to it! He will! And make sure that you are always in wudu when you are in the Haram. It is a pure place and you must be pure while you are there. If you break your wudu while you are in the Haram, then go and do wudu again immediately!"

❂   ❂   ❂

It is customary to kiss the Black Stone each time that you pass it while doing tawaf of the Ka'aba. If this is not possible, then it is customary to touch it and then kiss your hand. If this is not possible, then it is customary to salute it from a distance and then kiss your hand. These actions are not acts of worship of the Black Stone itself. They are a means whereby all the Muslims from every age are united at the same point and place.

In the same way, all the Muslims in every age always face the Ka'aba when doing the prayer, wherever they may be, but this does not mean that the Ka'aba is in itself an object of worship. Only Allah is worshipped. The Ka'aba is a focal point for the Muslims, and it is the means by which all Muslims are clearly identifiable: The Muslims are those who, when they do the prayer, which is the same prayer that the Prophet Muhammad did, face the Ka'aba in Makka.

❁ ❁ ❁

During most of the year, it is relatively easy to either kiss or touch the Black Stone each time that you pass it during tawaf, but at the time of the Hajj, it is literally impossible for every pilgrim to do so, and accordingly it is enough to salute it from a distance. However, I did want to begin and end my first set of seven tawafs by kissing the Black Stone, the very same Black Stone that the Prophet Muhammad had put in position when the Ka'aba was being rebuilt during his lifetime, and which he himself had kissed when doing tawaf of the Ka'aba, may the blessings and peace of Allah be on him. Accordingly I decided to follow the advice of the old man whom I had met in London. The situation was just as he had described, and I did just as he had said.

Bearing the old man's words of wisdom in mind, I headed out into the sea of people, and when I had reached the point where I could go no further, I came to a standstill, asked Allah to take me to the Black Stone, and then did nothing. Slowly but inexorably the moving weight of the people behind me pushed me closer and closer towards the Black Stone, until suddenly I was there, flattened up against it. I kissed it, feeling its cool smooth black surface against my lips and scenting the same perfume that I had last scented in the East London Mosque, and then tried to move away, but was unable to do so, so eager were the people behind me to be where I was. For what seemed like several minutes, I was pinioned against the smoothed, hollowed out, sweetly perfumed stone which was now set in silver, until a sudden side eddy of people gently pushed me away from it and back into the main flow of the whirlpool. Allahu Akbar!

❁ ❁ ❁

It is said that the Black Stone was originally pure white, and that it came from the Garden, and that it was originally placed in position by the Prophet Ibrahim when he first built the Ka'aba. After being touched by millions upon millions of Muslims ever since that time, it is said that it was gradually blackened and worn smooth and hollow by so much contact with people, just as rocks are coloured and worn away after constant contact with running water. There are others who say that it was originally a meteorite. Whatever its original state, the Black Stone is now very hard, very black, and very smooth.

Immediately around the corner in which the Black Stone is set is Al-Multazam, the area between the Black Stone and the richly decorated and ornamented door that leads into the interior of the Ka'aba. Should you ever be allowed through that door into the inside of the Ka'aba, you may pray in whatever direction you wish. It is said that whatever dua you make at Al-Multazam will be answered, although, as the Prophet Muhammad once said, whenever you make a dua Allah does one of three things: Either He answers it straight away, or He delays answering it until the time is right, or He rewards you for having turned to Him in your dua, rather than to other than Him.

Just as I had been detained at the Black Stone, so I was kept from moving away from Al-Multazam, which was where the flow of people carried me as soon as I had rounded the corner in which the Black Stone is set. As a result I ended up making more and more duas, requesting all that I wanted for both myself and my relations and friends and everyone that I had met and all the Muslims and everyone else, while trying to include every event and eventuality both past and future, in this world and the next, until there was nothing left to say.

Some of the pilgrims at Al-Multazam were weeping uncontrollably as they stood close against the wall with their arms outstretched above their heads, imploring and sobbing unrestrainedly, but I avoided becoming emotionally distraught. I would have been embarrassed to draw attention to myself in this manner, although of course I was aware that people do not only weep out of self-pity and remorse, or because of or for other people, but simply for Allah, either out of yearning to see His face, or because they have been given a sudden insight into the nature of Reality, the impact of which makes them weep in a manner over which they have no control.

Having made all the duas that were possible, I managed to slip away from Al-Multazam and continue my first tawaf of the Ka'aba. It is customary to do the first three tawafs rapidly, and the next four at an ordinary walking pace, but right now it was so crowded that I had very little control over the speed at which I could move, and all that I could do was to go with the flow. After about forty minutes, I was still only about a quarter of the way around! All around me were pilgrims of every shape and size and age, all there for Allah, and all immersed in the dhikr of Allah, and although I was adrift in a sea of people, I felt no sense of danger nor fear of being crushed. I was not at all afraid of losing my balance and being trodden underfoot. In this sea of humanity, I was completely and perfectly at peace.

● ● ●

Years later, I was to read that the Prophet Muhammad had once said that a time would come when the very rich would go on the Hajj to have a holiday, and the merchants to do business, and the very poor to beg, but at this point in time I was oblivious to the possibility of any Muslim having such intentions when coming to Makka for the Hajj. All that I could see was a very glorious and noble celebration of life, immersed in the worship of Allah, so that the celebration and the worship were not separate, but one and the same thing.

● ● ●

As I rounded the second corner of the Ka'aba which towered high above the pilgrims that encircled it, I came upon the Hijr, a semi-circular unroofed enclosure whose low marble wall outlines the site of the first foundations of the original Ka'aba built by the Prophet Ibrahim, peace be upon him.

There was a small passage way between the two ends of the semi-circular wall and the present wall of the Ka'aba, but I decided to go the long way round, round the outside of the Hijr, partly because it was easier to do so, partly because I wanted to follow in the footsteps of the Prophet Ibrahim, partly because some people were doing voluntary prayers behind the shelter of the low wall and I did not wish to disturb them, and partly because I had read somewhere that at least seventy prophets are buried within this area and I did not wish to walk over their graves.

As I swung wide round the Hijr, I was able to have a better view of the Ka'aba which, once you are next to it, is really a very large building. The lower ends of its finely embroidered black covering, which is called the kiswah, were furled neatly up, secured with thick strong ropes that made them look like the sails of some large galleon, revealing the large well-finished solid blocks of the finest stone with which the Ka'aba is constructed, carefully and firmly cemented together with no ordinary mortar, and creating the overall impression of a structure which is not of this world. The simplicity of the building, for it is simply a very large cube, adds to its beautiful majesty, and the baraka and peace that pervades every atom in and around it is almost tangible.

Once I had circled round the Hijr, glimpsing the golden water outlet high up on its roof, mid-way between the second and third corners, as I did so, I edged back in towards the third corner of the Ka'aba. Although it is best to keep your eyes lowered while doing tawaf, and to busy your self with the dhikr of Allah, with your attention on your heart, I could not help being curious and looking around me at the mighty spectacle, for it was not like anything else that I had ever experienced in my life up until now. I had seen and been in large crowds at sports events and open air pop festivals, but there the resemblance ended, for the behaviour and the intentions of the people who swirled round the Ka'aba like the cloud formation of a hurricane or the star pattern of a galaxy were so completely different. At the Ka'aba, the main focus of attention is not a ball or a person or a personality, it is Allah, and the air is not filled with the sound of music, but with the sound of dhikru'llah. The Prophet Muhammad said that even if you do tawaf around the Ka'aba without attention, you are wading in mercy, and if you do tawaf with attention, doing dhikr, then ten wrong actions are removed and ten right actions are added with each step that you take.

As I approached the fourth corner of the Ka'aba, the Yamani corner as it is called, because it faces south towards the Yemen, I moved in close to touch it and salute it, since this is what the Prophet Muhammad used to do. I later learned that the reason why the Prophet used to greet the corner in which the Black Stone is set, and the Yamani corner, is because they stand on the original foundations of the Ka'aba which was built by the Prophet Ibrahim. Whereas he did not greet the other two corners, which face the Hijr, because they fall short of the original foundations. It is also recorded that the small semi-circular wall of the Hijr was built specifically so that those doing tawaf would go around it, and in so doing encircle all of the original foundations of the first Ka'aba.

There was not such a rush and crush of people trying to reach the Yamani corner, and accordingly I had no difficulty in approaching it, making contact with the wall of the Ka'aba well before it and then gradually drawing closer and closer as the people in front of me moved round, until I could reach out and touch it with my right hand, placing the fingers that had done so on my lips immediately afterwards.

Then on, on and around in the great sweeping current of people, the white of our ihrams and the marble beneath our feet contrasting boldly with the black of the kiswah, and above us the blue of the desert sky, as I headed once again towards the corner in which the Black Stone is set. This time around, I did not try to kiss it or even touch it, but, skirting round the large crowd of people who were trying to do so, I saluted the Black Stone with my right hand from a distance and then kissed my hand. Then, tucking in one finger of my left hand in order to keep count of my first tawaf, I launched out into the second, and then the third, tucking in one more finger each time a tawaf was completed.

With each succeeding tawaf, I felt more relaxed and found it easier to concentrate my attention on doing dhikr, which consisted mainly of the talbiya and various other small dhikrs such as:

> **La ilaha illa'llah, wahdahu la sharika lah,**
> **lahu'l-mulku wa lahu'l hamd,**
> **wa huwa ala kulli shay'in qadir.**

Which means:

> There is no god but Allah, alone, without any partner.
> The Kingdom belongs to Him and Praise belongs to Him,
> And He has power over everything.

And:

> Subhana'llahi wa'l-hamdulillahi
> wa la ilaha illa'llah wa'llahu akbar
> wa la howla wa la quwwata illa bi'llahi'l-aliyyu'l-adheem.

Which means:

> Glory be to Allah and Praise belongs to Allah,
> And there is no god except Allah and Allah is greater,
> And there is no power and no strength but through Allah,
> the High, the Great.

And:

> La ilaha illa'llah wa'llahu akbar,
> wa subhana'llahi wa bihamdihi wa'staghfiru'llah,
> wa la howla wa la quwwata illa bi'llah.
> Huwa'l-Awwalu wa'l-Akhiru wa'dh-Dhahiru wa'l-Batin.
> Biyadihi'l-khayr. Yuhiyy wa yumiyt.
> wa huwa ala kulli shay'in qadir.

Which means:

> There is no god except Allah and Allah is greater,
> Glory be to Allah and by His Praise:
> and I seek forgiveness from Allah:
> and there is no strength
> and there is no power
> except by Allah.
> He is the First and the Last
> and the Outwardly Manifest and the Inwardly Hidden.
> Good is in His hand. He gives Life and He gives Death.
> And He has power over everything.

When I was moving between the Yamani corner and the corner in which the Black Stone is set, I would recite:

> Rabbana atina fi'd-dunya hasanatan
> wa fi'l-akhirati hasanatan
> wa qina adhaba'n-nar.

Which means:

> O our Lord, give us good in this world,
> And good in the next world,
> And protect us from the punishment of the Fire.

(Qur'an: 2. 201)

And:

> Rabbana faghfir lana dhunubana
> wa kafir anna saiyatina
> wa tawaffana ma'al-abrar.

Which means:

> O our Lord, so forgive us our wrong actions,
> and cover over our bad actions,
> and make us die the death of the righteous.

(Qur'an: 3.193)

But above all, I repeated the talbiya over and over again:

> Labayk, Labayk, Allahumma Labayk.
> La sharika lak, Labayk.
> Inna'l-hamdu wa'n-ni'mata laka wa'l-mulk.
> La sharika lak.

Which means:

> I am totally at Your service, I am totally at Your service,
> O Allah I am totally at Your service.
> You have no partner, I am totally at Your service.
> Surely the Praise and the Blessing are Yours and the Kingdom.
> You have no partner.

As I circled the Ka'aba again and again, in an ever changing pattern of people, immersing my self in the remembrance of Allah, I marvelled at all the different people who were there, ranging from the very young to the very old. A few people who were too weak to do the Hajj on foot were being carried round on wooden litters, and I marvelled at the dexterity and strength of the carriers who, with the litters balanced firmly on their broad shoulders, were able to thread their way through the mass of people without losing their passengers in the process.

The people who were nearest to me were constantly changing. At one moment I would be aware of a frail-looking man who sailed through the crowd as if he were surrounded by an invisible bodyguard, space all around him, touching no-one, his eyes down and his lips moving incessantly in dhikr, nothing distracting him from the remembrance of Allah. A moment later, there would be a group of women from Africa, all in high spirits and smiling, holding on to each other and virtually dancing round the Ka'aba. I would look up again, to notice a group of very serious-looking middle-aged people who were all trying to defy the natural flow around them by sticking together while they read out prayer after prayer from the thick books in which their heads were buried. A few moments later, and there would be another large group also trying to stick together, but this time being led round by a mutawwif who was reciting all the duas for them in a loud voice so that they could all try and hear what he was saying. I would steer my course to either one side of them or the other, and soon I would be in different company again. There were so many different people, both men and women, of every age, and so many different groupings of people, from so many different countries and cultures and walks of life, all there for Allah, and all remembering and worshipping and calling upon Allah in the way that was easiest and most natural for them. It was beautiful to behold such diversity, and rather than becoming a distraction, it only served to increase one's awe of the One who is the source of all created forms.

And as I swam round the Ka'aba, going with the flow, with one tawaf following the next so fluently that I was glad that I had been keeping a careful count of each tawaf with my fingers, one truth became clear to me, a truth that was to become even clearer during the next five days: Even in this vast gathering of Muslims – whose fundamental understanding of the nature of existence and whose way of life were basically the same – let alone in the whole wide world – where there are so many different people with very varied beliefs and lifestyles – each one of us is completely alone, in the presence of Allah. People may clutch at each other, or at books, or at the Black Stone, or at some of all the rites and rituals that there are in life, or at the beliefs or ideas that make them do so, but in Reality there is nothing to hold on to except Allah. You can only really make a lasting pact with Allah, and not with any thing or any one else.

This realisation was not always easy to accept, for it left me feeling about as helpless and as substantial as a plankton in the middle of the ocean. And the existence of all the other plankton in the sea did nothing to diminish the feeling of complete insignificance that this realisation caused. Like a baby clutching for its mother's bosom, I wanted to latch on to something more tangible, but in this shifting ever-changing sea of people, I simply could not. One of the meanings of the Arabic word 'Al-Hajj' is 'The Difficult Journey', and this difficulty is experienced not only outwardly but also inwardly.

As soon as I just let go, however, and relaxed into the present moment, then it was easy, and, like a plankton, I let the current of the ocean carry me and support me. There was always the next step to take, and in this crowd, even taking the next step required awareness and attention. If you went too fast, you were likely to tread on other people's heels. If you went too slow, other people were likely to tread on yours. Step by step, moment by moment, immersed in constant dhikr with the tongue and the heart, I circled the Ka'aba, as the sun rose higher and higher in the sky above the mass of pilgrims who constantly swirled round the still black cube.

○ ○ ○

As I came to the end of my seventh tawaf, I edged in towards the Black Stone once again, and having used the same approach as before, I soon found myself momentarily before the Black Stone once again. This time around, I only just had time to kiss it swiftly before the current of people pulled me away, like a piece of straw that the river bumps up against a rock before rapidly sweeping it on further downstream.

Having completed my Tawaf al-Qudum as it is called, that is the tawaf that you first do on arrival in the Haram, the next action that was required of me was to pray two rakats at what is called 'Al-Maqam Al-Ibrahim' which in Arabic literally means 'The Standing-Place of Ibrahim', and which is the place where the Prophet Ibrahim is said to have stood in prayer during and after the building of the Ka'aba.

○ ○ ○

Set back a few yards from the Black Stone was a small ornate glass and metal pagoda-like edifice that must have been about eight feet high. I steered away from the Black Stone through the flow of people towards this waymark and was soon right next to it. It was very strongly constructed, and the glass panes were thick. I peered through one of the larger panes of glass, and there inside, at ground level, was a grey stone with a very large human footprint clearly embedded in its surface. The footprint is said to be that of the Prophet Ibrahim, and people try to do their two rakats at the end of their tawaf as close to this spot as possible, believing that this is the exact place where Ibrahim used to stand in prayer, peace be upon him, although I was told a few years later that in fact he used to stand much closer than this, so that when he went into prostration, with his forehead on the ground, the top of his head would be virtually touching the wall of the Ka'aba.

Of course at this time of the year, at the height of the Hajj, it was virtually impossible to do two rakats anywhere near the Ka'aba, and even as far back as this little pagoda, which has since been removed to allow a freer flow of people. There were a few optimists attempting to pray their two rakats in the lee of the little pagoda, but it must have been impossible to concentrate, as the inexorable oncoming sweep of the people doing tawaf swept around them, breaking their qiblah incessantly and often making them lose their balance.

Lining up the pagoda with the Black Stone, I moved slowly away and back from the Ka'aba until I was virtually under the arches and domes of the enclosed part of the mosque. Finding a clear space in front of a pillar, I did my two rakats where no one could break my qiblah, as close to Al-Maqam Al-Ibrahim as was possible under the circumstances. The Prophet Muhammad once said that if the one who passes in front of a man praying knew what he was bringing upon himself, it would be better for him to stop for forty than to pass in front of him, and I did not want to pray anywhere where it would be virtually impossible for someone not to break my qiblah. Having done the two rakats, I made some dua, asking Allah to give me a taste of what the Prophet Ibrahim's inward state was like, and then paused for reflection.

○   ○   ○

When I had first embraced Islam some four years earlier, I had known next to nothing about it, other than the fact that the community of Muslims whom I had joined were more knowledgeable and radiant and better behaved than any other human beings that I had ever met during my life up until then. I had embraced Islam in the hope of acquiring that knowledge and radiance and courteous behaviour, and as time passed my hopes were gradually fulfilled, as, little by little I learned about and tried to embody the teachings of the Prophet Muhammad, may the blessings and peace of Allah be on him.

Understanding was not always instant, or complete, but I usually found that once I had actually done something that was part of the Prophet's teaching, then I could understand it. The meaning of the Hajj was something that had always eluded me, and whenever I read about it, I could not understand it, or see the point of it. For three and a half years, I had had no desire to go on the Hajj, other than the feeling that I ought to do so because it is one of the five pillars of Islam, and then, once I did sincerely wish to do the Hajj, I had soon found myself on the way to Makka.

Now that I was here, actually doing the Hajj, it made perfect sense, and as soon as I did anything that was required of me, its meanings approached me from every direction. At this point in time, doing the Hajj was clearly the best and most natural course of action in the world. There was nowhere else that I wished to be, and there was nothing else that I wanted to do. As far as I was concerned, I was in exactly the right place at exactly the right time, doing exactly the right thing.

By now, I was beginning to feel thirsty, for I had been out under the hot sun in continual movement and invocation of Allah for at least two hours. It was clearly time to visit the well of Zamzam before doing the next preliminary rite of the Hajj, which is to go back and forth seven times between two small hills called Safa and Marwa, and slowly I made my way towards the steps which lead down to the taps from which the water of Zamzam flows so abundantly.

❂   ❂   ❂

The story of how Zamzam came into existence is well-known to the Muslims, for many of the rites of the Hajj are derived from the events that took place at that time, and indeed it would be true to say that virtually all the rites of the Hajj derive from the pattern of worship of the Prophet Ibrahim, a pattern of worship which was confirmed and perpetuated by all the prophets who came after him, especially the Prophet Muhammad. This, briefly, is the story of how the well of Zamzam came into existence:

○   ○   ○

The Prophet Ibrahim was travelling with his wife Hagar and their baby son Ismail in the region in which Makka now stands. Ibrahim, who is often called 'Al-Khalil' which in Arabic means 'the Intimate Friend', because he had conversations with Allah, was told to leave Hagar and Ismail where the Haram of Makka now stands, and to travel on alone. After Ibrahim had left, and once their supplies of food and water had run out, Hagar became anxious for the well-being of Ismail. There were two small hills nearby. Putting Ismail down, Hagar ran between them seven times, looking for help, but there was only empty desert wherever she looked. She ran back to where Ismail lay, and lifting her hands in prayer, she asked Allah for help. When she looked down, water was welling up out of the ground from where the baby Ismail had kicked it. Swiftly she made a wall of mud to contain it. The Prophet Muhammad once said that if Hagar had not made a wall round the water when Zamzam first welled up out of the ground, then it would have become a river!

A little later on, some birds in the sky spotted the new supply of water and began to circle round it. A passing caravan spotted the birds, and, knowing that they must be circling around water, headed in that direction until they reached the water, the mother and the child. The water was so good and plentiful that they decided to settle there. Later on, Ibrahim returned, and built the Ka'aba with the help of Ismail near the well which was called Zamzam, making dua for the people who were to come after them and who would worship Allah there, as is recorded in the following verses of the Qur'an:

And when We made the House [the Ka'aba]
a resort for mankind and a sanctuary,
[saying]: 'Take as your place of worship
the place where Ibrahim stood' [to pray].
And we imposed a duty upon Ibrahim and Ismail,
[saying]: 'Purify My House for those
who go around it and those who meditate in it
and those who bow down and prostrate' [in worship].
And when Ibrahim prayed:
'My Lord, make this a region of security
and bestow upon its people fruits,
such of them as believe in Allah and the Last Day,'
He answered: 'As for him who rejects,
I shall leave him in contentment for a while,
then I shall compel him to the punishment of the Fire,
a hapless journey's end.'
And when Ibrahim and Ismail were raising
the foundations of the House,
[Ibrahim prayed]: 'Our Lord, accept this from us.
Surely only You are the Hearer, the Knower.
Our Lord, and make us Muslim to You,
and from our offspring a nation which is Muslim to You,
and show us our ways of worship, and turn to us.
Surely only You are the One Who Turns, the Compassionate.
Our Lord, and raise up in their midst
a messenger from among them
who shall recite to them Your revelations
and will give them knowledge
of the Book and the Wisdom
and will make them grow.
Surely only You are the Mighty, the Wise.'
And who leaves the way of Ibrahim
except the one who fools himself?
And certainly We chose him in this world,
and surely in the next world he is among the righteous.
When his Lord said to him: 'Submit!'
he said: 'I have submitted to the Lord of the worlds.'

(Qur'an: 2.125-131)

Thus Makka was born, and its future was guaranteed. Indeed one old man later said to me, as we sipped tea at a cafe just outside the Haram, "We are only here because of the dua that Sayyedina Ibrahim once made, alehi salem."

◆ ◆ ◆

Having reached the steps that lead down to Zamzam, I waited patiently amongst the crowds of pilgrims for a chance to reach one of the taps that lined the small underground room at the bottom of the steps, and after a while, inching forward whenever it was possible, I was finally close enough to reach out and fill my right hand with the lovely pure cool tangy water of Zamzam that tastes like no other water that I have ever tasted. Again and again I reached out my cupped hand to fill it with the bubbling water that gushed out of the taps. All around me, people were doing likewise, some drinking it, some doing wudu in it, and some drenching themselves in it.

Having quenched my thirst with the best water in the world, I made my way back up the crowded steps to ground level, and headed for Safa and Marwa, the same two small hills that Hagar had once run between in desperation, looking for help for herself and Ismail. Ever since that time, it has always been one of the rites of the Hajj to go between these two hill-tops, quickening one's pace mid-way between the two, and pausing a while on each hill-top to make dua each time that one comes to rest on them, until, like Hagar, one has been between the two hills seven times.

Since it is customary to start the sa'y, as the going back and forth between Safa and Marwa is called, at Safa, I made my way to Safa, asking three people along the way in order to make absolutely sure that I was not making a mistake. Things had changed since Hagar's time. The ground between the two hills is now paved with white marble, like the rest of the Haram, and the whole area is roofed over and walled in, although the numerous archways along the way ensure easy access and good ventilation.

A one-way system between the two hills was in operation, which was just as well, for as with the tawaf, so with the sa'y, the sheer flow of people was tremendous. Thousands and thousands of slowly moving people filled the space between the two hill-tops, all dressed in white, all going at their own pace, ordered but not regimented, with the air filled with the sound of dhikr and duas spoken out loud and shining with the light that shimmered from the chandeliers that hung high above them. Here and there, as with the people doing tawaf, I could see those who were too weak to walk being carried shoulder high in wooden litters, their apparently tireless carriers moving purposefully but carefully through the crowd. It was an extraordinary sight.

I clambered up the clean boulders that are at the top of Safa, and after pausing momentarily to survey this amazing scene, I began my sa'y by repeating the following dhikr three times:

> **Allahu akbar, Allahu akbar, Allahu akbar.**
> **La ilaha illa'llah, wahdahu la sharika lah,**
> **lahu'l-mulku wa lahu'l hamd,**
> **wa huwa ala kulli shay'in qadir.**

Which means:

> **Allah is greater, Allah is greater, Allah is greater.**
> **There is no god but Allah, alone, without any partner.**
> **The Kingdom belongs to Him and Praise belongs to Him,**
> **And He has power over everything.**

Having made some duas, I set off for Marwa, increasing my pace but not running – as is customary – for a short interval about mid-way between the two hills, and busying my lips and heart with dhikru'llah, until I reached my destination.

At Marwa, I did virtually the same as I had done at Safa, clambering up the clean hard boulders that still remain at its top and repeating the same dhikr three times before making yet more duas, and then setting off once again, back to the point from where I had just come, slowly going with the steady flow of people, and speeding up during the midway stretch which was conveniently marked by flashing green lights. Having reached Safa, I would do the same once again, repeating the same dhikr as before three times, making even more duas, and then launching back out into the stream of people that was heading back the other way. Again, as with the tawaf, I kept good count of each crossing between the two waymarks by tucking in a finger each time one was completed.

As when doing the tawaf, it is best not to stop and talk with anyone while doing the sa'y, but at one point my eyes met those of another European and instinctively we smiled and, since there were not many of us about, we could not help exchanging a quick greeting. He was an Italian Muslim, from Rome, and I almost asked him for his address, but then thought no, and with a quick 'As-salaamu-alaikum – Wa alaikum as-salaam' we were both on our way again, travelling in different directions between Safa and Marwa.

After what seemed a long time, although it was difficult to measure time in such a place, I arrived at Marwa for the fourth time, my seven crossings between the two hill-tops now completed, and having repeated my dhikr once again and squeezed out still more duas, I looked around for someone with a pair of scissors.

❁ ❁ ❁

If I had been visiting the Haram at any other time of the year, and had only come for a visit, which is called an Umrah, and not to do the Hajj, then up until this point, my actions on first entering the Haram would have been exactly the same. On completing the sa'y between Safa and Marwa, however, I would have had the hair on my head – other than my beard and moustache and eyebrows – completely shaved off. However, since I was doing the Hajj, my hair would not be completely shaved off until right at the end of the rites of the Hajj, and right now, all that was necessary was for me to have a lock of hair snipped off.

❁ ❁ ❁

There were several men with scissors nearby Marwa, and one of them kindly did me the honours, snipping off a small lock of hair from the back of my head with a huge pair of very sharp scissors, and giving me a broad open smile. The preliminary rites of the Hajj were now completed, and I was ready to leave for Mina!

Gratefully I made my way over to the spot where Muhammad Abdal-Bari had arranged for the people in our group to meet, stopping off en route at Zamzam for a much needed drink. Although the Hajj was taking place during the cool time of the year, for it was now mid-November, it was still very hot during the day, and right now it must be about mid-day, since the preliminary rites must have taken me around four hours to complete.

When I reached our meeting-place, it was to find everyone there except Abdal-Jalil. Naturally Muhammad Abdal-Bari and Uthman and Muhammad Qasim had completed their preliminary rites some days earlier, and had been doing tawaf of the Ka'aba whenever they could do so ever since, for this is one of the best forms of dhikr that there is. It was good just to sit there quietly, after all the movement and dhikr and duas of the last few hours, waiting for the time of dhur to arrive, and watching the incessant swirl of people passing us by as they swung round and round the stillness of the Ka'aba which we were careful always to have in our line of vision, for it is a courtesy never to turn your back on the Ka'aba while you are actually in the Haram. As I gazed at this wonderful living spectacle, I could not help but silently repeat some words that I had memorised many many years before:

at the still point, there the dance is,

(The Four Quartets of T.S. Eliot)

Just when I least expected it, the adhan for dhur suddenly filled the air, and as we sat and listened to it, repeating each phrase quietly as it filled the air around us, the main swirl of the people doing tawaf continued to flow round the Ka'aba. After the last 'La ilaha illa'llah' of the adhan had filled the air and died away, many of those who were in the sheltered part of the mosque rose to their feet to do their sunnah prayers, but still the main flow of people continued to wheel round the Ka'aba, until, as the qadqamatis salat which signalled the start of the prayer was given, it finally came to a halt, as everyone dispersed and arranged themselves in concentric circles facing the Ka'aba in preparation for the prayer, all the women making their way to the areas which are set aside for the women.

For four years I had been doing the prayer, facing in the direction of the Ka'aba wherever I happened to be, without ever really appreciating what it was that I was facing. I had seen photographs of the Ka'aba and heard people describe what it is like to pray with the Ka'aba actually in sight, but nothing that I had seen or heard could have prepared me for this.

In the vast silence that now filled the Haram, everything was still except for the white doves that circled in the sky above us.

Every possible space was filled with a human being, and the Ka'aba loomed high above us, almost completely filling my field of vision when I looked at it. Normally during the prayer, your gaze is directed towards the point on which your forehead will come to rest when in prostration – for the Prophet Muhammad once said that if you look up while doing the prayer, you will go blind – but when you are actually in the Haram, you are permitted to direct your gaze at the Ka'aba itself, and this was what I now did.

"Allahu Akbar!" The imam's voice sounded clearly over the public address system. "Allahu Akbar!" echoed thousands and thousands of voices, all as one voice, and so the prayer began. This was worship of Allah as I had never before experienced it, and I sank deep into the prayer, annihilated in the concentrated stillness that filled the air of the Haram, with the black cube of the Ka'aba filling my gaze, with the hot blue sky above us, and the still white sea of ihrams lapping all around at its edges. How different this was, both inwardly and outwardly, to doing the prayer by oneself in a small room in England on a cold mid-winter's day!

The prayer took its beautifully majestic simply defined course and came to an end, followed almost immediately by the funeral prayer for someone who had just died, but already, with the closing 'As-salaamu-alaikum' of the prayer, there were people circling the Ka'aba once again, as the human whirlpool reformed once again, predictably and unhurriedly, and swirled inevitably back into motion.

○   ○   ○

Abdal-Jalil still had not reappeared, so the four of us waited a little longer, talking about what was past and what was to come, and what had always been. I was told that ever since the Conquest of Makka by the Prophet Muhammad, may the blessings and peace of Allah be on him and his family and his companions and his followers, there had always been at least someone doing tawaf of the Ka'aba, except during the prayer, twenty-four hours a day for the last fourteen hundred years. I was told that there are never any bird droppings on the Ka'aba or in the Haram from the myriads of white doves and pigeons that continually circle and swoop over it. And I was told that Zamzam never dries up, its flow increasing at the time of the Hajj to cater for between one and two million extra people, and then decreasing but not ceasing for the rest of the year.

After a while, Abdal-Jalil appeared out of the crowd, looking a changed man, as all of us did, for it is impossible to be exposed to such baraka without being immediately affected and transformed by it. The time of the prayer had arrived while he was still doing his sa'y between Safa and Marwa, and so he had been unable to complete it until the prayer was over. Now that we were all free to leave for Mina, we left the Haram and returned to Abdal-Hamid's mother's house to have a rest before setting out on the next stage of the Hajj.

● ● ●

On our return, another meal awaited us and we tucked into it hungrily. Abdal-Hamid's mother and sister were the epitome of hospitality and generosity, may Allah bless their whole family in this world and in the next, and together with Abdal-Hamid, who was doing the Hajj with us, they provided us with the traditional hospitality and knowledge that has always been extended by the generous Makkans to those pilgrims who come from far off places.

As we sat and ate in their small sitting room, I was filled with gratitude at the way things had turned out. Not only had Allah brought us to Makka just in time to do the preliminary rites of the Hajj, but also we had been given the best of hosts. Each stage of the journey had unfolded so beautifully and majestically, mercy on a knife-edge, for although we hoped for the best, there was never a time when we felt that we deserved the best, and accordingly it was always such a pleasant surprise when we were unexpectedly given the best.

I knew that had we been staying at the lodgings provided by the mutawwif to whom we had been officially assigned during our clearance at pilgrim city in Jeddah by Abdal-Wahhab, then we would not have received such a warm welcome. In these present times, when modern communications and travel facilities have made Makka far more accessible to the millions of Muslims who are now spread across the world, the official mutawwif's task has now become the almost impossible one of fitting as many pilgrims as possible into what limited accommodation there is available, and trying to explain what the rites of the Hajj are to those pilgrims who have arrived without having adequately prepared themselves for the Hajj.

Fortunately, all the people in our group knew what we had to do during each stage of the Hajj, but we still received valuable insights and knowledge from Abdal-Hamid along the way, and in the meantime we had been given the best of resting places and hosts while we were actually in Makka.

After the meal was over, we all stretched out on the cushioned divans that bordered the room and slept soundly until asr, after which we had tea together, and then it was time to leave for Mina. First of all, however, there was a long discussion as to whether we should walk to Mina or catch a taxi there.

Both Abdal-Jalil and I found it a trifle irksome to even have to discuss the matter, when it was clearly so much more enjoyable to walk through the relative cool of the late afternoon and the early evening than to pay through the nose to be stuck in a traffic jam. We were fit from our travels in the Sudan, and accustomed to making decisions swiftly and acting on them. Now that we were part of a larger group – most of whom were probably still adjusting to their completely new surroundings – we felt like wild horses that have suddenly been caught and corralled. However, knowing that the hand of Allah is over the hand of the Amir, we had our say and then awaited Muhammad Abdal-Bari's decision, thankful that in the end he decided on the obvious.

MINA

By the time we left Abdal-Hamid's mother's house and began to follow the wide busy road that winds up and out of Makka towards Mina, it was growing late, and when we stopped after about a mile to buy a drink, I found that the few rials that were all that were left of the money that Shaykh Al-Fattih had given us in Omdurman, and which I had rolled into the waist band of my ihram, had worked their way loose and must have fluttered somewhere to the ground. Abdal-Jalil and I accordingly had no money, but this did not bother us, for we knew that Allah would provide for us from where we did not expect. At the same time, I did wish that I had at least some money to spend on the others, since I did not want to become a burden on their finances. As the Prophet Muhammad once indicated, the hand that gives is better than the hand that receives.

Muhammad Qasim was also in the same position as us, for although he had come with a money bag filled with money, which was slung around his neck and shoulder once he had put on his ihram, the strap had been cut with a razor while he was doing tawaf, and the money bag stolen by a light-fingered thief. Thus only two people in our small group actually had any money, Uthman and Muhammad Abdal-Bari. On this occasion it was gentle Uthman who kindly paid for the drinks.

Apparently this kind of occurrence does happen from time to time, since clearly no-one in ihram has any pockets in which to put their money, and money bags on straps are easy game for practised thieves in the crowds of people who are packed together during the tawaf. My relief at not having to worry about losing a money belt that I did not possess was only equalled by my surprise that anyone could actually come to the Haram at such a time simply to steal, when there were people there who had spent weeks and months crossing continents and oceans simply to do the Hajj in obedience to Allah!

❂   ❂   ❂

The mountains which border Makka are steep, with whitewashed houses creeping up their sides and holding on against all odds, and as we made our way up the steep wide road and gained height, we reached a point where we could see the Haram far below, the slowly turning wheel of pilgrims still turning round the still hub of the Ka'aba, as latecomers swiftly completed the preliminary rites of the Hajj in order to reach Mina in time.

Meanwhile, the sky had darkened and the sun had set, and by the time we finally walked into Mina, which is about five miles out of Makka, it was dark. There was hardly anyone about and most of the people must have gone to sleep, many of them squeezed into the rows of tents which had been put there for them by their mutawwifs. Although all of us had been allocated the same mutawwif, we had no idea where his tents were, for none of us had made contact with him on our arrival in Makka, simply because we had all gone straight to Abdal-Hamid's mother's house.

After searching for our mutawwif's tents in the darkness for a few minutes in vain, we stopped, wondering where we could spend the night. Remembering our experience in Alexandria, I said that there was bound to be a hole-in-the-wall somewhere – in this case, a hole-in-a-tent – and after another apparently pointless and unnecessary discussion as to whether there would be one or not if we looked for it, and if there was one whether or not we should go through it, we set off to find one. Soon I spotted a large empty space through a half-open flap of a tent occupied by some Nigerians, and, zipping in quick before anyone could have second thoughts – those deadly killers of spontaneity – I asked a half-awake Nigerian if we could shelter the night there. Of course we could!

Fortunately there was a water supply nearby, and having done wudu, we quietly prayed maghrib and isha together, doing travelling prayers, and then lay down in our ihrams on the plastic matting that covered the ground. The night air was quite chilly, and after the day's exertions I felt a little dishevelled and dusty, but I also felt tired and sleepy, and nothing could prevent me from sleeping. I fell into a deep dreamless sleep, waiting expectantly for the new day to dawn, for it would be the climax of the Hajj, and of the journey that had first begun weeks and weeks ago.

ARAFAH

We awoke next morning at dawn. It would have been impossible not to have done so, for the whole of Mina was on the move. Today was the 9th of Dhu'l-Hijjah, the Day of Arafah as it is called, the day on which all those who are doing the Hajj have to make their way to the plain of Arafah, which is about ten miles away from Mina, and stand in prayer from mid-afternoon until sunset on, if it is possible, a small hill called the Jebel Ar-Rahma, which in Arabic means the Mount of Mercy. It is said that Adam was re-united with Hawwa on the Jebel Ar-Rahma after years of wandering about on the earth apart from each other, after their expulsion from the Garden of Adnin, and it was from the Jebel Ar-Rahma that the Prophet Muhammad addressed the Muslims on the Day of Arafah during his farewell pilgrimage.

❂   ❂   ❂

Having prayed subh, we waited until the sun had risen, and then set out for the plain of Arafah, surrounded by thousands and thousands of pilgrims who were doing likewise. As with the way between Safa and Marwa, so with the road to Arafah, things had changed a great deal since the time of the early prophets. A wide dual carriageway had been built all the way from Makka to the plain of Arafah, and it was now the scene of an almighty traffic jam, as hundreds and hundreds of cars and coaches all converged upon the same point.

The rough desert terrain on either side of the dual carriageway was also completely packed with people on the move, striding out on foot, with the six of us among them, walking steadily through the early morning sun, clouds of dust hanging everywhere in the still air, and yet to breathe, the air seemed pure and fresh, and although it was another hot desert day, there was a coolness in the air which could only be ascribed to the rahma of Allah.

As had been the case ever since we had first rolled into Makka a little over twenty-fours earlier, the spectacle of so many different people gathered together and united by one intention was both breath-taking and absorbing, and I tried not to let my attention become too distracted by everyone around me. As had been the case ever since I had first put on my ihram in Jeddah, I tried to maintain a steady repetition of the talbiya, sometimes quietly and sometimes out loud:

> Labayk, Labayk, Allahumma Labayk.
> La sharika lak, Labayk.
> Inna'l-hamdu wa'n-ni'mata laka wa'l-mulk.
> La sharika lak.

Which means:

> I am totally at Your service, I am totally at Your service,
> O Allah I am totally at Your service.
> You have no partner, I am totally at Your service.
> Surely the Praise and the Blessing are Yours and the Kingdom.
> You have no partner.

As we progressed towards the plain of Arafah, pausing momentarily to have a drink from a tap that suddenly appeared unexpectedly, protruding out from a rough concrete block by the roadside, I tried to imagine what it must have been like in the time of the Prophet Muhammad, may the blessings and peace of Allah be on him, when there was neither a tarmac road nor the sound of car and coach engines, just the sounds that a large number of camels make, with thousands of the Prophet's companions, both men and women, reciting the talbiya out loud in the midst of the silence of the desert on this best of days, for as the Prophet once said, "Hajj is Arafah."

❂ ❂ ❂

After walking for what seemed like a few hours, we finally arrived at the mosque which is on the edge of the plain of Arafah, and there, or rather near it, for it was already filled and overflowing with people, we prayed dhur and asr together in the form of travelling prayers. After we had finished the prayer, we all had a cup of tea from a nearby stall, except for Abdal-Hamid who was fasting. By now we were all hungry, and Abdal-Hamid, probably sensing this, shared out the few packets of biscuits and cheese that he had been carrying with him. It was probably the food that he had brought to eat once the sun had set and his fast was ended, may Allah reward him.

Once our simple meal was over, we made our way towards the myriad of white tents that had been pitched near the base of the small hill that was clearly Jebel Ar-Rahma. Along the way, Muhammad Abdal-Bari spotted a large plastic jerry-can that had clearly been abandoned, and on finding that it had been used to carry water, he asked me to hang on to it, and half fill it with water when the opportunity to do so arose. At the time it seemed to me to be a totally unnecessary measure to take, since there were many water supply points dotted about the place, where we could quench our thirst whenever the need arose. However, since Muhammad Abdal-Bari was now our Amir, I did as I was asked, and spent the rest of the day lugging our water supply about the place with us. It was not until night eventually came, that his idea's worth was proved, and I was forced to admit silently to myself that perhaps it had been a good idea after all.

By the time we were in among the tents, we were all feeling hot and thirsty and hungry, and since it was not yet mid-afternoon – the time at which the standing in prayer on the plain of Arafah commences – we decided to try and find a tent that had some spare room in it for us. After looking into a couple of the large tents which were completely full, we discovered one tent where there appeared to be quite a lot of free space. The pilgrims who were sheltering there from the heat of the early afternoon sun turned out to be from Egypt. Abdal-Hamid asked everyone's permission for us to enter, and it was immediately granted. Gratefully the six of us moved into the one remaining empty space and laid down thankfully to have a short rest and a snooze.

We had only been there for about a quarter of an hour, all stretched out on the ground and fully relaxed, when a sudden puff of wind found its way into the tent and lifted it up, just long enough to free one of the supporting poles, which slowly keeled over, in slow motion, and suddenly landed heavily on an old man's leg before anyone could do anything to stop it. I leapt to my feet and stretched my arms up to hold the canvas as it slowly began to collapse and float downwards, while Abdal-Jalil grabbed the pole and slotted its top end back into its hole in the canvas. Then, together, we lifted the canvas right up and jammed the pole back into an upright position.

Meanwhile, Muhammad Abdal-Bari was bending over the old man, asking him if he was alright and patting him reassuringly on the shoulder. The old man responded strangely, almost shrugging off Muhammad Abdal-Bari's concern and immediately busying himself with lighting some charcoal in a small clay cooker and putting on some water to boil. Within minutes, he had prepared some tea and offered each one of us a generous glassful. As we all sipped the hot sweet refreshing tea, he explained something in Arabic to Abdal-Hamid, who first looked serious, and then smiled, and then laughed.

Apparently after we had first come inside the tent and settled ourselves down, the old man had been thinking, 'Who are these people? What are they doing here? This is not their tent. They are taking up our space. Why don't they leave us in peace and go and find their own tent?' It was just as he was having these thoughts that the pole had crashed down onto his leg, and, perceiving this as a warning from Allah, he had quickly made us some tea and made us welcome – just as he should have done when we had first entered the tent! We all smiled and laughed as Abdal-Hamid translated the old man's words for us, and told him that he had been quite right, we should not really have just arrived like that, but thankyou for making us welcome. With peace restored, we all settled down to rest a little while longer in the beautiful cool shade of the tent, sallying forth out into the forest of tents every so often to do this and that.

One of the things that I realised that afternoon was that if you really want something, first make a dua asking Allah for it, and then go and look for it, and insh'Allah you will find it! This happened clearly when looking for the tent, the toilet, some food, a drink of cool water, and especially a way through to the Jebel Ar-Rahma.

Once the heat of the day was beginning to wear off and it was mid-afternoon, we decided to go and try to find a place to stand on the Jebel Ar-Rahma itself, rather than somewhere around its base, only to find about a million other pilgrims trying to do exactly the same thing. As we made our way in the general direction of the

Jebel Ar-Rahma, we soon discovered that all the pilgrims were being channelled into a large river of people which was meant to flow round, and then up, and then down the other side of the small rocky hill which, now that we were closer, looked much larger than before, with some quite large boulders on its sides and summit.

Naturally, once anyone was on the Jebel Ar-Rahma, they did not wish to leave it again, and accordingly the river of pilgrims had by now almost stopped flowing upwards and was collapsing back down on itself, creating some nasty scenes and side-currents, as some of the less patient pilgrims tried to force their way up through the short-cuts that led up the side of the hill and which were barred by the inevitable uniformed officials. It was in one of the sudden commotions caused by these tussles that our group was unexpectedly divided in two, as we all tried to avoid becoming involved in any kind of argument or conflict. There was a sudden flurry of people, some propelled by the people who were being pushed uncontrollably by the sheer weight of numbers around them, and, after taking instinctive avoiding action, Muhammad Abdal-Bari, Muhammad Qasim and I found that the others had simply disappeared. After a few minutes, we gave up looking for them, and turned our attention back to the Jebel Ar-Rahma.

Silently I made a dua to Allah, asking for another hole-in-the-wall opening up to the top of the Jebel Ar-Rahma, while Muhammad Qasim and I did our best to restrain Muhammad Abdal-Bari from losing his fiery Irish temper with yet another unyielding official. Indeed there was so much baraka and rahma in the air, that it simply was not worth allowing ourselves to become angry anyway, since this would have distracted us from the incredible uniqueness of this particular day of our lives. The Prophet Muhammad once said, indicating the special qualities of the Day of Arafah:

> "Shaytan is not considered more abased or more cast out or more contemptible or more angry on any day than on the Day of Arafah. That is only because he sees the descent of the Mercy and Allah's disregard for great wrong actions."
>
> (Al-Muwatta of Imam Malik: 20.81.254)

Slowly we walked back the way we had come, to where the crush of people was not so great, and then I saw it, an empty tent with an opening in its far side. Calmly, and unobserved by any of the officials, we entered the tent as if it were our own, walked nonchalantly across to the opening, and then swiftly stepped through it, to find ourselves faced by a large ditch full of water, and beyond it, the slopes of Jebel Ar-Rahma.

The water appeared to be surprisingly clean, and, having paused to do wudu, we waded through the water and clambered up the slope ahead of us. When we were near the top of Jebel Ar-Rahma, it began to become crowded, and accordingly we each selected a boulder on which to stand, and began to make our dua of a lifetime. The Messenger of Allah, the Prophet Muhammad, may the blessings and peace of Allah be on him and on his family and on his companions and on his followers, once said:

> The most excellent dua is the dua on the Day of Arafah, and the best of what I and the prophets before me have said is: 'La ilaha illa'llah, wahdahu la sharika lah'.
>
> (Al-Muwatta of Imam Malik: 20.81.255)

Which means:

> 'There is no god but Allah, alone, without partner.'

There I stood, on the Jebel Ar-Rahma, as it gradually became more and more crowded, no longer repeating the talbiya, for its time was up, but making dua after dua as they flowed into and out of my heart and onto my tongue.

Although my attention was on and in my heart, I could not help but look out across the plain of Arafah from my vantage point from time to time. It was an extraordinary sight. Thousands upon thousands of pilgrims, all dressed in white, enveloped the Jebel Ar-Rahma and the area around it in a sea of white, washing round the large island of white tents and hundreds of parked coaches and cars, while the sun slowly sank westwards through a cloudless blue sky on a hot day that was cool and vibrant and radiant with baraka and rahma.

There must have been about a million and a half people there, each with their own particular destiny and story, all gathered there from across the face of the world to share this time and place for a few hours, just on that afternoon, on that day, in that month, in that year, the 9th of Dhu'l-Hijjah in the 1397th year after the Hijrah, the Hijrah being the journey in which the Prophet Muhammad and his sincere companion Abu Bakr travelled in the way of Allah from Makka to Madina, where the first Muslim community became truly established.

It was probably the nearest actual living experience to the Last Day – when everyone who has ever lived will be brought back to life and gathered together before being sent to either the Garden or the Fire – that I had ever experienced in my life. One of the names of the Last Day is Al-Yawm al-Qiyamah, which in Arabic means 'the Day of Standing', since everyone will be standing there before Allah on That Day, just as everyone was standing here before Allah right now on the Jebel Ar-Rahma and on the plain of Arafah.

I had not been standing there long, just relaxing and feeling good as I tried to take everything in and make the best use of my time on the Jebel Ar-Rahma, when, with a sudden tug of alarm at my heart, I suddenly remembered a four-year-old debt that I had not settled before leaving London at the start of our difficult journey. My heart sank, for one of the conditions for an acceptable Hajj is that when you do the Hajj, you have no debts hanging over your head.

It was not as if it was a debt that I had tried to ignore. I had just simply forgotten that it existed, until now, for the homoeopathic doctor who had treated me when I was very poor and who had said 'Pay me back when you can', had never reminded me of the money that I still owed him. All that I could do for the time being was to resolve to repay the debt after I had returned to England, insh'Allah – which I eventually did, ten years later! – and to ask Allah to overlook it. Although it was disquieting to be suddenly reminded of this forgotten debt, there was nothing else I could do about it now, so I tried to forget it for the time being and to busy myself with dhikru'llah instead, as the sun sank slowly lower and lower in the sky.

◉   ◉   ◉

For about three hours I just stood there, like everybody else, outwardly the same and with only Allah knowing what was in each of our hearts, in the Mercy and at the Mercy of Allah, and as I stood there, making all the duas I had already made at the Ka'aba again and making all the fresh duas that I could possibly think of, I paused to reflect on the meaning of it all.

During the rites of the Hajj, I had gone round in circles round the Ka'aba; I had gone back and forth between here and there between Safa and Marwa; and now I was just being still standing still here on the Jebel Ar-Rahma. And this, I reflected, is all that we ever do in life. Either we stay still in one place, or we go back and forth between two places, or we go round in circles, these simple fundamental patterns of movement and no movement interacting with each other in a myriad of different forms and combinations to form the beautifully intricate pattern of individual and collective destinies which are for ever unfolding and never quite exactly repeating themselves during each moment of existence.

Silently I stood there, filled with awe, as I reflected on the beauty and the majesty and the sheer intricacy of the creation which is alive and changing with each passing moment, never to be the same again. My awareness turned from the creation to the Creator, to the Reality in Whom everything that appears to exist has its reality, to the One Who pervades every atom in the cosmos without being contained by any thing – Who is beyond space, to the One Who has no beginning or end in time – Who is beyond time, to the One Who is not only the Inwardly Hidden but also, if we could only understand, the Outwardly Manifest, to Allah.

How little we know! Our knowledge is restricted by place and time. We have to imagine what things were like if we were not there, and even if we were present, our understanding is limited, not only by lack of perception but also because we can only really focus our attention on one thing at a time, and existence is multidimensional, both in the Seen and in the Unseen worlds. And as for the future, we can only imagine what lies ahead.

Allah knows it all, from the innermost depths to the outermost parts. He has always been present everywhere for as long as space and time exist, always present, before and beyond space and time, always present, with no beginning and no end. The whole creation from beginning to end is in the knowledge of Allah, from before time, for all time, beyond time.

ALLAH

Everything that had happened in my life up to this point dwindled away and faded like a dream. There was no past and no future, just the present moment, as I stood there in the presence of Allah, a frail human being dressed in two pieces of white cloth and a pair of plastic sandals, with no food and no money and no shelter, standing on a small rocky hill in the middle of the desert, in the middle of the world, in the middle of the universe, a helpless slave in the presence of his Lord.

MUZDALIFAH

As time passed, a feeling of expectancy began to fill the air. Soon it would be time to move on, as soon as the sun had dropped below the rocky edge of the horizon. I rejoined Muhammad Abdal-Bari and Muhammad Qasim, and we waited patiently on the rocky hillside for the sign to move. The sun was now out of sight, and there was that stillness in the air that always comes at dawn and dusk, in the interspace between darkness and light, but still the sea of white stayed where it was, only rippling here and there in expectancy, as orange and pink and red began to tint and tinge the fading blue of the western sky.

Suddenly, there was the blaring of a thousand horns, and the still white sea of pilgrims was transformed into a giant wave in slow motion, as everyone began to move once again. The Day of Arafah was over, and it was time to head for Muzdalifah, a place between the plain of Arafah and Mina that is neither here nor there, where all the pilgrims spend the night of the 10th of Dhu'l-Hijjah.

There was no need to ask anyone where Muzdalifah is, as a million and a half people surged in its direction, either on foot or on wheels, sending up clouds of dust in their wake. We had a clear view of this extraordinary sight from our vantage point near the top of Jebel Ar-Rahma, thousands and thousands of people on the move through the dusk, and it was like nothing else that I had ever seen, not even the African plain filled with a vast herd of buffalo that I had once witnessed as a young child.

We joined the flow of people down the side of the hill, staying close together, and soon we were on the flat and on the move, walking at a steady pace through the growing darkness, with thousands of pilgrims all around us, staying inwardly calm in the midst of all this motion, and doing dhikr. Once again, I was glad that we were on foot and not in a coach or a car. As well as not being stuck in a traffic jam, it just felt much better to be moving along through life at a walking pace, rather than being cooped up in a metal cage with restricted movement and vision.

◐ ◐ ◐

By the time we reached Muzdalifah, it was dark. The moon had not yet risen, but the stars were shining brightly and there were quite a few groups of people who had started small fires, and even some of those who had come by car who had small gas-lamps, so it was relatively easy to pick our way across the uneven desert floor between the small clusters of pilgrims that were scattered about as far as the eye could see. Having branched out a little away from the main crowd we tried to find the ideal spot at which to spend the night. "That looks like a good place over there," I would say, but when we got there, it would be much the same as the one we had just left. "How about over there then?" I would say, but on arrival we would find that it was no better. After this had happened several times, Muhammad Abdal-Bari smiled and said, "They're all the same, Ahmad! Let's just stay right where we are now!" And that is what we did.

It was at this point that I was glad that Muhammad Abdal-Bari had asked me to carry the half-filled plastic jerry-can of water around all day. There was enough water for each of us to quench our thirst and do wudu, with some left over for later on and the next morning. After doing wudu, the three of us prayed maghrib and isha together, doing travelling prayers, and then sat down for supper. We had hardly eaten anything since leaving Makka, and were all feeling a little weak from hunger and the day's travelling, but fortunately Muhammad Abdal-Bari had a tin of sardines and a packet of biscuits, and these we gratefully shared between us.

Once we had finished eating and had rinsed our fingers, we each collected 49 small pebbles, which would be used during the next three days when stoning the shaytans in Mina, and, having rolled them securely into the waistbands of our ihrams, we turned in for the night. It was easy enough to get comfortable by wriggling about a bit in the sand until it fitted the contours of your body, but it was a cool night, and no matter how you wrapped your ihram around your body, it did not do much to keep out the cold. I fell asleep feeling cold, and slept on and off for most of the night, never quite relaxed because of the cold.

It was still dark and before dawn when all three of us were on our feet, jumping about and trying to keep warm. Fortunately for us, a Saudi Arabian family had parked their van nearby while we had been asleep and had built a fire. Seeing us jumping about, the head of the family walked over and invited us to come and keep warm by their fire. Soon we were feeling much better, sitting near the warm flames of the fire, with glasses of Saudi tea in our hands, munching thankfully at the brittle pastries which had been given to us.

Dawn came, and having used the last of our water to do wudu, we prayed subh together, and then, having accepted the family's offer of a lift, we clambered into the back of the open van which was soon bumping along over the uneven terrain until it was back on the road that leads to Mina. We were now all feeling a little worse for wear, dusty and dishevelled and a little tired, and right then and there it was very good to be on wheels and not on foot, as we slowly moved along the road that was filled with cars and vans and coaches and myriads of pilgrims on the move once again.

As we crawled along, I quickly ran through in my mind what we would have to do once we had arrived in Mina. To begin with, we would have to stone the Jamrat al-Aqaba, one of three stone-built pillars that stand in Mina, using seven of the pebbles we had collected during the night. After this we would have to have our hair shaved off, either in Mina or Makka, and then finally we would have to do seven circuits of the Ka'aba, the Tawaf Al-Ifada as it is called.

After this, the rites of the Hajj would be completed, and we would be able to remove our ihrams and wash using soap and put on our everyday clothes again. However, we would have to return to Mina to spend the night there, and would also have to spend at least the next two days and nights there as well, and possibly a further day and a night if we wished. During these days, which are known as the Days of Tashriq, all that it would be necessary to do would be just to be there and to stone the three jamras each day, using seven stones for each jamra. It was for this reason that we had collected 49 pebbles during the night, since we would need 7 pebbles today, and two lots of 21 pebbles for the next two days. I still did not fully understand the meaning of stoning the jamras, which is often referred to as the stoning of the shaytans, but, no doubt, I reflected, it would become clearer when it actually came to doing it.

Many of the pilgrims would be sacrificing an animal today, probably either a sheep, or a cow, or a camel, in remembrance of the sacrifice that the Prophet Ibrahim was prepared to make – which was to sacrifice his son Isma'il in accordance with the dream that he had had – and of the sacrifice that he actually did make – which was to sacrifice a large ram instead in accordance with Allah's command. This had been a test from Allah to show that Ibrahim loved Allah more than anything or anyone else in the world, even his own family.

Since I was doing the simplest form of Hajj, Hajj Al-Ifrad as it is called, which in Arabic means 'Hajj By Itself', I was not obliged to sacrifice an animal, and since I did not have a single penny in the world, I could not afford to do so anyway. Had I been doing one of the other two forms of the Hajj, which involve doing an Umrah and the Hajj together, then it would have been obligatory for me to sacrifice an animal, and in the event of my not having one to sacrifice, it would have been necessary to fast ten days instead, three days during the time of the Hajj, and seven days once I had returned home.

Since neither Muhammad Abdal-Bari nor Muhammad Qasim nor I were wealthy enough to be able to afford an animal to sacrifice, all we had to do in Mina that morning was to stone the Jamrat Al-Aqaba, and then we would be free to make our way back down into Makka.

● ● ●

While I had been reflecting on what it was necessary to do next, the van in which the three of us were being carried had been going progressively more slowly, and finally it came to a halt. When we peered round the canvas that covered the back of the van, it was to see an apparently endless line of traffic up along the road ahead. The time had clearly come to start walking once again, and, now that the sun was just up and it was warmer and lighter, we did not mind having to do so. We jumped out of the back of the van, walked round to the front to thank our benefactors, and then joined the steady stream of pilgrims who were making their way to Mina on foot.

MINA

We stopped at the first makeshift wayside teastall that we came across, and Muhammad Abdal-Bari treated the three of us to a much needed glass of Liptons Tea each, which we sipped gratefully as the pilgrims passed us by in an apparently never ending stream. Then we were on our way once again, walking steadily with the flow of the crowd until, a couple of hours later, we had arrived in Mina and were on the edge of the huge crowd of pilgrims who were converging on the Jamrat al-Aqaba, a huge stone-built pillar that had been enlarged so that it could be stoned from more than one level. The other two jamras were further away and out of sight, but we would not have to find exactly where they were until the next day.

We now had to approach the Jamrat Al-Aqaba, the big shaytan, as it is sometimes called, and stone it seven times. This was easier said than done, for there were literally thousands of people all wanting to stone it, and the space in which this could be done was limited. If anyone tried to throw their stones from too far back the people in front of them were in danger of being hit, and for this reason, anyone who approached too close was in danger of being hit from behind. Accordingly it was necessary to approach carefully and to go no closer once the Jamrat Al-Aqaba was within easy throwing distance.

Having each removed seven stones from our waistbands, we began our approach, clutching them safely in our left hands. The slow flow of people took us along the top of a huge concrete ramp that was well above ground level, where there was another equally large flow of pilgrims, past a lone crippled beggar who was sitting on the concrete in mid-stream, surrounded by piles of paper money, and next to a flight of wide concrete steps down which you could go once you had completed your stoning of the jamra. From this point we could just make out the top of the Jamrat Al-Aqaba, rising above a sea of heads. Having agreed to meet back at this point, we merged into the crowd, one at a time, and headed toward the stone pillar.

◊ ◊ ◊

I had been told by one of the fuqara before I set out on the Hajj, that when it came to stoning the jamras, you were, in effect casting out the shaytan in your self, the negative aspects and defects in your self that had been revealed during the course of the Hajj as a result of the intense illumination to which the heart had been subjected, especially on the day of Arafah. Thus although the stones were thrown at the jamra, this did not mean that the inanimate stone-built jamra was an evil shaytan. Rather it was a means by which you could focus your attention on your self in such a way as to be aware of its less pleasant aspects so that they could be consciously rejected. This conscious rejection was given an outward expression in the form of throwing one stone at the inanimate jamra for each major defect that had been revealed and identified during the previous two days. By approaching the stoning of the jamras in this way, you were forced to look closely into your own heart and being, and to reflect deeply on your own personal experience during the Hajj, rather than being distracted by the outward spectacle that surrounded you wherever you looked.

Bearing all this in mind, I waded slowly through the crowd until I was within easy throwing distance of the Jamrat Al-Aqaba. The air was thick with stones, whizzing through the air and bouncing incessantly off the jamra. Slowly, one by one, I threw my seven small pebbles at the Jamrat Al-Aqaba, saying, 'Bismillah! Allahu Akbar!' – 'In the Name of Allah! Allah is Greater!' – with each one, just as it left my hand, and with each one I consciously rejected and cast out one of the negative aspects of my self that had become most apparent in that moment.

Having completed this process, I waded back through the crowd to our meeting point by the top of the concrete stairs, and as I slowly moved forward, I remembered being told that in spite of the vast numbers of stones that are thrown at the jamras during the Days of Tashriq, they never pile up, because there are angels that remove them before this can happen, and certainly, whenever I looked at the bases of the jamras during these three days, there never seemed to be all that many stones there.

Once the three of us were all back at the top of the stairs, we slowly descended them, and then headed on down the road to

Makka. Although we were completely surrounded by other pilgrims, and had been continuously for the last two days now, I still did not feel at all claustrophobic or hemmed in, but rather like a swimmer in water, relaxed and to some extent supported by this ever changing river of people. It was good to be alive!

The steady flow of people swept us inexorably down the road out of Mina towards Makka. In no time at all it was soon behind us, and it was only at this point that I suddenly realised that I had not seen one animal being sacrificed while we had been in Mina. Come to that, I had not seen one animal, alive or dead, since we had left Makka on the 8th of Dhu'l Hijjah. No doubt there was a special area nowadays where all the sacrifices took place, and clearly the flow of pilgrims had taken us past it without our noticing it, but nevertheless this must be one of the rites of the Hajj that had changed a great deal since earlier times.

How different it must have been in the time of the Prophet Muhammad, I thought, may Allah bless him and grant him peace, when many of the pilgrims rode camels, and when all the animals that were going to be sacrificed were garlanded and taken with the pilgrims to stand on or near the Jebel Ar-Rahma on the Day of Arafah. This was a practice that had now been rendered virtually impossible by the sheer weight of numbers of pilgrims now coming on the Hajj each year, and by the advent of technology and mechanised transport, and it was a pity that it had virtually disappeared.

There was nothing that could be done to change this state of affairs for the time being, however, and as these thoughts passed through my mind, we continued on our way down the road to Makka, still unaware of the exact location of the place where those who were sacrificing animals had to go. In a way I was glad that I was unable to sacrifice an animal myself. I would have liked to have done so, but only in the way that they used to do it in the time of the Prophet Muhammad, may the blessings and peace of Allah be on him and on his family and on his companions and on his sincere followers.

MAKKA

Although we had intended to walk all the way back into Makka, an open-backed van which was only half-filled with men suddenly halted ahead of us, when we were about half way there, and its smiling occupants welcomed us aboard. Thankfully we climbed up into the van, for it was growing quite hot now, even though the day was still relatively young, and off we went, with the wind tugging at our dusty ihrams.

The men in the back of the van were from the Yemen, and they were some of the sweetest men that I have ever met, with large full beards and laughing shining smiling eyes. As we bumped along the road to Makka, they repeated some of the recorded sayings of the Prophet Muhammad in which he extolled the fine qualities and virtues of the people of the Yemen, laughing and beaming as they pointed at themselves in delight and added, "We are from the Yemen!", without the slightest trace of pomposity or vanity.

Soon we were back in Makka again, standing just outside the Haram. It seemed as if we had been away for a lifetime. Right now it was time to have our hair shaved off, and, spotting a barber's shop just across the road we walked over and joined one of the queues that stretched back behind the four chairs within. Muhammad Abdal-Bari caught the eye of the barber, and said, "How much?" The barber, who was now well away in what must have been his busiest day of the year, hardly paused as he held up two fingers of one hand while continuing to shave away at yet another head with his other hand. We breathed a sigh of relief. Two rials each was very reasonable, and, more to the point, Muhammad Abdal-Bari could just afford to pay for the three of us.

When, however, the very large Nigerian in front of us pulled out some money to pay for his haircut, we realised that the cost of a haircut was not two rials but twenty, which meant that Muhammad Abdal-Bari could not even afford to pay for one haircut, let alone three. Even before we could begin to walk out of the room, the very large Nigerian suddenly and unexpectedly said to the barber, "And I will pay for these three brothers as well!" handing him over another sixty rials on the spot, as he beamed expansively at us. Gratefully we thanked him, and fifteen minutes later we were outside in the sun once again, completely bald for the first time in our life!

All that remained for us to do was the Tawaf Al-Ifada, and then the essential rites of our Hajj would be completed. After doing wudu in the spacious toilet and wudu area, we entered the Haram through the Bab As-Salaam, again immediately awed by the beautiful majesty and stillness of the Ka'aba, which again was completely surrounded by hundreds and hundreds of pilgrims doing tawaf, and having agreed to meet at our usual meeting place opposite the golden water outlet on the roof of the Ka'aba, we each launched into our final set of seven tawafs.

It was now very hot, and I felt completely shattered, both inside and out. I had not washed or groomed myself now for three days, for while you are in ihram you have to let everything be; you cannot trim your hair or cut your nails or wash with soap or use perfume; you cannot kill any living thing, even a louse or a fly, and even plants should not be picked or damaged in any way; you have to float through the Hajj like an insignificant piece of driftwood in the middle of the ocean, helpless and harmless and obedient to its will.

Dusty and dishevelled, I approached the Black Stone slowly, completely humbled and no longer excited as I had been the first time that I approached it, all those light years ago. The Haram was not as crowded as it had been on the 8th of Dhu'l-Hijjah, but there were still hundreds and hundreds of pilgrims there, most of the men with their heads shaved – although it is permissible just to have it cut short if that is what you wish – doing tawaf at a measured pace, their bodies tired but their hearts illuminated.

Following the same approach as before, I was soon washed up against the Black Stone, and having kissed it, I somehow managed to do seven circuits of the Ka'aba, trying my best to remember Allah with every breath, and growing thirstier and thirstier and more and more tired with each step. Finally, I was washed up against the Black Stone once more, and, having kissed it, I retreated back far enough to be able to do two rakats as near to the Maqam Al-Ibrahim as was possible. This time, I was able to pray in the area that was covered with small pebbles, for at that time the surface of the area of the Haram which is open to the sky had not yet been entirely paved with white marble as it is today.

I completed my two rakats with 'As-salaamu-alaikum', the best greeting in the world, made a short dua thanking Allah for the Hajj and asking that it be accepted, and then virtually collapsed with both exhaustion and relief, feeling about as real as a breath of wind. I was suddenly very, very tired, and very, very thirsty, and as if in answer to an unspoken prayer, a man with a large bucket of iced Zamzam water approached me. I looked up at him.

"I have no money to give you," I said, "but I am very, very thirsty."

"Bismillah," he replied, handing me a large metal beaker which was full to the brim with Zamzam. Thankfully I drained it in three very large sips, each one preceded by a soft 'Bismillah', and handed the empty beaker back. The man smiled and left, looking for another thirsty pilgrim, and I just sat there, weak and dusty and suddenly overcome with a flood of tears, suddenly fully aware of my complete and utter helplessness as the realisation dawned that it was Allah Who had made it all happen, every step of the way, from the first moment that the desire to do the Hajj had entered my heart, to the moment that I had first arrived in Makka, right up to now. I had never had any choice in the matter. Ma sha'Allah. What Allah wants happens:

> Surely His command when he intends something
> is that he says to it: 'Be!' – So it is.
> So glory to the One in whose hand
> is the dominion over all things.
> And to Him you will return.
>
> (Qur'an: 36.82-83)

I wept until there were no more tears to weep, doing my best to hide what was happening, and then, having regained my composure, I threaded my way through the crowds of pilgrims to our meeting place. Neither Muhammad Abdal-Bari nor Muhammad Qasim were there yet, and moments later the adhan for dhur reverberated majestically and beautifully through the air.

For the second time in my life, I did the prayer directly facing the Ka'aba, which, again, seemed to increase in size until it filled my entire field of vision, and again the prayer was immediately followed by the funeral prayer for someone who had died during the Hajj, although already the swirl of people doing tawaf was under way once more, and the deep full silence that had filled the Haram during the prayer was once again replaced by the hum of dhikr issuing from thousands of hearts and lips.

Many Muslims consider dying while travelling on the way to Makka to do the Hajj, or actually during the Hajj itself, as one of the best times to die, second only to dying as a martyr by being killed by a plague, or by a disease of the belly, or by drowning, or by a collapsing building, or while fighting in the way of Allah. Thus, for example, when Shaykh Muhammad ibn al-Habib, whose Diwan we had been singing wherever we travelled, knew that he was going to die, he gave away all his belongings, and set out across North Africa towards Makka with the intention of doing the Hajj, dying on the way there in Blida, Algeria, may Allah give him baraka and light in his grave, as in his life:

> Allah is the light of the heavens and the earth.
> The likeness of His light is as if there were a niche,
> and in the niche is a lamp,
> and in the lamp is a glass,
> and the glass as it were a brilliant star,
> lit from a blessed tree, an olive,
> neither of the east nor of the west,
> whose oil is well nigh luminous,
> though fire scarce touched it.
> Light upon light.
> Allah guides whoever He wants to His light.
> Allah sets up likenesses for man.
> And Allah knows all things.
>
> (Qur'an: 24.35)

There are many meanings in this ayah of the Qur'an – for as the Prophet Muhammad himself said, may the blessings and peace of Allah be on him, each ayah of the Qur'an has an outward meaning, and an inward meaning, and a gnostic meaning – but one of the accepted meanings of this fine metaphor is that the niche is the world, the heavens and the earth; the lamp is the person; the glass is the ruh, that is, the spirit; and the light that illuminates the glass is the secret of the ruh; and Allah guides whomever He wants to knowledge, and understanding, and gnosis, of that secret.

◉   ◉   ◉

I did not have long to wait, bewildered and dazed, before Muhammad Abdal-Bari and Muhammad Qasim appeared out of the moving crowd. Quietly and humbly we left the Haram and made our way to Abdal-Hamid's mother's house, not exultant and full of our selves as I had sometimes imagined we would be if we ever did manage to reach Makka in time and do the Hajj, but shattered and emptied of our selves, and illuminated.

We arrived to find Abdal-Hamid and Abdal-Jalil and Uthman already there, all washed and changed and positively glowing with light. We followed suit, and when it was my turn to use the shower room, I gratefully stood under the powerful cold rush of water that shocked me wide awake as it hit my hairless scalp with a direct force that I had never experienced before and washed away all the dust and sweat of the last three days. Having put the shampoo and soap to good use, I did a ghusl for good measure, and then put on my fresh clean floppy Sudanese underwear, the white robe that had been made for me in Cairo, a clean dark green turban from England, and a generous helping of the sandalwood oil that Shaykh Ahmad had given to us in El Obeid. I paused a moment before going into the sitting room to join the others. It was one of those precious moments when you really feel so amazingly and wonderfully glad to be alive.

Everyone was transformed, not only because our heads had been shaved, the borders of our white scalps peeping out beyond the parameters of our turbans and contrasting vividly with our sunburnt faces, but also because we were all shining brightly, inside and out, as if we had been caught in the full force of some benevolent atomic radiation. It was impossible to carry on where we had left off, which had been the last time we had all been together in this room, and I said little, as we discussed what had happened to each other after we had been separated on the Day of Arafah. As we talked, a very welcome hot steaming platter of rice and lamb was placed before us, followed by fresh fruit and then tea. Clean, replete, and relaxed, we all lay down on the divans to catch up with some much needed sleep.

We awoke at asr, and after doing the prayer and having some tea and biscuits, it was time to return to Mina once again. This time we decided to take a taxi van, and with our remaining 42 small pebbles safely transferred to our robe pockets, we were soon hurtling along the road that we had come along only that morning, now travelling in the opposite direction, and feeling as refreshed now as we had felt exhausted only a few hours earlier.

In no time at all we were back in Mina once again, for the third time in as many days, and after looking around, we found some space in a tent filled with friendly Algerians which was neither too close to nor too far from the jamras. For the next three nights, this became our temporary home, and we were made welcome by those whose tent it was.

MINA

During the next two days, the Days of Tashriq, as they are called, the days of feasting, during which no one is permitted to fast, I tried to feast not only on some of the meat from the animals which had been sacrificed on the first day of the Id Al-Adha as this festival is called, meaning in Arabic 'the Festival of the Sacrifice', but also to feast on the meanings of the Hajj itself. It was important to reflect on the meaning of all that had taken place during the rites of the Hajj, while everything was still fresh in my awareness and before other considerations, such as how was I going to get to Madina, and how was I going to get back to England, began to distract and preoccupy me.

Each of the outward actions of the rites of the Hajj had a deep inward meaning, and indeed every moment and every meeting had had its meaning, and although everyone had basically been doing the same actions, yet everyone's experience and perceptions and understanding of that experience were different. Certainly, whatever that experience was, each pilgrim had been utterly transformed by it. The Prophet Muhammad once said that whoever has an acceptable Hajj is purified of all their previous wrong actions. He also said, may the blessings and peace of Allah be on him and on his family and on his companions and on his followers, that the only reward for an accepted Hajj is the Garden.

❂ ❂ ❂

Part of the process of reflection on the meanings of the Hajj is the stoning of the three jamras, or the stoning of the shaytans as it is sometimes called, and the conscious appraisal and rejection of the negative aspects of one's self. The word shaytan, a'udhu bi'llahi min ash-shaytani'r-rajim, means in Arabic 'to be obstinate' or 'to be perverse'. It also means 'to distance' or 'to make something seem far away'.

Shaytan, who, the Qur'an tells us, is one of the jinn, and not a fallen angel, was cast out by Allah because he was obstinate in refusing to bow down before Adam with the angels when he was commanded to do so by Allah. His argument was that he was better than Adam, because he was created from fire whereas Adam was created from clay. Some say that he also said that his love for Allah was so great that he refused to bow down before anything or anyone other than Allah, although clearly if he really loved Allah so much, he would have done what his Beloved commanded him to do. Allah cast out shaytan, because of his pride and obstinacy:

> He said: 'So go from here for surely you are outcast,
> And surely my curse is on you until the Day of Judgement.'
> He said: 'My Lord, reprieve me until the Day of Rising.'
> He said: 'So surely you are one of those reprieved,
> until the Day of the Appointed Time.'
> He said: 'Then by Your might I surely will beguile them all,
> except your sincere slaves from among them.'
> He said: 'The Truth is and the Truth I speak,
> that I shall fill Hell with you
> and those of them who follow you, together.
>
> (Qur'an: 38.77-85)

One of the ways in which shaytan beguiles people, a'udhu bi'llahi min ash-shaytani'r-rajim, is by making the next world seem distant, even though it will be forever, and by making Allah seem far away, even though He is closer to us than our jugular vein. Once the inevitable is forgotten, and the Real appears to be unreal, then it is easy to be perverse and obstinate and proud, like shaytan. Many of the negative aspects of the self derive from this state of forgetfulness and lack of awareness.

❀ ❀ ❀

Each day, on the 11th and 12th of Dhu'l-Hijjah, shortly before dhur, we would go to stone the three jamras, throwing seven pebbles at each jamra, and saying 'Bismillah! Allahu Akbar!' as each pebble sped towards its target. The crowds were not nearly as great as they had been on the 10th of Dhu'l-Hijjah, and it was much easier to approach and withdraw from the jamras in safety. With each stone that I threw, I tried to 'cast out' a negative aspect or bad quality that I had recognised in my self by virtue of the light to which it had been exposed during the rites of the Hajj.

Other than this, there was nothing else that had to be done, other than simply to be there and do the prayer in its time. Since we were doing travelling prayers, this meant, in effect, that there were only three times of prayer each day: at dawn, in the afternoon once the time of dhur had commenced, and at night once the time of maghrib had commenced. After each prayer, in accordance with the practice of the Prophet, we would all glorify Allah with several loud takbirs:

**Allahu akbar, Allahu akbar, Allahu akbar.
La ilaha illa'llah.
Allahu akbar, Allahu akbar.
Wa lillahi'l hamd.**

Which means:

**Allah is greater, Allah is greater, Allah is greater.
There is no god except Allah.
Allah is greater, Allah is greater.
And to Allah is the Praise.**

We had begun to recite these takbirs after dhur on the first day of the Id, and would continue to do so after each prayer during the Days of Tashriq, until after subh on the fourth day, as indeed would the whole Muslim world, for the Id Al-Adha, like the Id Al-Fitr at the end of the fast of Ramadan, is celebrated by every Muslim wherever they are in the world, and not just by the Muslims who are on the Hajj.

I spent the days quietly, reflecting a great deal and not saying very much. Already I could feel the immediacy of the Hajj beginning to fade, and I spent much of the time consciously playing back my internal video tape of everything that had happened – not only since we had arrived in Makka but also ever since we had first set out from London – so as to fix it more firmly in my memory, a precious intangible treasure that I wanted never to forget or lose.

Mina itself looked like a vast campsite, with tents and encampments stretching out across the narrow valley floor and up the sides of the mountains that hemmed it in. The pilgrims, on the whole, had been allocated areas that corresponded to their nationalities, but this did not stop everyone from mixing freely, and it was good to be surrounded by so many kindred spirits from all over the world.

I did not do much visiting in actual fact, although on the second evening we did walk over to where most of the Moroccans were camped, in the hope of meeting a great wali whom we had heard had come on the Hajj. As it turned out, no one whom we asked had heard of him, and since none of us knew what he looked like, we might even have already met him during the last few days without even realising it! Having spent some time with some friendly and hospitable Moroccans, we returned to our tent to spend our last night in Mina.

After asr on the 12th of Dhu'l-Hijjah we were free to leave Mina, although had we wished, we could have stayed one more night, as many pilgrims would, and left late the next morning after stoning the jamras once more. We were just about to set off, when we met some Sudanese pilgrims who insisted that we come and visit them in their encampment a little way up the mountain side. Naturally we accepted their invitation, and after a while, we were sitting on carpets in a large circle of men in their large shady shelter, sipping hot sweet tea and listening to the Qur'an being recited by a man who recited it very sweetly from the depths of his heart. It was good to be among people from the Sudan again, and after the time that we had spent there, both Abdal-Jalil and I especially felt immediately at home in their company.

Their leader was a descendant of the Mahdi and was called Sadiq Al-Mahdi, a very noble and knowledgeable man, who, like all the leaders whom we had met in the Sudan, treated us with great courtesy and hospitality even though we were the least of people. The sun was beginning to hang low in the sky when we asked Sadiq Al-Mahdi's permission to leave. After the relative inactivity of the last forty-eight hours, I was looking forward to a good walk back into Makka, but Sadiq Al-Mahdi insisted that we have a lift in the back of his van, and Muhammad Abdal-Bari decided that it would be best to accept the offer, although, as I had foreseen, this meant that we were reduced to a slow crawl along a road that was packed with pilgrims leaving Mina.

One of my last memories of Mina on the 12th of Dhu'l-Hijjah, as the million and a half Muslims from all over the world who had been together for the last five days began to disperse and go their different ways, is that of Sadiq Al-Mahdi standing by his van just before we were about to set off, outlined against the blue sky in his immaculate white robe and turban, with the sun hanging low and red in the sky, and the air filled with dust and the sound of car engines and the hooting of hundreds of horns, and the pilgrims who were on foot moving wherever there was space to walk. Everywhere you looked, there were people in motion.

Sadiq Al-Mahdi gazed at the moving spectacle with us, looking a little wistful, as if he were picturing every Hajj that had ever taken place since the Farewell Hajj of the Prophet Muhammad almost fourteen centuries previously, may Allah bless him and grant him peace, and was a little saddened by some of the changes that had taken place, even though he knew that everything is by the command of Allah, both the good of it and the evil of it.

"There are so many, many Muslims around nowadays," I said, stating the obvious. The experience of the Hajj had really made me aware of just how many Muslims there are in the world, and I no longer had the feeling that I had felt back in England of just being one of a very small minority.

"Yes," replied Sadiq Al-Mahdi, and almost imperceptibly shook his head with a tinge of regret, "there are many Muslims, just as the Prophet foretold, salla'llahu alayhi wa sallam. He said that one day there would be many Muslims, but that they would be weak, like the flotsam that floats on the waters of a flood."

There was a slight bitterness in his voice and in his words, but the truth is often bitter, until you have swallowed it, and then the aftertaste is often sweet.

Slowly we crawled back down the road to Makka in the midst of thousands and thousands of Muslims on the move. Very few of us would ever taste anything like the depth and quality of knowledge and wisdom that the close companions of the Prophet Muhammad had enjoyed, but all the Muslims alive today have inherited some of that knowledge and wisdom in varying degrees, from the absolute acceptable minimum to the absolute possible maximum, and it was this inheritance, the living legacy of the Last Messenger of Allah – the Prophet Muhammad, may the blessings and peace of Allah be on him and on his family and on his companions and on all those who follow him and them with sincerity in what they are able until the Last Day – that had united all of us during the Hajj, so that, whatever our differences and shortcomings, we had been able to live with each other, even in difficult conditions, at peace with each other, at peace with our selves, at peace with Allah.

The Hajj was over.

The Difficult Journey had been completed.

And Life goes on – and nothing can stop it!

MAKKA

We finally rolled into Makka just before maghrib, and after doing the prayer in the Haram, we did tawaf of the Ka'aba until isha. This was the first time that I had been in the Haram at night time, and it was breathtakingly beautiful. The covered area of the mosque was illuminated with thousands of light bulbs that shone from the hanging chandeliers, and the open area of the mosque was also well-lit with tall lamp posts spaced strategically along its periphery. The Ka'aba shone out in the middle of it all, beautifully majestic in its black and gold embroidered kiswah, and, as always, a deep calm peace pervaded the air, despite the presence of thousands and thousands of pilgrims.

Although the rites of the Hajj were now completed, many of the pilgrims would not be departing immediately, and while in Makka, there is no better thing for a visitor to do than to do voluntary tawaf of the Ka'aba, which are always done in sets of seven followed by two rakats. Those who were obliged to leave almost straight after the Hajj was over, could not do so until they had done their farewell tawaf of the Ka'aba, the Tawaf Al-Wad'a as it is called, and accordingly the Haram was packed full that night, both with departing pilgrims who were doing their Tawaf Al-Wad'a, and with pilgrims who were staying on a little longer and wished to make the best use of their time.

It is customary to do the Tawaf Al-Wad'a just before you are about to leave Makka, and since we were not yet quite sure when we would be departing to visit the tomb of the Prophet Muhammad in Madina, we had naturally decided to delay doing our farewell tawaf until we knew for certain when we would be on our way again. As had often been the case throughout the journey, neither Abdal-Jalil nor I knew quite what was going to happen next, especially in our present penniless state, but I was certain that we would manage to get to Madina somehow, even if we had to hitch-hike or walk.

For the time being, I sank into the depths of the crowds of Muslims who were doing tawaf of the Ka'aba. It was the first of the three nights in the lunar month on which the moon is full, and now that it had risen sufficiently, it shone down on the ever-changing swirl of people swinging steadily around the Ka'aba, moving wherever it was possible to make a full circle. Everyone whose face I saw was radiant with light, whether they were serious or joyful, and now that everyone was out of ihram, the variety of different garments being worn was amazing. They were all loose and flowing and varied in colour from the very white to the very black to all the colours and patterns that you could imagine. Round and round the Ka'aba we flowed, in an amazing, wonderful, awe-inspiring celebration of life, swimming in mercy and glorifying Allah, some of the most fortunate people in the whole of existence:

> Successful indeed are the believers,
> Those who are humble in their prayers,
> And those who shun vain conversation,
> And those who are payers of the zakat,
> And those who guard their private parts,
> except with their wives
> or the [slaves] their right hands possess,
> for then they are not blameworthy
> – but whoever desires beyond that are transgressors –
> And those who are shepherds
> of their pledge and their covenant,
> And those who pay heed to their prayers,
> These are the ones who are the heirs,
> Those who will inherit Paradise,
> Who will live there for ever.
>
> (Qur'an: 23.1-11)

○ ○ ○

After isha, we all met at our usual meeting place and then returned to Abdal-Hamid's mother's house, to find that she and her daughter had washed and dried our ihrams for us while we had been in Mina, may Allah reward them with the Garden. There was also another welcome meal awaiting us, and gratefully we satisfied our hunger, before turning in for the night, stretched out on the divans that lined the walls of the room.

○ ○ ○

After breakfast the next morning, it was time to leave, for we did not wish to overstay our welcome and become a burden on the family who had been so kind to us. Muhammad Abdal-Bari had decided that we should go and stay in the quarters that were supposed to be provided for us by our officially designated mutawwif, and having said goodbye and thankyou to our most generous hosts, we made our way through the still very crowded streets of Makka, no longer echoing to the sound of the talbiya, to these quarters.

Our new abode was part of an enormous complex of small rooms that were packed with about ten people to a room. There was just enough space for each person to lie down full length on the concrete floor, with a bit of space over to store your few possessions, and the bareness of our room contrasted starkly with the descriptions in the Qur'an of the Garden which the sincere true believers will inherit:

> Reclining therein upon couches,
> they will not find any sun or bitter cold there.
> Its shade is close upon them,
> And its clustered fruits hang down.
> Goblets of silver are brought round
> for them and beakers [like] glasses,
> with glass [made] of silver,
> which they have measured to the measure.
> There they are given a drink
> from a cup whose mixture is Zanjabil,
> from a spring there which is called Salsabil.
> And waiting on them are immortal youths
> who, when you see them,
> you would think were scattered pearls.
> And when you see,
> then you will see bliss and a great kingdom.
> Their raiment will be of fine green silk
> and gold embroidery,
> and they will wear bracelets of silver,
> and their Lord will give them
> a pure drink to drink.
> Surely this is a reward for you
> and your endeavours have been accepted.
>
> **(Qur'an: 76.13-22)**

Despite being so cramped, the toilet facilities were adequate, and the building was near to the Ka'aba. It did not take us long to settle in, although the mutawwif was a little surprised to see us turning up after the Hajj rather than before it, and then we were free to do as we wished, walking the streets of Makka for some of the time, but spending most of it in the Haram, either doing tawaf, or reciting the Qur'an, or doing dhikr, or simply looking at the Ka'aba, and of course doing the prayer whenever its time came. The Haram is so peaceful, and your own heart is so at peace while you are there, that there is nowhere in the world where you would rather be while you are there.

We had moved into our new quarters on a Thursday, and by the time the day of the jumua dawned, our future had been clarified. For a start, Muhammad Abdal-Bari had announced that he no longer wished to be Amir of the group, and I did not blame him, for it is not an easy task or a light responsibility, and whatever the Amir decides, there is always going to be someone who does not agree with his decision.

In fact, in the circumstances, Muhammad Abdal-Bari's decision made things easier rather than more difficult, since Abdal-Jalil and I had completely different plans to those of Muhammad Abdal-Bari, Uthman and Muhammad Qasim, and wanted the same freedom of action that we had enjoyed during our travels before arriving in Makka. The three of them had flown to Jeddah together and would be flying back from Jeddah together, and had already made their own arrangements for the journey to and from Madina. The continued presence of Abdal-Jalil and myself in the party would only have complicated matters, especially as we were becoming a drain on their limited resources. Furthermore, I intended to travel overland back to England via Istanbul once my visit to Madina was completed, while Abdal-Jalil intended to make his way to the Gulf and somehow become a millionaire!

The different intentions in our hearts had replaced the one single intention that we had all shared while we were doing the Hajj, and Muhammad Abdal-Bari's decision to step down was just a reflection of this change, and a means by which we could all do what we wanted without any unnecessary friction arising between us.

At first Abdal-Jalil and I were left wondering about how we would manage to travel to Madina, but, as it turned out, the four ladies from our community in England, whom we had last seen in Jeddah all those millions of light years ago before the Hajj, had hired a taxi van to travel to Madina, and had asked us to travel with them as their escort. Thus we did not have to worry about how we were going to get there. The van was due to leave on the Saturday morning at about eleven o' clock, which meant that we would have plenty of time in which to do our farewell tawaf directly before leaving for Madina.

Our last two days in Makka passed all too quickly. When the time came for the jumua, we had under-estimated how soon we should leave in order to be able to find a place in the Haram itself, and accordingly we had to find a place in one of the main streets leading to the Haram. Every approach to the Haram was filled with people, and when the time came for the prayer, it must have been an amazing sight from above, as the concentric circles of worshippers surrounding the Ka'aba filled the Haram to capacity and then spilled out beyond the confines of the huge mosque walls into the streets of Makka itself; and then, of course right beyond the confines of Makka, a never ending rippling configuration of worshippers all over the world, all facing the Ka'aba, wherever they are, all standing and bowing and prostrating and sitting in prayer in time with the movement of the sun through the sky, so that it is always time for each of the five prayers somewhere in the world, and there is always at least someone there to do them – a ceaseless pattern of worship of Allah that began with one man and then slowly expanded, like the ripples that spread out when a stone is dropped in the midst of still water, with more and more people becoming a part of the pattern, until today it stretches out from the Ka'aba over the surface of the earth, and even on boats and ships crossing the seas and the oceans, right round the world!

After listening to the khutba which was broadcast out to the people in the streets by means of a very clear public address system, we did the prayer in the sunshine using a large piece of cardboard as our prayer mat, the whole city at a standstill, still and quiet, except for the sound of the Imam's voice reciting the Qur'an clearly and firmly, and the loud takbir each time he changed position in the prayer, echoed by hundreds of voices so that everyone praying would get the message and make the next movement in the prayer together after him. It was the largest jumua I had ever attended.

After the prayer, I was suddenly aware of a very strong presence behind me, and looking round, my eyes met those of a lovely old man from the Sudan who was, quite simply, shining. It was as if Allah had arranged the meeting here in Makka because we had been unable to meet in the Sudan. After a short conversation, we greeted each other once again, and then he melted back into the crowds of people from which he had appeared.

Once the crowds had abated, we made our way into the Haram, and spent the rest of the afternoon there, sitting in the shade at the edge of the covered area of the mosque. Since I was fasting that day, I did not want to be involved in much activity, and instead I just sat there, drinking in the profound peace of the place. I did not have any food or water with which to break my fast, but when the adhan for maghrib rang out, a man sitting next to me pulled out a bottle of Zamzam and offered it to me, a grain of wheat which had probably been dropped by a passing dove fell into my lap from the sky, and after the prayer a group of Muslims from Syria invited me back to their room for a meal! Al-hamdulillahi wa shukrulillah!

❂ ❂ ❂

The next morning we were up at dawn, and after praying subh in the Haram, the five of us shared our last simple breakfast together. Then Abdal-Jalil and I re-entered the Haram for the last time for the time being, and began our farewell tawaf, the Tawaf Al-Wad'a. As with my previous tawafs, I began and ended the set of seven circuits by kissing the Black Stone. All too soon they were completed, and all too soon I had done my two rakats at the Maqam Al-Ibrahim, and all too soon my duas were completed. After drinking my fill of Zamzam, I met Abdal-Jalil at our meeting place, and then we reluctantly and slowly left the mosque, not taking our eyes off the Ka'aba until it was out of sight.

❂ ❂ ❂

After a short walk, we were outside Abdal-Hamid's mother's house where we had arranged to meet everyone. The taxi van was there and so were Mansura and Saba and Rukaya and Rashida. We bid Muhammad Abdal-Bari and Uthman and Muhammad Qasim goodbye, saying that insh'Allah we would meet them in Madina, and thanked Abdal-Hamid and his mother and sister once again for all their help and hospitality, and then we were all aboard the taxi van and threading our way out through the streets of Makka, sad to be leaving and glad to be on our way again, for nothing lasts and life goes on!

❂ ❂ ❂

Soon we were speeding through the desert on a broad tarmac road, with the sun on our faces and the wind in our robes, feeling incredibly clean and fresh both inside and out, without a trace of anxiety or longing in our hearts, just looking forward to our visit to the tomb of the Prophet Muhammad in Madina, the illuminated city, the city which is illuminated by the presence of the ruh of the Last Messenger of Allah and of those of some of his family and companions and sincere followers, may the blessings and peace of Allah be on him and all of them and on all who follow in their footsteps.

And as we sped through the heat of the day, I reflected on the words of Shaykh Abdal-Qadir al-Murabit who once said:

> **The destination is just an excuse.**
> **What matters is the journey itself.**

And I reflected on the words of Shaykh Muhiyyi'din ibn Arabi, who once wrote:

> **Whoever engages in travel will arrive!**

How true they were. We had started out on the Difficult Journey, trusting in Allah, travelling in the way of Allah, and by Allah we had arrived! We had done the Hajj! And now we were on another journey, or you could say on the next stage of our life's journey, the Way Back, and, insh'Allah, we would arrive! Insh'Allah we would arrive, not only at the end of this particular journey, but again and again, at the end of each successive stage of our life's journey, until finally we reach our journey's end, and gaze upon the face of Allah:

Forgive us our Lord
And to You is the journey.

(Qur'an: 2.285)

ALLAH

In the Name of Allah the Merciful the Compassionate

Have we not expanded your breast for you,
And eased you of the burden
which weighed down on your back,
And exalted your fame?
So surely with hardship comes ease,
Surely with hardship comes ease.
So when you are finished, still try,
And direct your love to your Lord.

(Qur'an: 94.1-8)

GLOSSARY OF ARABIC TERMS

abd : man as slave of his Lord.

Adam : the first man, created from clay, peace be on him.

adab : correct behaviour inward and outward, inner courtesy coming out as graciousness in right action.

adhan : the call to prayer.

Adnin : the Garden of Eden.

ahlan wa sahlan : 'you are with your parents and at your home', the equivalent in Arabic of saying 'make yourself at home'.

ahl as-suffa : the people of the bench. The poor and needy amongst the companions of the Prophet Muhammad, may Allah bless him and grant him peace, who lived on a verandah in a courtyard next to the house of the Prophet in the mosque in Madina.

ahlu'l-dhimma : non-Muslims living in Muslim territory and under the protection of Muslim rule by virtue of the fact that they have agreed to pay the jizya tax.

ahwal : plural of hal.

akhira : the next world, what is on the other side of death, the world after this world in the realm of the Unseen. See dunya.

alayhi sallam : 'on him be peace'.

al-hamdulillahi wa shukrulillah : 'praise to Allah and thanks to Allah'.

alim (plural - ulama) : a man of knowledge. In this context a man learned in Islam who acts on what he knows.

Allah – ta'ala : Allah – the Most High, the Lord of all the worlds. Allah, the supreme and mighty Name, indicates the One, the Existent, the Creator, the Worshipped, the Lord of the Universe. Allah is the First without beginning and the Last without end and the Outwardly Manifest and the Inwardly Hidden. There is no existent except Him and there is only Him in existence.

amir : one who commands, the source of authority in any given situation.

Ansar : the 'Helpers', the people of Madina who welcomed and aided the Messenger of Allah, may Allah bless him and grant him peace, when he made hijrah to Madina.

aql : intellect, the faculty of reason.

Aqsa : the furthest, in this context referring to the Masjid al-Aqsa, the mosque in Jerusalem which stands where the Temple of Solomon once stood.

Arafah : a plain 15 miles to the east of Makka on which stands the Jebel Ar-Rahma. One of the essential rites of the Hajj is to stand on Arafah, on or near the Jebel Ar-Rahma, between the times of asr and maghrib , making dua.

ard : the earth.

arif : the gnostic. Shaykh Abdal-Qadir al-Murabit once wrote: 'Gnosis, the central knowledge, for it is knowledge of the self, is a proof to the one who knows it and this is its glory and its supremacy over all others. By it its possessor knows the universe, how it is set up and its underlying laws in their action, their qualities and their essences. His knowledge of the Universe is his own self knowledge, while his knowledge of his own self is direct perception of his own original reality, the adamic identity. Everything he has comes from Allah. He never sees anything but he sees Allah in it, before it, after it. There is only Allah in his eyes as there is only Allah in his heart.'

arkan : the five indispensable pillars of Islam which are the shahada, the salat, the zakat, the fast of Ramadan, and, if you are able to do it, the Hajj.

arwah : plural of ruh.

asida : a thick pasty porridge made from durra.

asr : afternoon, and in particular the obligatory afternoon prayer which can be prayed at any time between mid-afternoon and a little before sunset.

as-salaamu-alaikum wa rahmatullahi wa barakatuhu : 'peace on you and the mercy of Allah and His blessing'.

astaghfiru'llah : 'I ask Allah for forgiveness'.

a'udhu bi'llahi min ash-shaytani'r-rajim : 'I seek protection in Allah from the outcast shaytan'. See shaytan.

awliya : plural of wali.

ayah : a sign, a verse of the Qur'an. There are 6,666 ayat in the Qur'an.

ayat : plural of ayah.

ayat al-kursi : the 'Throne' ayah, Qur'an: 2.255.

ayat an-nur : the 'Light' ayah, Qur'an 24.35.

ayn : the source.

❂ ❂ ❂

Bab As-Salaam : The Door of Peace. The name of one of the entrances to the Haram in Makka and of one of the entrances to the mosque of the Prophet Muhammad in Madina, may the blessings and peace of Allah be on him.

badl (plural - abdal) : Shaykh Abdal-Qadir al-Murabit once wrote: 'The abdal are those exalted gnostics who by the perfection of their slavery to Allah remain in constant contemplation of His Presence. The proof of this station is when it is attested that he has been seen at the Ka'aba while others confirm his presence elsewhere. Thus the word badl means substitute for he appears to use a substitute body.'

Badr : a place near to the coast of the Red Sea about 95 miles to the south of Madina where, in the second year after the Hijrah, in the first battle fought by the newly established Muslim community, the 313 outnumbered Muslims led by the Messenger of Allah, may Allah bless him and grant him peace, and helped by thousands of angels in the Unseen, overwhelmingly defeated 1000 Makkan idol-worshippers.

bani Adam : the tribe of Adam, mankind in a genetic sense.

baqa : going on in Allah. It is the state described in the sublime statement of Shaykh Ahmad ibn Ata'illah: 'O Allah, You have commanded me to return to created things, so return me to them robed in lights and the guidance of inner sight, so that I may return from them to You just as I entered in to You from them, with my secret protected from looking at them and my himma raised above dependence on them. For truly, You have power over everything.' Shaykh Abdal-Qadir al-Murabit once wrote: 'The man of baqa is outwardly slave, inwardly free, outwardly dark, inwardly illuminated, outwardly sober, inwardly drunk. He is the barzakh of the two oceans – the shari'ah and the haqiqah. Separation does not veil him from gatheredness and gatheredness does not veil him from separation.'

Baqi : the cemetery of the people of Madina where many of the family of the Messenger of Allah, may Allah bless him and grant him peace, and his companions are buried.

baraka : a blessing, any good which is bestowed by Allah, and especially that which increases; a subtle beneficent spiritual energy which can flow through things and people or places. It is experienced in certain places more strongly than in others, and in some places and objects overpoweringly so. Its highest realm of activity is the human being. Purity permits its flow, for it is purity itself, which is Light. Density of perception blocks it. It is transformative, healing and immeasurable. Shaykh Abdal-Qadir al-Murabit once wrote: 'Whoever denies baraka denies that Allah is the Living who does not die. To the Muslim, baraka is at the Black Stone, the Rowdah, on the Laylat al-Qadr. To the mumin, baraka is in the mosque, at the tombs of the awliya – without shirk or bida for there is no need to do anything to experience it – and in the presence of the salihun. To the muhsin, baraka is in every tree and every stone and every flower and every face and every star. Tabaraka'llah.'

Glossary of Arabic Terms 279

baraka'llahu fi'k : 'may the blessing of Allah be on you.'

barzakh : an interspace.

bayt al-mal : the 'house of wealth', the treasury of the Muslims where income from the zakat and other sources is gathered for re-distribution.

Bayt al-Maqdis : the 'Pure House', a name of Jerusalem.

bid'a : innovation, changing the original teaching of the Prophet Muhammad, may Allah bless him and grant him peace.

Bismillahi'r-Rahmani'r-Rahim : 'In the Name of Allah the Merciful the Compassionate'.

brique : a water container for use in the toilet and when doing wudu.

burnus : a hooded cloak.

❂   ❂   ❂

Dajjal : the false Messiah whose appearance marks the imminent end of the world, the antithesis of Jesus. The science of recognising Dajjal is very intricate and carefully delineated. The manifestation will appear both as a person, and as a certain historical situation, and as a series of cosmic phenomena. Dajjal will affect the masses and cause chaos.

Da'wud : the Prophet David, peace be on him.

deen : the life-transaction, submission and obedience to a particular system of rules and practices; a debt of exchange between two parties, in this usage between the Creator and the created. Allah says in the Qur'an, **'Surely the deen with Allah is Islam.'** (Qur'an: 3.19).

dhat : the Essence, being the Essence of Allah. Shaykh Muhammad ibn al-Habib says in his Diwan:

> **Recognise the beauty of the Essence**
> **in every manifest action.**
> **Were it not for it,**

the existence of the Existent would not have been established.

dhalim : a person who is unjust and oppressive.

dhikr : remembrance, mention. In a general sense all ibada is dhikr. In common usage it has come to mean invocation of Allah by repetition of His names or particular formulae. The five pillars of Islam are its foundation. Recitation of Qur'an is its heart, and invocation of the Single Name, Allah, is its end.

dhikru'llah : remembrance of Allah, invocation of Allah.

dhimma : obligation or contract, in particular a treaty of protection for non-Muslims living in Muslim territory.

dhimmi : a non-Muslim living under the protection of Muslim rule.

Dhu'l-Hijjah : the twelfth month of the Muslim lunar calendar, the month of the Hajj; one of the four sacred months in which fighting is prohibited.

Dhu'l-Qada : the eleventh month of the Muslim lunar calendar; one of the four sacred months in which fighting is prohibited.

dhur : noon, and in particular the obligatory mid-day prayer which can be prayed at any time between noon and mid-afternoon.

dinar : gold coinage; one dinar is 4.4 grams of gold.

dirham : silver coinage; one dirham is 3.08 grams of silver.

diwan : A collection of qasidas primarily concerned with the declaration of haqiqat, a description of the tariqah and confirmation of the shari'ah. Shaykh Abdal-Qadir al-Murabit once wrote: 'From a linguistic viewpoint the writings in the Diwani Canon are set in a structural framework which, both thematically and verbally, contains an encoded message. This coding is manifest both in the specifics of its vocabulary – in a complex set of recurrent terms – in a series of metaphoric transfers which operate from the mithal (likeness) to the subject, as well as in the deep structure of the language which attempts to dismantle step by step the subtle awareness of the one following the signal, both through the signal itself and ALSO the effect of the signal on the re-tuned sensibility of the subject. In short, the meanings and the effect of the meanings are geared to achieve a profound inward change in the perception and subtle awareness of the subject. One might say that this is surely the desired effect of any poem, say a piece by Lord Byron, but it is not the case. For, if we are to be precise, we must now abandon the word sensibility, for the matter at issue is not the feeling-life of the subject, indeed the allaying of emotion would be the most successful condition for taking in the deep effect of Diwani singing. It is said that the beginner is made turbulent by the singing of Diwan while the great are made serene. For what is desired from the Diwani activity, which is called in Arabic quite simply sama'a (or listening), is the descent on the heart of warid, or spiritual breakthrough; of drinking (shurb) and drunkenness (sukr). The wine of this intoxication flows in the singing of these Diwans. (For detailed analysis of these terms see: **The Hundred Steps** – Shaykh Abdal-Qadir As-Sufi Ad-Darqawi: Diwan Press 1979).

'Thus a whole technique is contained in the Diwani Canon in the same way that a spiritual technique is contained in the Koan collections like the Mumonkan and the Blue Cliff Record which has gathered the Koan literature of the Zen Masters. Both these methods aim at creating 'hayra' or bewilderment as a point of breakthrough from the prison of the rational mind, but the Diwani literature has in it, and we should say the sufic sciences have in them, a much richer transformative energy. That is to say, the Diwani technique opens the seekers to a flowing and delightful condition in which the most exalted and purest experience of Divine Love is known. It is this love between the slave and the Lord, between Majnun and Layla, the lover and the Beloved that is the purpose and only meaning of sama'a as a practice. And the practice of sama'a is based on the technical apparatus of the Diwans ... Any 'study' of these works in a university setting is futile. This is the wine-list. The tavern is elsewhere.'

djelaba : a long loose robe either with or without a hood.

dua : making supplication to Allah.

duha : the forenoon, and in particular the voluntary morning prayer of duha.

dunya : the world, not as cosmic phenomenon but as experienced. It derives from a root describing those grapes which appear on the vine but which when you stretch out to pick them prove to be out of reach. Dunya takes on its actuality through attachment. When the heart is liberated, dunya disappears and akhira – the next invisible world – appears. Dunya is vanishing and moving away, the next world is appearing and approaching.

durra : millet, sorghum.

❂   ❂   ❂

fajr : dawn, first light, and in particular the post-dawn sunnah prayer.

fana : annihilation in Allah. Shaykh Abdal-Qadir al-Murabit once wrote: 'It is the meaning-death, based on the cessation of the attributes, even life itself. It is arrived at by the most fine process of withdrawal from the sensory by the means of the Supreme Name until even the Name, the last contact with awareness, disappears. From the death of the Original Void the secrets and the lights emerge. The seeker will pass through the heavens, each with its own colour and meanings. Light upon light. Until the great tajalli which unveils the secret and INDICATES Allah.'

faqih (plural - **fuqaha**) : a scholar of fiqh who by virtue of his knowledge can give an authoritative legal opinion or judgement.

faqir (plural - **fuqara**) : the poor; these are the men of knowledge. Shaykh Abdal-Qadir al-Murabit once wrote: 'There is no higher company. As they are the least of men and make no claims they are the elite and the two worlds are their property. With them is the maqam al-Mahmud, for the Messenger, blessings and peace of Allah be upon him, has said: "Look for me among the poor, for I was only sent among you because of them," and "Poverty is all my glory," and "Allah loves the poor."'

fard : obligatory acts as defined by the shari'ah. This is divided into fardun'ala'l-ayan which is what is obligatory for every adult Muslim, and fardun'ala'l-kifaya which is what is obligatory on at least one of the adults in any Muslim community.

Fatiha : 'The Opening', the opening surah of the Qur'an.

fatwah : an authoritative legal opinion or judgement given by a faqih.

fi sabili'llah : 'in the way of Allah'.

fidya : a ransom, compensation paid for rites missed or wrongly practised in ignorance or ill-health.

fiqh : science of the application of the shari'ah.

fitrah : the first nature, the natural, primal condition of mankind in harmony with nature.

fuqaha : see faqih.

fuqara : see faqir.

furqan : the faculty of being able to discriminate between what is valuable and what is worthless, between what is fruitful and what is unfruitful, between what is good and what is bad for your self and others. To embody the sunnah and follow the shari'ah is furqan. One of the names of the Qur'an is 'Al-Furqan'.

❂ ❂ ❂

ghawth : a qutb who heals. A granter of requests, his followers always range in their thousands. He is characterised by vast generosity.

ghayb : the realms of the Unseen.

ghusl : the full ritual washing of the body with water alone to be pure for the prayer. It is necessary to have a ghusl on embracing Islam, after sexual intercourse or seminal emission, at the end of menstruation, after child-birth, and before being buried, when your body is washed for you. It is necessary to be in ghusl and in wudu before you do the salat or hold a copy of the Qur'an. See tayyamum.

❂ ❂ ❂

hadd (plural - hudood) : the limits, Allah's boundary limits for halal and haram. The hadd punishments are the specific fixed penalties laid down by the shari'ah for certain specified crimes.

hadith : reported speech, particularly of, or about, the Prophet Muhammad, may Allah bless him and grant him peace.

hadith qudsi : those words of Allah on the tongue of His Prophet, may Allah bless him and grant him peace, which are not part of the Revelation of the Qur'an.

hadra : presence. In this context, the invocation of 'Hayyu'llah' – 'the Living-Allah', usually done standing, which increases awareness of the Presence of Allah.

hady : an animal offered as a sacrifice on the Hajj.

haik : a large piece of cloth, usually woven from cotton or wool, that is draped over the head and about the body as a protective outer garment.

Hajj : the yearly pilgrimage to Makka which every Muslim who has the means and ability must make once in his or her life-time, and the performance of the rites of the Hajj in the protected area which surrounds the Ka'aba. The Hajj begins on the 8th of Dhu'l-Hijjah, the twelfth month in the Muslim lunar calendar. It is one of the indispensable pillars of Islam. Shaykh Abdal-Qadir al-Murabit once wrote: 'The root, HJJ means 'to struggle with', to make a spiritual journey'. It means 'Hajj' for it is its own root. 'An argument', 'a single Hajj, a year'. In the Hajj, a man or woman experiences life and the self within such a determined and patterned geometric activity that though there may be near to two million people, outwardly all engaged in the same practice at the same time, inwardly each has his own unique struggle with the nafs to surrender once and for all the fantasy of selfhood, and the fantasy of otherness on which the world and all its ravishingly beautiful and terrible commotion is based. The Hajj is 'a year', a complete cycle of existence.'

Hajj al-Ifrad : Hajj 'by itself', the simplest way to do the Hajj, in which it is not necessary to do an Umrah as well, or to sacrifice an animal or fast instead.

Hajj al-Qiran : the 'joined' Hajj, where the pilgrim does an Umrah and then does the Hajj, without changing out of ihram between the two. A person doing the Hajj al-Qiran must either sacrifice an animal or fast instead, three days during the time of the Hajj, and a further seven days after returning home.

Hajj at-Tamattu : the 'interrupted' Hajj, where the pilgrim does an Umrah and then changes out of ihram until it is time to change back into ihram to do the Hajj. A person doing the Hajj at-Tamattu must either sacrifice an animal or fast instead, three days during the time of the Hajj, and a further seven days after returning home.

Hajjat'al-Wad'a : the final 'Farewell Hajj' of the Prophet Muhammad, may Allah bless him and grant him peace.

hajrat al-aswad : the 'Black Stone', a stone which some say fell from heaven, set into one corner of the Ka'aba in Makka by the Prophet Ibrahim, peace be upon him, which the pilgrims, in imitation of the Prophet Muhammad, may Allah bless him and grant him peace, kiss, so unifying all the Muslims throughout the ages in one place.

hakim : a wise man, particularly a doctor.

hal (plural - ahwal) : state. Your inward state is always changing.

halal : permitted by the shari'ah.

halwa : a kind of sweet. See tahnia.

al-hamdulillahi wa shukrulillah : 'praise to Allah and thanks to Allah'.

haqiqat: the realities. Shaykh Abdal-Qadir al-Murabit once wrote: 'Haqiqat, the realities, are the inward illuminations of knowledge which flood the heart of the seeker. It is the realm of meanings, as shari'ah is the realm of the senses. As the one is the science of the outward, the other is the science of the inward. There is no way to its experience but by submission to the fact of being human, being mortal, an in-time creature. Once shari'ah is submitted to, then the seeker on the Path realises that he has come from non-existence and is going to non-existence.'

Haqq : the Real, the Truth, Allah.

haram : forbidden by the shari'ah; also a protected area, an inviolable place or object. See Haram.

Haram : a protected area in which certain behaviour is forbidden and other behaviour necessary. The area around the Ka'aba in

Makka is a Haram, and the area around the Prophet's Mosque, in which is the Prophet Muhammad's tomb, may Allah bless him and grant him peace, in Madina, is a Haram. They are referred to together as the Haramayn.

Haramayn : the two Harams, of Makka and Madina.

hasan : an adjective describing a married person, from the noun hisn, a fortress. A person who has been made hasan by marriage (muhsan) has the full hadd punishment of death inflicted on them if they commit adultery.

hasbuna'llahu wa ni'm'al-wakil ni'm'al-mowla wa ni'm'al-nasir : 'Allah is enough for us and He is the best guardian, the best protector and the best helper'.

Hawwa : Eve, the first woman, the partner of Adam, peace be on them.

Hawd : the watering-place of the Prophet Muhammad, may Allah bless him and grant him peace, whose drink will refresh those who have crossed the Sirat before entering the Garden.

Hayy : the Living, Allah.

Hijaz : the region along the western seaboard of Arabia, in which Makka, Madina, Jeddah and Ta'if are situated.

Hijr : the semi-circular unroofed enclosure at one side of the Ka'aba, whose low wall outlines the shape of the original Ka'aba built by the Prophet Ibrahim, peace be upon him.

hijrah : emigration in the way of Allah. Islam takes its dating from the Hijrah of the Prophet Muhammad, may Allah bless him and grant him peace, from Makka to Madina, in 622 AD.

hikma : wisdom.

himma : yearning. It is by the heart's yearning that the goal is reached. All human action is based on himma only the force is directed onto the illusory palimpsest of the world. Once the faculty is directed at the non-objective it reaches its goal which is not other than the source from which the himma has come.

howliya : a very large gathering of dhikr attended by several Shaykhs and their fuqara and anyone else who wants to be there.

hudud : plural of hadd.

● ● ●

ibada : an act of worship.

Ibrahim : the Prophet Abraham, peace be on him.

Id : a festival. There are two main festivals in the Muslim year, on the first day of each of which Id prayers are prayed.

Id Al-Adha : the 'Festival of the (greater) Sacrifice', a four-day festival at the time of the Hajj; it starts on the 10th day of Dhu'l-Hijjah, the day that the pilgrims sacrifice their animals.

Id Al-Fitr : a three-day festival after the end of the month of fasting, Ramadan; it starts on the first day of Shawwal.

idda : a period after divorce or the death of her husband for which a woman waits before remarrying to ensure that there is no confusion about the paternity of children.

idhn : permission, given by the teacher to the student. It is itself a station of knowledge and a door to the freedom of the student. It is used not for existential matters, but for entering realms of knowledge and for adopting certain practices which are useless if adopted without it. Idhn is from Allah and His Messenger, may Allah bless him and grant him peace.

ihram : the conditions of clothing and behaviour adopted by someone on Hajj or Umrah.

ihsan : the state of being hasan; being absolutely sincere to Allah in oneself; it is to worship Allah as though you see Him, knowing that although you do not see Him, He sees you. It is the core of gnosis. You imagine that you are observing the cosmos as a subject. The reality is that you are being observed. When you discover that your watching and the being watched are not two realities but one and that your aspect in it is non-existent you have arrived.

ijtihad : to struggle, to exercise personal judgement.

ikhlas : sincerity, pure unadulterated genuineness. The one who has ikhlas is the one in whose sight there is always meeting with his Lord.

ila : a vow by a husband to abstain from sexual relations with his wife. If four months pass and the husband decides to continue to abstain, then the ila is considered a divorce.

ilm al-huruf : the science of the letters. Shaykh Abdal-Qadir al-Murabit once wrote: 'The root of the word in arabic means the cutting edge of a sword. It also means an edge, a rim, a brink. The letters are actions. The letters cut the undifferentiated stillness. They are edges, rims, brinks. They delineate. Make forms. They are therefore both the means to the deep coding of all animate forms and all inanimate forms.'

Ilya : a name for Jerusalem.

Imam : the one who leads the prayer, an eminent scholar.

iman : acceptance, belief, trust, in the Real, a gift from Him. Iman is to believe in Allah, His angels, His books, His Messengers, the Last Day and the Garden and the Fire, and that everything is by the Decree of Allah, both the good and the evil.

Injil : the original Gospel which was revealed to the Prophet Jesus, peace be on him.

insan al-kamil : the 'perfect man'. Shaykh Muhammad ibn al-Habib writes in the introduction to his Diwan: 'Allah the Exalted has destined for this noble path in every age one who sets right its deviations and manifests its secrets and its lights. He is the Shaykh who unites the haqiqah and the shari'ah with the idhn of Allah and His Messenger and all the perfected of Allah. He is the unique man of Muhammad of whom there is only one in every age. If there are numerous Shaykhs in his age, he rules over them all, whether they are aware of it or not. Many have laid claim to the station of uniqueness with falsehood and lies because they seek leadership and desire to possess this passing world. The pretender is unaware that whoever claims what is not in him is exposed by the witnesses of the test, since in their presence a man is either exalted or humiliated. True Shaykhs are satisfied with the knowledge of Allah and depend only on Allah. All that emanates from them speaks of the baraka of Allah. He, may He be exalted, said:

"**As for the baraka of your Lord – declare it.**"

Shaykh Abdal-Qadir al-Murabit once wrote: 'The Perfect Man is not perfect in any other way than that his gnosis is perfect and by it his life is preserved by Allah. On being asked if such a man was free from committing wrong actions, Imam Junayd gave the profound answer: "The decree is from before endless time."'

insh'Allah : 'if Allah wills it', 'God willing'.

iqama : the qadqamati's-salat, the call which announces that the obligatory prayer is just about to begin.

Isa : the Prophet Jesus, peace be on him.

isha : evening, and in particular the obligatory night prayer which can be prayed at any time between nightfall and a little before dawn.

Islam : peace and submission to the will of Allah, the way of life embodied by all the prophets, given its final form in the prophetic guidance brought by the Prophet Muhammad, may the blessings and peace of Allah be on him. The five pillars of Islam are the affirmation of the Shahada, doing the Salat, paying the Zakat, fasting the month of Ramadan, and doing the Hajj once in your lifetime if you are able.

isnad : the written record of the names of the people who form the chain of human transmission, person to person, by means of which a hadith is preserved. One of the sciences of the Muslims which was developed after the Prophet Muhammad's death, may Allah bless him and grant him peace, is the science of assessing the authenticity of a hadith by assessing the reliability of its isnad.

istislam : greeting the Black Stone and the Yemeni corner of the Ka'aba during tawaf by kissing, touching or saluting with outstretched hand.

itikaf : seclusion, while fasting, in a mosque, particularly during the last ten days of Ramadan.

❀ ❀ ❀

Jabarut : the source world, the world of divine light and power. Shaykh Abdal-Qadir al-Murabit once wrote: 'The kingdom of power. This is the kingdom of lights. Shaykh al-Akbar notes: "With Abu Talib it is the world of Immensity. With us it is the middle world." By this he indicates that the mulk is opposite the jabarut and it is precisely the realm of lights, the Divine Presence that creates the split between the two worlds on which creational reality is based. That means that Light is the barzakh, the inter-space between the visible and the invisible. In reality existence is one, the three kingdoms are one kingdom with one Lord. It is by the setting up of the limits and the barriers and the differences that the universal metagalactic existence is able to come into being. That which sets up barriers, and is the barriers, is none other than the One Reality in its sublime perfection unrelated to any form. The barriers are not realities in themselves yet without them nothing would be defined and no-one could define them.'

Jahannam : a name for Hell.

Jahiliyya : the time of Ignorance, before the coming of Islam.

Jahim : the fire of Hell.

jamra (plural - jimar) : a small walled place, but in this usage a stone-built pillar. There are three jamras at Mina. One of the rites of the Hajj is to stone them. Stoning the jamras is sometimes referred to as stoning the shaytans.

Jamrat Al-Aqaba : one of the three jamras at Mina. It is situated at the entrance of Mina which faces in the direction of Makka.

janaba : the impure state in which a person requires a ghusl before prayer is permissible again.

Jebel Ar-Rahma : the Mount of Mercy which is on the plain of Arafah and where it is said that Adam was re-united with Hawwa after years of wandering about the earth after their expulsion from the Garden of Adnin.

Jebel Murra : the 'Mountains of Time', situated in the far west of the Sudan.

○   ○   ○

Jibril : the archangel Gabriel who brought the Revelation of the Qur'an to the Prophet Muhammad, may the blessings and peace of Allah be on him.

jihad : struggle, particularly warfare to defend and establish Islam. Inwardly the greater jihad is the fight against the kufr in your own heart. Until your heart is purified, you are your own worst enemy. Outwardly the lesser jihad is the fight against the kufr around you.

jinn : unseen beings created of smokeless fire who co-habit the earth together with mankind. Some are Muslims, some are kaffirun, and some are the followers of shaytan, a'udhu bi'llahi min ash-shaytani'r-rajim.

Jinnah : the Garden, the final destination and resting place of the Muslims in the akhira once the Last Day is over. Jinnah is accurately described in great detail in the Qur'an and hadith.

jizyah : the annual tax paid by all adult males of the ahlu'l-dhimma who are guaranteed the protection of the Muslims in return.

jumua : the day of gathering, Friday, and particularly the jumua prayer which is prayed instead of dhur by all those who are present at the mosque to do the prayer.

○ ○ ○

Ka'aba : the cube-shaped building at the centre of the Haram in Makka, originally built by the Prophet Ibrahim, peace be on him, and rebuilt with the help of the Prophet Muhammad, may Allah bless him and grant him peace; also known as the House of Allah. The Ka'aba is the focal point which all Muslims face when doing the salat. This does not mean that Allah lives inside the Ka'aba, nor does it mean that the Muslims worship the Ka'aba. It is Allah Who is worshipped, and He is not contained or confined in any form or place or time or concept.

kaffara : prescribed way of making amends for wrong actions, particularly missed obligatory actions.

kaffir (plural - **kaffirun**) : a person who commits kufr, the opposite of a mumin.

karama (plural - **karamat**) : miraculous gifts and favours which Allah gives to His awliya. Miracles are events in the phenomenal world that imply a break in the causal chain.

Kawthar : it is said that it is a river in the Garden, abundant blessing, intercession, and the Hawd of the Prophet Muhammad, may Allah bless him and grant him peace.

khalifa (plural - **khulafa**) : someone who stands in for someone else; in this usage, the leader of the muslim community who stands in as the representative of Allah.

khalil : intimate friend, the kunya used to describe the Prophet Ibrahim, peace be on him, because he conversed with Allah.

khalwa : Shaykh Abdal-Qadir al-Murabit once wrote: 'Khalwa, retreat, is the withdrawal from the world in the concentrated act of invocation of the Supreme Name in order to arrive at the vision of the Face. Its guide is the Shaykh. It is at this maqam that the words of Shaykh Moulay Abdal-Qadir Al-Jilani must be obeyed utterly. Ignorant people misquote them implying a false social control of the Shaykh over the murid. This is not so. It is within the context of this maqam that he says: "Be with your Shaykh as a dead body in the hands of the washer."'

Khandaq : 'the Ditch'; in the fifth year after the Hijrah the Makkan idol-worshippers, assisted by the Jewish tribes of Banu Nadhir, Banu Ghatfan and Banu Asad, marched on Madina with an army of ten thousand soldiers. The Messenger of Allah, may Allah bless him and grant him peace, ordered a ditch to be dug on the unprotected side of Madina and to be manned constantly. The enemy were halted by this unexpected tactic, and then driven away by awful weather, mutual distrust and low morale, without any major engagement having taken place.

kharaj : taxes imposed on revenue from land or the work of slaves.

khayal : this means imagination, but not in the popular sense. Rather it is that faculty in the human brain which perceptually and experientially 'solidifies' and gives reality to the phenomenal world, both externally and internally.

khidma : service.

Khidr : the Prophet Khidr, peace be upon him. It is said that he is the prophet who has never died, and that he appears to people disguised as a person in need, in order to test their generosity.

khul : a form of divorce in which a woman seeking divorce returns her dowry, or part of it, or even more than it, as a ransom for her freedom.

Khulafa Ar-Rashidun : the rightly-guided khalifs, Abu Bakr, Umar, Uthman and Ali, may Allah be pleased with all of them.

khutbah : a speech, and in particular a standing speech given by the Imam before the jumua prayer and after the two Id prayers. At the jumua there are two khutbas separated by a short sitting pause.

kiswah : The huge embroidered black and gold cloth that drapes the Ka'aba.

kohl : antimony powder used both as a decoration and as a medicine for the eyes.

ksar: a large walled fortress, found mainly in the deserts of North Africa.

kufr : to cover up the truth, to reject Allah and His Messenger, may the blessings and peace of Allah be on him. Shaykh Abdal-Qadir al-Murabit once wrote: 'Kufr means to cover up reality: kafir is one who does so. The kafir is the opposite of the mumin. The point is that everyone knows 'how it is' – only it suits some people to deny it and pretend it is otherwise, to behave as if we were going to be here for ever. This is called kufr. The condition of the kafir is therefore one of neurosis, because of his inner knowing. He 'bites his hand in rage' but will not give in to his inevitable oncoming death.'

kunya : a respectful and affectionate way of calling people as the 'Father of so-and-so' or the 'Mother of so-and-so'.

❁   ❁   ❁

labayk : 'at your service'; it is part of the talbiya.

la ilaha illa'llah : 'there is no god except Allah'.

layla : night; also one of the names used to indicate the Beloved.

laylat'al-fuqara : the 'night of the fuqara', meaning the gathering of dhikr attended by the fuqara with their Shaykh or one of his muqaddems, usually on the laylat'al-jumua.

laylat'al-jumua : the night before the day of the jumua, Thursday night.

laylat'al-qadr : the 'Night of Power', concealed in one of the odd nights in the last ten days of Ramadan; the night on which the Qur'an was first revealed by Jibril to the Prophet Muhammad, may Allah bless him and grant him peace, and which the Qur'an itself describes as **'better than a thousand months'**. (Qur'an: 97.3).

li'an : mutual cursing, an oath taken by both the wife and the husband when the husband accuses his wife of committing adultery and she denies it. He makes three oaths that he is truthful and a fourth that the wrath of Allah will be on him if he is lying. The wife can free herself of guilt and thus punishment by avowing herself to be innocent three times and making a fourth vow that the wrath of Allah will be on her if she is lying. A couple who make li'an are automatically and irrevocably divorced and can never be remarried.

lubb : a core. This term is used in the Qur'an to indicate people who have great understanding in the core of their being, the heart.

luh : a writing board, commonly used by those who are learning the Qur'an by heart.

lutf (plural - lata'if) : subtlety, the all-pervading texture of the universe that cannot be grasped or defined. Its opposite is kathif, or thickness.

● ● ●

Madina : the City, often called Madina al-Munawarra – the Illuminated, or the Enlightened, City – where the revelation of the Qur'an was completed and in which the Prophet Muhammad died and is buried, may Allah bless him and grant him peace. The first Muslim community was established in Madina al-Munawarra, and Allah says in the Qur'an that this is the best community ever raised up from amongst mankind. Their hearts and actions were illuminated and enlightened, may Allah be pleased with all of them, by Allah and His Messenger, and today Madina is still illuminated by the presence of the arwah of those of them who are buried there, especially the Messenger of Allah, may the blessings and peace of Allah be on him and them.

maddrasah: a traditional Muslim place of learning based on memorisation and study of the Qur'an and the hadith.

madh-hab: a school of fiqh. There are four main sunni madh-habs, the Hanafi, Maliki, Shafi'i, and Hanbali madh-habs.

Magians: Zoroastrian fire-worshippers.

maghrib: the west, the time of sunset, and in particular the maghrib prayer which can be prayed at any time between just after sundown and before the stars appear in the sky.

mahdi: one who is rightly guided; also the name of the Muslim leader who will fight the Dajjal until the return to this world of the Prophet Jesus, peace be on him, who will kill the Dajjal and his followers by a miracle.

majlis: an assembly.

mahr: the dowry given by husband to wife on marrying.

mahram: a person with whom marriage is forbidden.

Makka: the city in which the Ka'aba stands, and in which the Prophet Muhammad was born, may Allah bless him and grant him peace, and where the revelation of the Qur'an commenced.

makruh: disapproved of without being forbidden.

mala'ika: the angels, who are made of light and glorify Allah unceasingly. They are neither male nor female. They do not need food or drink. They are incapable of wrong action and disobedience to Allah. They do whatever Allah commands them to do. Everyone has two recording angels with them who record their actions and none of this escapes the knowledge of Allah.

Malakut: the angelic world, the kingdom of Unseen forms. Shaykh Abdal-Qadir al-Murabit once wrote: 'This is both the kingdom of the source-forms of the creational realities, crystals, atoms, organisms, and the kingdom of the spiritual realities, the Lote-tree, the

Balance, the Throne and so on. It is the realm of vision as the mulk is the realm of event. As the characteristic of the mulk is fixity or apparent fixity so the characteristic of the malakut is flux and transformation or apparent flux. In fact one could say that the reality of the two worlds is opposite that, for indeed the solid forms are all in change, while the visions are all unfolding the fixed primal patterns on which all the visible world is based.'

mamnu'a : what is prohibited in acts of worship in the shari'ah.

ma'rifa : gnosis, the highest knowledge of Allah possible for a man or woman. It is to directly witness the Light of the Names and Attributes of Allah manifested in the heart. See arif.

maqam : a station. Shaykh Abdal-Qadir al-Murabit once wrote: 'The maqam is arrived at when the slave is established in a degree of adab in his khidma, service to Allah, and when he has acquired a firm place in certainty inwardly. Stations first manifest, fleetingly, as ahwal (plural of hal), then they become fixed in the murid. This is likened to dyeing cloth, so that it is dipped in the same colour and dried, dipped and dried, until the colour at a certain point becomes fixed. Once the dye is fixed the maqam is established.

Maqam Al-Ibrahim : The Station of Ibrahim. The place where the Prophet Ibrahim stood which marks the place of prayer following tawaf of the Ka'aba.

Maqam al-Mahmud : The praiseworthy station, of remembering and worshipping Allah in every waking moment, while others sleep.

marhaban : welcome!

Marwa : see Safa and Marwa.

Maryam : Mary, the mother of Jesus, peace be on her and him; the only woman to be mentioned by name in the Qur'an.

ma salaama : 'with peace'.

ma sha'Allah : 'what Allah wants' happens.

Masih ad-Dajjal : the anti-Messiah; see Dajjal.

Masih ibnu Maryam : the Messiah, Jesus son of Mary, peace be on them. See Isa. The Qur'an states that he was a prophet – and not the son of God – and was not crucified.

masjid : a place of sajda, a mosque.

Masjid Al-Aqsa : the 'Furthest Mosque' in Jerusalem, which stands where the Temple of Solomon once stood.

Masjid Al-Haram : the 'Protected Mosque', the name of the mosque built around the Ka'aba in the Haram at Makka.

Masjid An-Nabiyyi : the 'Prophet's Mosque', the name of the mosque in which is the Prophet Muhammad's tomb, may Allah bless him and grant him peace, in Madina.

mawlana : 'our master', a term of respect.

mawqif (plural - **mawaqif**) : a standing or stopping place. There are two places where those doing the Hajj must 'stop', Arafah and Muzdalifah.

Mika'il : the archangel Michael.

mimbar : steps on which the Imam stands to deliver the khutba on the day of the jumua.

Mina : a valley five miles away from Makka on the road to Arafah, where the three jamras stand. It is part of the rites of the Hajj to spend the night before the Day of Arafah in Mina, and to spend three nights in Mina during the Days of Tashriq.

minza : a sitting room.

miqat (plural - **mawaqit**) : one of the designated places for entering into ihram for Umrah or Hajj.

Mi'raj : the Night Journey of the Prophet Muhammad, may the blessings and peace of Allah be on him, from Makka to Jerusalem and then through the realms of the seven heavens beyond the limit of forms, the sidrat al-muntaha, to within a bow-span's length or nearer to the Presence of the Real.

miskin (plural - **masakin**) : the utterly bereft in poverty, the helplessly needy.

mithal : a likeness; a metaphor. Shaykh Abdal-Qadir al-Murabit once wrote: 'It has a different texture of meaning in tasawwuf than it does in ordinary usage. According to this teaching there are different modalities of experiencing reality; one of these is by thinking about it, and that in turn has different forms or qualities. The use of abstract thought is a function of intellect. The use of analogue, however, is a higher mental operation and involves, as it were, an extra dimension. If you like, abstract thought is linear and diagrammatic or structural.

The mithal when used is like leaving the drawing explanation behind and constructing a hologram in space. This function in turn is superseded by a higher zone of intellection which calls, quite literally, for the invention of, as it were, a special language so that the mithal itself has to be extended into the active language structure. Then a kind of high, hermeneutic coding takes place. The outward expression of this is so fine that the 'song' in no way can even suggest the experience of the listener.'

Mizan : the Balance. Shaykh Abdal-Qadir al-Murabit once wrote: 'Its meaning is the justice and harmony of all creation and therefore of time/space and therefore of us and events. It is the meaning of the Garden and the Fire, of the balance between the matrices. It is what was called in the ancient Tao-form of Islam in China, yin/yang. It is the secret of the contrary Names. It is what we are born and die on, and which turns our acts and intentions into realities to be weighed on the Day of the Balance.'

muadhdin : someone who calls the adhan, the call to prayer.

mubashirat : good news, good dreams.

mudd : a measure of volume, one both hands cupped full, a double handed scoop.

mufsida : what invalidates acts of worship in the shari'ah.

Muhajirun : Companions of the Messenger of Allah, may Allah bless him and grant him peace, who accepted Islam in Makka and made hijrah to Madina.

Muhammad ar-Rasulu'llah : 'Muhammad is the Messenger of Allah', may the blessings and peace of Allah be on him.

Muharram : the first month of the Muslim year, which is based on the lunar calendar, and one of the four inviolable months during which fighting is prohibited, haram, from which its name is derived.

muhrim : a person in ihram.

muhsan : a person who has hasan.

muhsanat : the feminine of muhsan. As well as meaning a person guarded by marriage, it also refers to a chaste unmarried free woman, who is sexually protected, as opposed to an unmarried slave woman over whom her master has sexual rights.

muhsar : a person detained from the Hajj by an enemy or an illness.

muhsin : someone who possesses the quality of ihsan, and who accordingly only gives reality to the Real. Only the muhsin really knows what tawhid is. Shaykh Abdal-Qadir al-Murabit once said: 'The difference between the kafir and the Muslim is vast. The difference between the Muslim and the mumin is greater still. The difference between the mumin and the muhsin is immeasurable.' This is not only in inward state, but also in outward action.

mujiza : an evidentiary miracle given to a Prophet to prove his prophethood.

Mulk : the phenomenal world, the universe. Shaykh Abdal-Qadir al-Murabit once wrote: 'The visible realm. The mulk is what is experienced in the sensory (hiss) and in illusion (wahm). Of its nature mulk is both solid, sensory and pure-space, illusory. This is now confirmed by kafir science. The amazing interlocking substantiality of Mulk veils most people from the meaning-realm onto which it opens the intellect, thus it is designated kingdom for it is a realm of reality, seemingly complete in itself. It is not real, but it is made WITH THE REAL, in the language of Qur'an. Thus to understand it we must penetrate its imprisoning solidity.'

Multazam : the area between the Black Stone and the door of the Ka'aba where it is recommended to make dua.

❂   ❂   ❂

mumin (plural - **muminun**) : someone who possesses the quality of iman, who trusts in Allah and accepts His Messenger, may Allah bless him and grant him peace, and for whom the akhira is more real than dunya. The mumin longs for the Garden so much, that this world seems like the Fire by comparison. Shaykh Abdal-Qadir al-Murabit once wrote: 'One who trusts that existence is inwardly as it is. He takes his evidence from inside himself. His first acceptance of the knowledge of existence is dependant on his accepting a fellow human being. Thus to be muslim you must be able to trust the other. When you are given certainty, that is, confirmation, you trust yourself and then you are mumin. A muslim is one who accepts his existence outwardly, and does not try to defy his cosmic situation. He is a frail boat within the ocean. The mumin allows to dawn on him that outwardness is only one dimension of existence, and that his inwardness must contain the other. He sets out to develop this capacity. He discovers the ocean within the boat. This takes him to the station of being muhsin, a man of ihsan. He then smiles and declares, "What a wonderful thing this is – the boat within the ocean and the ocean within the boat!"'

munafiq (plural – **munafiqun**) : a hypocrite; the hypocrites outwardly profess Islam on the tongue, but inwardly reject Allah and His Messenger, may Allah bless him and grant him peace, and side with the kafirun against the Muslims. The deepest part of the Fire is reserved for the munafiqun.

Munkar and Nakir : the two angels who question your ruh in the grave after your body has been buried, asking, 'Who is your Lord? Who is your Prophet? What is your Book? What was your Deen?'

muqaddem : The deputy of a Shaykh who has the idhn to act and teach on his Shaykh's behalf.

murid : the student of a Shaykh of instruction. Its root is irada, meaning will, for he must hand over his will to the teacher in order to discover who he is. Shaykh Muhammad ibn al-Habib writes in the introduction to his Diwan: 'Murid is derived from will (irada) and it depends on sincerity (ikhlas). The true meaning of murid is one who has stripped himself of his own will and accepted what Allah wills for him, which is the worship of Allah ta'ala, for as He said, **"I have not created jinn and men except to worship Me."**

When the murid is weak in disciplining his self – since the inner rule belongs to the self and shaytan – he places himself under the rule of the Shaykh and in the protection of his power. He, in his turn, will help the murid to obey and worship Allah through his himma which operates by the idhn of Allah and through his words which are made effective by the gift of Allah. So a murid must cling to whoever of the Shaykhs of the age are well disposed towards him.' Shaykh Muhammad ibn al-Habib also writes: 'The murid will gain a master in accordance with his own sincerity and strength of resolution. Allah is the one to ask for help.'

Shaykh Abdal-Qadir al-Murabit once wrote: "The Shaykh does not 'do' anything. He recognises those Allah loves. This recognition has wisdom in it for him and for you. Shaykh Ahmad al-Badawi of Fez, Allah be merciful to him, said: "One glance from the Shaykh wipes out a thousand wrong actions." This is very difficult for the people of thought-forms to understand and easy for the people of the states. This concerns the inner zone of the **lubb** or core of the human self's awareness. Its mithal is the sun's rays. If you sit in the sun you become sunburned. If you sit with the Shaykh you become purified, later intoxicated, and finally annihilated. As one who is first warmed, then burned and at the end blinded by the rays of the sun. In this zone is the innermost reality and the secrets of 'keeping company' . . . Your service to the Shaykh is a tremendous thing. Greater than it is his service to you. Wrong feelings against the Shaykh endanger the murid by confusion and the illusion that the nafs is other, and there is no other. Abu'l-Abbas al-Mursi, Allah's mercy be upon him, said: "The one who says 'why?' to his Shaykh will never be happy." Never forget the object of the contract with the Shaykh is to move you from ilmi nafsika to ilmi rabbika from knowledge of your nafs to knowledge of your Lord.'

Musa : the Prophet Moses, peace be on him.

mushrik (plural - **mushrikin**) : one who commits shirk.

muslim : someone who follows the way of Islam, not abandoning what is fard, keeping within the hudud of Allah, and following the sunnah, in what he or she is able. A Muslim is, by definition, one who is safe and sound, at peace in this world, and promised the Garden in the next world.

mustahab : what is recommended, but not obligatory, in acts of worship in the shari'ah.

mut'a : temporary marriage under strict conditions, allowed in the early days of Islam but later prohibited.

mutawwif : a resident of Makka who welcomes pilgrims to Makka, feeds them, shelters them and, if necessary, teaches them the courtesies and meaning of the rites of the Hajj and the Umrah.

Muzdalifah : a place between Arafah and Mina where the pilgrims returning from Arafah spend a night in the open between the 9th and 10th days of Dhu'l-Hijjah after praying maghrib and isha there.

●   ●   ●

nabi : a prophet, a rightly guided man sent by Allah to guide others. Altogether there have been one hundred and twenty-four thousand prophets, beginning with Adam, peace be on him, and ending with Muhammad, the Seal of the Prophets, may the blessings and peace of Allah be on him and on all of them.

nabidh : a drink made by soaking grapes, raisins, dates and so on in water without their being allowed to ferment.

nafila : a voluntary act of ibada.

nafl (plural - **nawafil**) : a gift, from the same root as anfal, meaning booty taken in war; it means a voluntary act of ibada.

nafs : the illusory experiencing self. You as you think you are. When the nafs is impure, it is an illusory solidification of events obscuring a light, the ruh. When it has been completely purified, the nafs is the ruh. Shaykh Abdal-Qadir al-Murabit once wrote: 'Shaykh al-Akbar defines nafs as, "What is caused of the attributes of the slave." So it is that the self is imprisoned by the very elements it imagines liberate its actions. The more the self does the more it builds up an illusory continuity and history. Event consolidates the myth of the self. This is why Shaykh al-Kamil says that, "everything in the nafs is dreadful." It is irrelevant to imagine you can 'forge' a good nafs. It is a more terrible idol than the bad one. The nafs is the great idol which, while it sets up the other idols cannot smash itself. This is why one takes the Shaykh. His function is simply to serve as a mirror self which will help one escape the deceptions of the self which are self-perpetuating.'

Nar : the Fire of Jahannam, the final destination and place of torment of the kafirun and munafiqun in the akhira once the Last Day is over. Some of those Muslims who neglected what is fard in the shari'ah and who did grave wrong action without making tawba will spend some time in the Fire before being allowed to enter the Garden, depending on the forgiveness of Allah Who forgives every wrong action except shirk if He wishes. Nar is accurately described in great detail in the Qur'an and hadith.

nasiha : good advice, sincere conduct.

nawafil : what is voluntary in acts of worship in the shari'ah.

nifaq : hypocrisy. See munafiq.

nikah : marriage.

nisab : the minimum amount of wealth of whatever kind from which zakat can be deducted.

Nuh : the Prophet Noah, peace be on him.

nur : light. The Qur'an states:

> **Allah is the light of the heavens and the earth.**
>
> **(Qur'an: 24.35)**

nuri-Muhammad : the ruhani Light of Muhammad, may Allah bless him and grant him peace.

❖ ❖ ❖

'oud : a type of tree whose oil is used as a perfume, and whose wood is burned as a form of incense.

❖ ❖ ❖

qabr : the grave, experienced as a place of peace and light and space by the ruh of the mumin who sees his or her place in the Garden in the morning and in the evening; and experienced as a place of torment and darkness and no space by the ruh of the kafir who sees his or her place in the Fire in the morning and in the evening. After death there is a period of waiting in the grave for the ruh until the Last Day arrives, when everyone who has ever lived will be brought back to life and gathered together. Their actions will be weighed in the mizan, and everyone will either go to the Garden or to the Fire, for ever.

qadr : the decree of Allah, which determines every sub-atomic particle in existence, and accordingly whatever appears to be in existence. One of Allah's names is Al-Qadir, the Powerful, the One Who does what He wants, the One Who has power over everything. The Prophet Muhammad, may the blessings and peace of Allah be on him, once said:

"Everything is by decree."

(Al-Muwatta of Imam Malik: 46.1.5)

qadqamati's-salat : the call which announces that the obligatory prayer is just about to begin:

Allahu akbar, Allahu akbar.
Ash-shadu an la ilaha illa'llah.
Ash-shadu anna Muhammad ar-Rasulu'llah.
Haya ala's-salat.
Haya ala'l-falah.
Qadqamati's-salat.
Allahu akbar, Allahu akbar.
La ilaha illa'llah.

Which means:

Allah is greater, Allah is greater.
I bear witness that there is no god except Allah.
I bear witness that Muhammad is the Messenger of Allah.
Come to the prayer.
Come to success.
The prayer has been established.
Allah is greater, Allah is greater.
There is no god but Allah.

qasida : a verse, in this context from the Diwan of one of the Shaykhs of Instruction. They contain the ultimate 'means' by which ma'rifa is approached. These have never been studied or translated in this society, where they have been brilliantly rendered meaningless by pseudo-poetics, who have projected onto them an aesthetic value they never sought nor can tolerate. The whole science of Diwan method remains to be explored.

qiblah : the direction faced in prayer, which, for the Muslims, is towards the Ka'aba in Makka. Everyone has a direction in life, but only the Muslims have this qiblah.

qudrat : power, in the sense of determining one's existence. Qudrat is, in truth, with Allah.

Qur'an : the 'Recitation', the last revelation from Allah to mankind and the jinn before the end of the world, revealed to the Prophet Muhammad, may Allah bless him and grant him peace, through the angel Jibril, over a period of twenty-three years, the first thirteen of which were spent in Makka and the last ten of which were spent in Madina. The Qur'an amends, encompasses, expands, surpasses and abrogates all the earlier revelations revealed to the earlier messengers, peace be on all of them. The Messenger of Allah said, may Allah bless him and grant him peace, that each verse of the Qur'an has an outward meaning and an inward meaning and a gnostic meaning. The Qur'an is the greatest miracle given to the Prophet Muhammad by Allah, for he was illiterate and could neither read nor write. The Qur'an is the uncreated word of Allah. Whoever recites the Qur'an with courtesy and sincerity receives knowledge and wisdom, for it is the well of wisdom in this age.

Quraysh : one of the great tribes in Arabia. The Messenger of Allah, may Allah bless him and grant him peace, belonged to this tribe.

quru : a woman's becoming pure after menses, used particularly in reference to the idda of divorce.

qutb : the Pole or axis of the Universe. Shaykh Abdal-Qadir al-Murabit once wrote: 'This term is only understood by the one who has attained to it. An approximation would be to say that in him gnosis is complete inwardly so that outwardly his gnosis radiates as a sun over all the other gnostics. The proofs of the qutb are these: that he is surrounded by a circle of gnostics as a King is visibly recognisable by his Court, that the deen of Islam revives around him bringing life to the people, and thirdly that he names his successor before his death.'

rahma : mercy, the mercy of Allah.

Rajab : the seventh month in the Muslim lunar calendar, one of the four sacred months in which fighting is prohibited.

rak'a (plural – **rak'at**) : a unit of the prayer (salat - see below), a complete series of standing, bowing, prostrations and sittings.

Ramadan : the month of fasting, the ninth month in the Muslim lunar calendar, during which all adult Muslims who are in good health fast from the first light of dawn until sunset each day. During the first third of the fast you taste Allah's mercy; during the second third of the fast you taste Allah's forgiveness; and during the last third of the fast you taste freedom from the Fire. The Qur'an was first revealed in the month of Ramadan during the laylat al-qadr. Ramadan is one of the indispensable pillars of Islam.

rami : the act of throwing the small pebbles at the jamras in Mina.

raml : 'hastening' in the tawaf, a way of walking briskly, moving the shoulders vigorously, usually done during the first three circuits in a set of seven, but not in the remaining four.

rasul : a 'Messenger', a prophet who has been given a revealed book by Allah. Every Messenger was a prophet, but not every prophet was given a revealed book.

ratib: a wird.

Rowdah : the part of the Prophet's Mosque between his grave and the mimbar. He said, may Allah bless him and grant him peace:

> "What is between my house and my mimbar is one of the meadows of the Garden, and my mimbar is on my watering-place (al-Hawd)."
>
> (Al-Muwatta of Imam Malik: 14.5.10)

riba : usury, which is haram, whatever form it takes.

ridwan : the sublime serenity of dynamic contentment that fills the heart and remains.

rikaz : treasure buried in the pre-Islamic period which is recovered without great cost or effort. Zakat is exacted from such finds.

riwaya : a reading or transmission of the Qur'an or another text.

ruh : the spirit which gives life, formed from pure light; the angel Jibril.

ruhani : pertaining to the ruh.

ruku : bowing, particularly the bowing position of the prayer (salat – see below).

ruqya : recitation of verses of the Qur'an for treatment of, and protection against, illness.

❀ ❀ ❀

sa' : an hour, usually used to denote 'the Hour', when the world ends and the Last Day begins.

saa : a measure of volume, equal to four mudds.

sadaqa : giving in the way of Allah, a gift to another or others without any other motive than the giving. It is giving to the needy, in any form, including sharing wisdom, giving a helping hand, giving away clothing, food and money, and giving shelter. The smallest sadaqa is to come out to your brother or sister with a smiling face.

Safa and Marwa : two hills situated quite close to the Ka'aba. It is part of the rites of Umrah and the Hajj to walk seven times between the two hills, increasing your pace each time you come to a certain point, but not breaking into a run, and then slowing down again.

Safar : the second month in the Muslim lunar calendar.

sahaba : the Companions of the Prophet, may Allah be pleased with them.

sahih : healthy and sound with no defects; often used to describe an authentic hadith. The two most reliable collections of hadith by al-Bukhari and Muslim are both called Sahih.

sahur : the early morning meal taken before first light when fasting.

sajda : the act of making prostration, particularly in the prayer (salat – see below).

sakina : the presence of Allah sometimes made clear by a sign; also the feeling of peace of mind and security that comes from a heart at peace.

salafi : adjective from as-salaf, the 'early years', and used generally to describe the early generations of the Muslims, particularly the sahaba, the companions of the Messenger of Allah, may the blessings and peace of Allah be on him and them.

salat : the prayer, particularly the five daily obligatory ritual prayers of the Muslims which are called maghrib, isha, subh, dhur and asr. They consist of fixed sets of standings, bowings, prostrations and sittings in worship to Allah. The Muslim day begins at maghrib, because the first day of a new month is only determined when the new moon is sighted shortly after sunset. It is necessary to be in ghusl and in wudu before you do the salat. Salat is one of the indispensable pillars of Islam.

salih (plural - salihun) : a spiritually developed man. By definition, one who is in the right place at the right time.

salla'llahu alayhi wa sallam : 'may Allah bless him and grant him peace', meaning the Prophet Muhammad.

Samad : the Real in its endless effulgence of creative energy, by which the whole universe of endless forms emerge from the possible into the existent. It is the richness whose wealth is every form in creation. Allah is in need of nothing and everything is in need of Him.

samawati : the heavens.

sa'y : the main rite of Umrah and one of the rites of the Hajj. Sa'y is proceeding between the two hills of Safa and Marwa seven times.

sayyedina : 'our master', a term of respect.

○   ○   ○

Shaban : the eighth month in the Muslim lunar calendar, and one of the four sacred months in which fighting is prohibited.

shafaq : the redness in the sky after sunset.

shahada : to witness, to bear witness that there is no god but Allah and that Muhammad is the Messenger of Allah. The shahada is the gateway to Islam and the gateway to Jinnah. It is easy to say, but to act on it is a vast undertaking which has far-reaching consequences, in both inward awareness and outward action, in this world and in the akhira. Continual affirmation of the shahada is one of the indispensable pillars of Islam.

shahid (plural – shuhada) : a witness, a martyr in the way of Allah.

Sham : the territory north of Arabia which is now divided into Syria, Palestine, Lebanon and Jordan.

shari'ah : a road, the legal and social modality of a people based on the revelation of their Prophet. The last shari'ah in history is that of Islam. It abrogates all previous shari'ahs. It is, being the last, therefore the easiest to follow, for it is applicable to the whole human race wherever they are.

sharif : a descendant of the Prophet Muhammad, may Allah bless him and grant him peace.

Shawwal : the tenth month of the Muslim lunar calendar.

shaykh : the one who guides you from knowledge of the self to knowledge of your Lord. Shaykh Abdal-Qadir al-Murabit once wrote: 'Without a Shaykh a man can not defeat his nafs. The more he fights himself the more powerful the self becomes. Attention confirms nafs. The activator of the nafs will either be outside or inside the nafs. If it is activated from inside this is the work of Shaytan, the whisperer, who instigates wrong action. That is why, following the word of Moulay Abdal-Qadir al-Jilani, the murid must make himself like a dead body in the hands of the washer in relations with the Shaykh. Abu Yazid, Allah's mercy on these great awliya', said: "He who does not have a Shaykh for a Master will have Shaytan as a Master." This is why, 'keeping company' is a necessary condition of the Path. How can the doctor heal the patient unless the patient is brought before him? At the heart of the matter, however, there is no rule over the murid. The murid must want what the Shaykh wants, in that is his cure. Murid is one who has surrendered his irada – his will – to the Shaykh in order to come quickly out of the fantasies of the khayal (the faculty investing the solid objects with their 'reality') and the kufr, the covering, that is the self.

> **"Fear Allah
> and He will give you discrimination."**

That means not by you but by Him. Then separation does not veil you from gatheredness and gatheredness does not veil you from separation.'

Shaykh Muhammad ibn al-Habib writes in the introduction to his Diwan: 'Explaining the attributes of the teaching Shaykh, I said in one of my qasidas ending in ta':

> 'La ilaha illa'llah' banishes all temptations
> along with the instructions of a Shaykh
> who knows the Reality.
>
> His signs are:
> a light which shines outwardly,
> and a secret which appears inwardly, with himma.
>
> He elevates you with a glance even before he speaks,
> and from this glance
> comes a robe of honour.
>
> By it I mean the secrets
> which flow rapidly into the heart of the murid
> who seeks the truth without shirk.
>
> His doing-without among creatures is the staff of his journey,
> and his occupation is
> seeking isolation of the Beloved by vision.
>
> His speech is by idhn
> from the Best of the Community
> upon whom the glorious truthful ones depend.

> If you obtain the goal
> of finding such a one
> then set out and offer up the self without delay.
>
> Do not consider anything
> except what I have described here,
> for it is enough and in it is every happiness.'

Shaykh Muhammad ibn al-Habib also writes: 'There has always been agreement in this community of Muhammad that the first thing required of a murid once he has become aware of his state of distraction is that he should rely on a Shaykh of good counsel and guidance who knows the defects of the self, its motives, and the remedies for its ailments, and who has done with the putting right of his own self and its desires. He will give the murid insight into the faults of his self and draw him out beyond the perimeter of his senses. Whoever has no Shaykh to direct him will most certainly be directed by shaytan to the path of destruction.'

shaytan (plural - **shayatin**) : a devil, particularly Iblis (Satan), a'udhu bi'llahi min ash-shaytani'r-rajim. Shaytan is part of the creation of Allah, and we seek refuge in the perfect word of Allah from the evil that He has created.

shirk : the unforgiveable wrong action of worshipping something or someone other than Allah or associating something or someone as a partner with Him; the opposite of tawhid which is affirmation of Divine Unity. Shirk is idol-worship. Shaykh Abdal-Qadir al-Murabit once wrote: 'Idol-worship means giving delineation to the Real. Encasing it in an object, a concept, a ritual or a myth. This is called shirk, or association. Avoidance of shirk is the most radical element in the approach to understanding existence in Islam. It soars free of these deep social restrictions and so posits such a profoundly revolutionary approach to existence that it constitutes – and has done for fourteen hundred years – the most radical rejection of the political version of idolatry, statism. It is very difficult for programmed literates in this society to cut through to the clear tenets of Islam, for the Judaic and Christian perversions stand so strongly in the way either as, rightly, anathema, or else as ideals. The whole approach to understanding reality has a quite different texture than that known and defined in European languages, thus a deep insight into the structure of the Arabic language itself would prove a better introduction to the metaphysic than a philosophical statement. The uncompromising tawhid that is affirmed does not add on any sort of 'god-concept'. Nor does it posit an infra-god, a grund-god, or even an over-god. Christian philosophers were so frightened by this position that when they met it, to stop people discovering the fantasy element in their trinitarian mythology they decided to identify it with pantheism in the hope of discrediting it. That they succeeded in this deception is an indication of how far the whole viewpoint has been kept out of reach of the literate savage society. Let it suffice here to indicate that there is no 'problem' about the nature of Allah. Nor do we consider it possible even to speak of it. No how, who or what or why. It is not hedging the matter in mystery. It is simply asking the wrong questions! The knowledge of Allah is specifically a personal quest in which the radical question that has to be asked is not even "who am I?" but "Where then are you going?"' See Allah.

shuhada : plural of shahid.

siddiq : a man of truth. Sincerity is his condition, not his adopted position.

sidrat al-muntaha : 'the lote-tree of the furthest limit', the place where form ends.

sirah : the historical study of the Prophet Muhammad's life, may the blessings and peace of Allah be on him.

Sirat : the narrow bridge which must be crossed to enter the Garden.

Sirat al-Mustaqim : 'the Straight Path' of Islam.

siyam : fasting, from food and drink – and making love if you are married – during daylight, from the first light of dawn until sunset.

subh : morning, and in particular the obligatory dawn prayer which can be prayed at any time between first light (fajr - see above) and just before the sun rises.

subhana'llah : 'glory to Allah'.

Suffa: a verandah attached to the Prophet's Mosque in Madina where poor Muslims used to sleep.

sujud: the position of prostration, particularly in the prayer (salat – see above).

Sulayman: The Prophet Solomon, peace be on him.

sultan: king, ruler.

sunnah (plural - **sunan**): a form, the customary practice of a person or group of people. It has come to refer almost exclusively to the practice of the Messenger of Allah, Muhammad, may Allah bless him and grant him peace, but also comprises the customs of the First Generation of Muslims in Madina. It is a complete behavioural science that has been systematically kept outside the learning framework of this society. The Messenger of Allah, may Allah bless him and grant him peace, said:

> "I have left two matters with you. As long as you hold to them, you will not go the wrong way. They are the Book of Allah and the Sunnah of His Prophet."
>
> (Al-Muwatta of Imam Malik: 46.1.3)

surah: a large unit of Qur'an linked by thematic content, composed of ayat. There are 114 surahs in the Qur'an.

Surah Ya Sin: the heart of the Qur'an.

Surat'al-Fatiha: the opening surah of the Qur'an, the surah of both Opening and Victory:

> Bismillahi'r-Rahmani'r-Rahim
>
> Al-hamduli'llahi rabbi'l-alameen,
> Ar-Rahmani'r-Rahim,
> Maliki yawmi'd-deen.
> Iyyaka na'budu wa iyyaka nasta'een.
> Ihdina's-sirat al-mustaqim,
> sirat alladheen an'amta alayhim
> ghayri'l-maghdhubi alayhim wa la'dh-dhalleen.
>
> Amin

Which means:

In the Name of Allah the Merciful the Compassionate

Praise to Allah, Lord of the Worlds,
the Merciful the Compassionate,
King of the Day of the Life-Transaction.
Only You we worship and only You we ask for help.
Lead us on the Straight Path,
The path of those whom You have blessed,
Not of those with whom You are angry,
and not of those who are astray.

Amen

(Qur'an: 1.1-7)

Recitation of Surat'al-Fatiha is an integral and essential part of the salat which means that every Muslim recites the Fatihah at least twenty times a day – and often many times more. It is thus the most often daily repeated statement on the face of the earth today:

Surat'al-Ikhlas : the surah of Sincerity:

Bismillahi'r-Rahmani'r-Rahim

Qul Huwa'llahu Ahad
Allahu's-Samad
Lam yalid wa lam yuwlad
Wa lam yakun lahu kufuwan Ahad.

Which means:

In the Name of Allah the Merciful the Compassionate

Say: He is Allah the One
Allah the Everlasting
No one is born from Him and He is not born from anything
And there is nothing like Him.

(Qur'an: 112.1-4)

The Prophet Muhammad, may the blessings and peace of Allah be on him, said that Surat'al-Ikhlas is equal to one third of the

Qur'an. Its recitation gives you the freedom of action that only accompanies true sincerity.

Surat'al-Kahf : the surah of the Cave. It is said that its recitation is a protection against the Dajjal.

sutra : an object placed in front of a man praying so that people will pass beyond it and not 'break' his qiblah and concentration.

○ ○ ○

tabaraka'llah : 'blessed is Allah.'

Tabuk : a town in northern Arabia close to Sham. In the ninth year after the Hijrah, the Messenger of Allah, may Allah bless him and grant him peace, hearing that the Byzantines were gathering a large army to march against the Muslims, led a large expedition to Tabuk, on what was to be his last campaign, only to find that the Byzantine army had withdrawn back into its own territory.

tahajjud : voluntary prayers in the night between isha and fajr.

tahnia : a very sweet snack made principally from ground sesame seeds and honey or sugar and sometimes nuts; also called halwa.

Ta'if : an important town in the mountains, fifty miles to the east of Makka.

tajalli (plural - tajalliyat) : self-manifestation. Shaykh Abdal-Qadir al-Murabit once wrote: 'The tajalli is the unveiling of a spiritual reality in the realm of vision. It is a direct-seeing into the nature of existence, a showing forth of the secrets of the One in the celestial and terrestrial realms.' And: 'A divine manifestation witnessed by the inner eye of the seeker. Outer experience is event, inner experience is vision. Mulk, the kingdom of outwardness, is the realm of event. Malakut, the kingdom of inwardness is the realm of vision. Jabarut, the kingdom of the source, is the realm of annihilation. Mulk is the realm of darknesses, malakut of lights, and jabarut of light upon light.'

takbir : the saying of Allahu akbar – Allah is greater. The prayer (salat – see above) begins with a takbir.

○ ○ ○

talbiya : the call that the pilgrims make to their Lord on the Hajj:

> Labayk, Labayk, Allahumma Labayk.
> La sharika lak, Labayk.
> Inna'l-hamdu wa'n-ni'mata laka wa'l-mulk.
> La sharika lak.

Which means:

> I am totally at Your service, I am totally at Your service,
> O Allah I am totally at Your service.
> You have no partner, I am totally at Your service.
> Surely the Praise and the Blessing are Yours and the Kingdom.
> You have no partner.

tanzih:tashbih : Shaykh Abdal-Qadir al-Murabit once wrote: 'Tanzih is from NZH which means 'to keep something away from anything contaminating or impure'. It is to disconnect Allah from the forms, affirming that His Reality is beyond any association with the forms. It must be balanced with tashbih from ShBH meaning 'to make or consider something similar to some other thing' which affirms that He participates in the form-world, seeing is His and hearing is His.'

taqlid : garlanding sacrificial animals, especially hadys on the Hajj. In reference to fiqh, it means the following of previous authorities and the avoidance of ijtihad.

taqwa : being careful, knowing your place in the cosmos. Its proof is the experience of awe, of Allah, which inspires a person to be on guard against wrong action and eager for actions which please Him.

tarawih : extra night prayers in the month of fasting, Ramadan, in order to recite the Qur'an as fully as possible, or completely.

tarbush : a small round brimless hat, usually made from wool or felt, and either worn by itself or as the base of a turban.

tariqah : the Way.

tasbih : from the root SBH which means 'to swim', 'to glide through the stars', 'to glorify'; in this context a string of 99 beads and an 'alif', making 100, used to keep count when doing specified amounts of particular dhikrs, such as, for example, 20,000 'La ilaha illa'llah'; or 1,000 'Surat'al-Ikhlas'; or 666 'Allah'; or 313 or 454 'hasbuna'llahu wa ni'm'al-wakil'; or 100 'astaghfirullah'; or 41 'Surah Ya Sin'; or 100 prayers on the Prophet, may Allah bless him and grant him peace, such as, for example:

> Allahumma salli ala sayyedina Muhammidan
> abdika wa rasulika'n-nabiyyi'l-ummiyy
> wa ala alihi wa sahbihi wa sallim.

Which means:

> O Allah, bless our master Muhammad,
> Your slave and Your Messenger, the unlettered Prophet,
> and his family and his companions and grant them peace.

Generally speaking, such dhikrs need to be given with idhn by a Shaykh to his murid for them to be truly effective, for they are used like spiritual medicines. The Shaykh is the doctor and the murid is the patient. Only the Shaykh understands the nature of the illness and knows its cure, which varies from one person to another. However, no one needs idhn to recite the Qur'an, since we are commanded by Allah in the Qur'an to recite whatever is easy for us of it, and Allah also commands us in the Qur'an to ask blessings on the Prophet Muhammad, may the blessings and peace of Allah be on him and on his family and on his companions and on all who follow him and them with sincerity in what they are able until the Last Day.

tashahhud : to say the shahada. In the context of the prayer (salat – see above) it is a formula which includes the shahada. It is said in the final sitting position of each two rak'a cycle.

tashriq : the Days of Tashriq are the 11th, 12th and 13th of Dhu'l-Hijjah, the month of the Hajj, when the pilgrims sacrifice their hadys and stone the jamras at Mina. Since these are days of feasting, the Muslims are not permitted to fast during them.

taslim : giving the Muslim greeting of 'As-salaamu-alaykum' – 'Peace be on you'. The prayer (salat – see above) ends with a taslim.

tassawuf : Sufism. Shaykh Abdal-Qadir al-Murabit once wrote: 'Its preferred etymology is that it derives from suf, wool. Shaykh Hassan al-Basra said, "I saw forty of the people of Badr and they all wore wool." This means that the sufi – tasawwafa has put on the wool. This is distinct from those who confirm the way of Islam with the tongue and by book learning. It is taking the ancient way, the primordial path of direct experience of the Real. Junayd said, "The sufi is like the earth, filth is flung on it but roses grow from it." He also said, "The sufi is like the earth which supports the innocent and the guilty, like the sky which shades everything, like the rain which washes everything." The sufi is universal. He has reduced and then eliminated the marks of selfhood to allow a clear view of the cosmic reality. He has rolled up the cosmos in its turn and obliterated it. He has gone beyond. The sufi has said "Allah" – until he has understood. All men and women play in the world like children. The sufi's task is to recognise the end in the beginning, accept the beginning in the end, arrive at the unified view. When the outward opposites are the same, and the instant is presence, and the heart is serene, empty and full, light on light, the one in the woollen cloak has been robed with the robe of honour and is complete. The Imam also said, "If I had known of any science greater than sufism I would have gone to it, even on my hands and knees."'

tawaf : circling the Ka'aba; tawaf is done in sets of seven circuits, after each of which it is necessary to pray two rak'as, preferably at or near the Maqam al-Ibrahim.

Tawaf Al-Ifada : the tawaf of the Ka'aba that the pilgrim must do after coming from Mina to Makka on the 10th of Dhu'l-Hijjah. It is one of the essential rites of the Hajj.

Tawaf Al-Qudum : the 'Tawaf on Arrival', the tawaf of the Ka'aba that the pilgrim must do on first entering the Haram in Makka. It is one of the essential rites of both the Hajj and the Umrah.

Tawaf Al-Wad'a : the 'Tawaf of Farewell', the farewell tawaf of the Ka'aba which every visitor to Makka should do before leaving. It should be connected directly to the trip of departure, and whoever stays on afterwards should do it again.

tawba : returning to correct action after error, turning away from wrong action to Allah and asking His Forgiveness, turning to face the Real whereas before one turned one's back.

tawhid : the doctrine of Divine Unity, Unity in its most profound sense. Allah is One in His Essence and His Attributes and His Acts. The whole universe and what it contains is One unified event which in itself has no reality. Allah is the Real. Shaykh Abdal-Qadir al-Murabit once wrote: 'Our Imam said, "It is a meaning which obliterates the outlines and joins the knowledges. Allah is as He always was. Tawhid has five pillars: it consists of the raising of the veil on the contingent, to attribute endlessness to Allah alone, to abandon friends, to leave one's country, and to forget what one knows and what one does not know." His greatest statement on tawhid, which Shaykh al-Akbar has called the highest of what may be said on the subject is, "The colour of the water is the colour of the glass." Commenting on this Shaykh Ibn Ajiba said, "This means that the exalted Essence is subtle, hidden and luminous. It appears in the outlines and the forms, it takes on their colours. Admit this and understand it if you do not taste it." Tawhid is itself a definition whose meaning is not complete for the one who holds to it until he has abandoned it or rather exhausted its indications and abandoned it for complete absorption in the One.' And: 'True tawhid is based on complete understanding and appreciation of the self. Until you know you do not exist you cannot know that only He exists. This idea is itself a veil over knowledge of this, and its final enemy.' The Prophet Muhammad said, may the blessings and peace of Allah be on him, 'Whoever knows their self, truly knows their Lord.'

Tawrah : the Torah which was revealed to the Prophet Moses, peace be on him.

tayyamum : purification for prayer using clean dust, earth or stone, when water for ghusl or wudu is either unavailable or would be detrimental to health. Tayyamum is done by striking the earth or rubbing the stone with the palms of the hands and then wiping the face and hands and forearms.

Uhud : a mountain just outside Madina, much loved by the Messenger of Allah, Muhammad, may Allah bless him and grant him peace, where three years after the Hijrah, the Muslims lost a battle against the Makkan idol-worshippers when some of them disobeyed the Prophet's orders. Many great companions, and in particular the uncle of the Prophet, Hamza, the 'lion of Allah', were killed in this battle.

ulama : plural of alim.

Ummah : the body of the Muslims as one distinct and integrated community.

Umm al-Muminin : 'Mother of the Believers', an honorary title given to the wives of the Prophet, may Allah bless him and grant him peace.

Umm al-Qur'an : 'Mother of the Qur'an', the opening surah of the Qur'an which is called Al-Fatiha; also said to be its source in the Unseen.

Umrah : the lesser pilgrimage to the Ka'aba in Makka and the performance of its rites in the protected area which surrounds the Ka'aba. You can go on Umrah at any time of the year.

❀ ❀ ❀

wa alaikum as-salaam : 'and on you be peace'.

wahy : revelation.

wajib : a necessary part of the shari'ah but not obligatory.

wali : a guardian, a person who has responsibility for another person; used particularly for the person who 'gives' a woman in marriage. Also someone who is a 'friend' of Allah, thus possessing the quality of wilaya.

warid (plural - waridat) : what descends on the awareness of the student while performing dhikr or sitting in the company of the Shaykh. Shaykh Abdal-Qadir once wrote: 'The warid is sometimes described as the unwinding of the talisman, for its effect is at the core of self experience and it is a kind of un-doing. The warid is the first stage of awakening. In the warid the experienced field of reality is at last tasted as being with less and less separateness. It is the first oncoming of gatheredness. The objects are recognised but can no longer be distinguished. Action may still be possible but not speech. It is as if the body's contours – not the intellect's – were the perimeter of one's vision, so that the room or place where you are is part of your body which you can feel and recognise as shimmering and melting – that is, its melting and yours are one event. Here there is no compassion for the other, but compassion is itself the reality of the state, without other. This is the first hint that the self/universe is one cosmic situation. Anything can unlock it, a glance from the Shaykh, the action of another faqir, or a mithal sung in the Diwan.'

wasila : something which makes something else take place. Also the highest station with Allah on the Last Day, reserved for the Prophet Muhammad, may the blessings and peace of Allah be on him.

wilaya : friendship, in particular with Allah. Wilayat, the condition of the wali, refers uniquely to the gnostic station of a person. The station of the wali is the station of knowledge of the Real by direct seeing. The greatest wali is like a drop compared to the ocean of the Prophet Muhammad, may the blessings and peace of Allah be on him.

wird (plural - awrad) : A unit of dhikr constructed to contain in it certain patterns of knowledge and self awakening. They are medicines, and their recitation makes them effective in altering the self-form of the student. Some wirds can last hours, others only a few minutes.

wudu : ritual washing of the hands, mouth, nostrils, face, forearms, head, ears and feet with water alone so as to be pure for the prayer. You must already be in ghusl for wudu to be effective. You should ensure that your private parts and under-clothes are clean before doing wudu. Once you have done wudu you remain in wudu until it is broken by any of the conditions which make it necessary to have a ghusl, emission of impurities from the private parts – urine, faeces, wind, prostatic fluid, or other discharge – loss of consciousness by whatever means – usually by sleep or fainting – physical contact between man and woman where sexual pleasure is either intended or experienced, touching your penis with the inside of your hand or fingers, and leaving Islam. It is necessary to be in ghusl and in wudu to do the salat and to hold a copy of the Qur'an. See tayyamum.

wuquf : stopping at Arafah and Muzdalifah. See mawqif.

Yahyah : the Prophet Yahyah, peace be on him, often referred to as John the Baptist.

yaqin : certainty. It has three stages:

> ilm al-yaqin – knowledge of certainty.
> ayn al-yaqin – source of certainty.
> haqq al-yaqin – truth of certainty.

The Raja of Mahmudabad defined them thus:

> You are told there is a fire in the forest.
> You reach the fire in the forest and see it.
> You are the fire in the forest.

Yathrib : the ancient name for Madina al-Munawarra, the Illuminated City, before Islam.

yawm : a day.

Yawm Al-Arafah : the 'Day of Arafah', the 9th of Dhu'l-Hijjah. One of the essential rites of the Hajj is to pray dhur and asr together on the plain of Arafah and then to stand there, either on the Jebel Ar-Rahmah or as near to it as possible, between the times of asr and maghrib making duas to Allah.

Yawm Al-Jumua : the day of the jumua.

Yawm Al-Qiyama : the 'Day of Standing', the Last Day, also known as 'Yawm Al-Ba'ath' – the Day of Rising; 'Yawm Al-Hashr' – the Day of Gathering; 'Yawm al-Qiyama' – the Day of Standing; 'Yawm al-Mizan' – the Day of the Balance; 'Yawm al-Hisab' – the Day of Reckoning; 'Yawm ad-Deen' – the Day of the Life Transaction; and 'Yawm al-Akhira' – the Day of the Next World. It will be followed by Eternity, either in the Garden or in the Fire, forever.

Yawm As-Sabt : the 'Day of the Sabbath', Saturday.

Yemeni corner: the corner of the Ka'aba facing south towards the Yemen.

Glossary of Arabic Terms   323

Zabur: the Psalms which were revealed to the Prophet David, peace be on him.

Zakariyya: the Prophet Zacchariah, peace be on him, who looked after Maryam in the Temple of Solomon when she was a child, peace be on her, and who was the father of the Prophet Yahyah, peace be on him.

zakat: the wealth tax obligatory on Muslims each year, usually payable in the form of one fortieth of surplus wealth which is more than a certain fixed minimum amount, which is called the nisab. Zakat is payable on accumulated wealth, merchandise, certain crops, certain live-stock, and subterranean and mineral wealth. As soon as it is collected it is redistributed to those in need, as defined in the Qur'an and hadith. Zakat is one of the indispensable pillars of Islam.

zakat al-fitr: a small obligatory head-tax imposed on every responsible Muslim who has the means for himself and his dependants. It is paid once yearly at the end of Ramadan before the Id Al-Fitr.

Zamzam: the well in the Haram of Makka which has the best water in the world!

zahid: the one who does without. It does not mean ascetic. The one who is zahid no longer needs or desires the thing he does without, so his avoiding it eases his way and does not result in a struggle or denial.

zawiyya: a corner, the building used as a meeting place by the Shaykhs of Instruction.

zuhud: doing without. See zahid.

BIBLIOGRAPHY

The Qur'an : the uncreated word of Allah.

The Meaning of the Glorious Qur'an : A translation of the Qur'an into English by Muhammad Marmaduke Pickthall.

A Dictionary and Glossary of the Qur'an : John Penrice. Curzon Press 1979.

Al-Muwatta of Imam Malik : A translation by Aisha Abdar-Rahman Bewley. Diwan Press 1982.

The Foundations of Islam of Qadi Iyad : A translation by Aisha Abdar-Rahman Bewley. Diwan al-Amir Publications 1982.

Ash-Shifa of Qadi Iyad : A translation by Aisha Abdar-Rahman Bewley. Madinah Press 1990.

The Diwan of Shaykh Muhammad ibn al-Habib : Diwan Press 1978.

Diwans of the Darqawa : A translation by Aisha Abdar-Rahman Bewley. Diwan Press 1980.

The Meaning of Man of Sidi Ali al-Jamal of Fez : A translation by Aisha Abdar-Rahman Bewley. Diwan Press 1978.

The Darqawi Way of Shaykh Moulay al-Arabi ad-Darqawi : A translation by Aisha Abdar-Rahman Bewley. Diwan Press 1979.

Qur'anic Tawhid : Shaykh Abdal-Qadir al-Murabit. Diwan Press 1981.

The Book of Strangers : Ian Dallas. Victor Gollancz 1972.

The Way of Muhammad : Shaykh Abdal-Qadir al-Murabit. Diwan Press 1974.

The Hundred Steps : Shaykh Abdal-Qadir al-Murabit. Diwan Press 1979.

Self-Knowledge : Shaykh Abdal-Qadir al-Murabit. Diwan Press 1978.